When Husbands Come Out of the Closet

About the Author

Jean S. Gochros, PhD, holds her doctorate in social work. She is a member of the National Association of Social Work, the Academy of Certified Social Workers, and is a Diplomate in Clinical Social Work. She is certified as a sex educator and therapist by the American Association of Sex Educators, Counselors and Therapists (AASECT), and is a former chair of the Hawaii Chapter of that association.

With over twenty-five years experience as a therapist, she has taught on marriage and sex related issues across the country and overseas, and has written on these topics for both the professional and popular press. She presently divides her time between private practice and her work in a Hawaii Department of Health AIDS antibody testing and counseling clinic, where she provides individual counseling and runs a support group for people who are infected with the AIDS virus.

When Husbands Come Out of the Closet

Jean Schaar Gochros, PhD

Harrington Park Press
New York • London

ISBN 0-918393-61-2

Published by

Harrington Park Press, Inc., 10 Alice Street, Binghamton, New York 13904-1580
EUROSPAN/Harrington, 3 Henrietta Street, London WC2E 8LU England

Harrington Park Press, Inc., is a subsidiary of The Haworth Press, Inc., 10 Alice Street,
Binghamton, New York 13904-1580.

The Haworth Press, Inc., 10 Alice Street, Binghamton, NY 13904-1580
EUROSPAN/Harrington, 3 Henrietta Street, London WC2E 8LU England

Cover design by Marshall Andrews.

Library of Congress Cataloging-in-Publication Data

Gochros, Jean S.
  When husbands come out of the closet / Jean Schaar Gochros.
    p. cm.
  Bibliography: p.
  Includes index.
  ISBN 0-918393-61-2
  1. Bisexuality in marriage — United States. I. Title.
HQ74.G63   1989b
306.7'65 — dc19

88-36884
CIP

This book is dedicated to the men and women who participated in and/or supported the study on which this book is based. The husbands knew full well that they would have less than a favorable press; the honesty, courage and concern they showed in their willingness to participate did not go unappreciated by their wives and must not go unappreciated by readers.

And the wives themselves? No researcher could have had a more enthusiastic, supportive, tireless, candid, or thoughtful group of "subjects." They are a testament to the courage, resilience, strength, and compassion of women, and I feel privileged to have known them.

CONTENTS

Foreword

There are not many good things that can be said of AIDS. It is a disease that robs people of not only their lives but before that, their dignity and savings. Of those it touches, it also invades their privacy and that of their families. It exposes to public scrutiny an individual's sexual life and erotic pleasures.

Perhaps the few positive outcomes of the AIDS epidemic, however, is that it allows sexual behavior to be more openly and candidly discussed and sex education is indeed increasing. Both factors have simultaneously brought to public awareness the large and active reality of homosexuality and alerted the public to bisexuality, the erotic attraction to both males and females.

This book is about wives whose husbands are bisexual. It is about women who find the men they live with are erotically attracted to other men — sometimes more so than to them or other women. Sometimes the men reveal their secret and sometimes the women find out despite attempts at secrecy.

While several other books have dealt primarily with the men and their dilemmas in such relationships, this volume is less involved with the men themselves. And it is not specifically concerned with AIDS, although such issues are discussed. Rather this book is primarily about the women involved in the literally millions of such marriages. These are women who, often without a previous hint of such concern, are confronted with the reality that such an intimate part of their husband's life was completely secret from them. And their marriage and families may be severed as a result.

These women, like the men they have married, are your neighbors, friends, fellow workers and members of your own family. They pray as Roman Catholic and Mormon, or Buddhist and Baha'i and every other religion. Some of these women profess no religion at all.

They work as politicians, physicians, lawyers and laborers, tailors and teachers. To all outward appearances, the couples discussed in this book are no different from the other married couples you see around you. And you and your marriage may be one of them.

I have said that such couples number in the millions. That is not an idle guess. According to statistics that are seemingly as true today as when first reported by Alfred Kinsey and his colleagues, some 1 in 10 husbands is bisexually active. The ramifications of this type of living arrangement, trying to deal with its emergence as a factor to be reckoned with by spouses, and the emotional costs and benefits to each as well as their families, is the subject our author tackles. And she does so with skill and sensitivity.

The book begins with vignettes that speak to the emotions of wives coming to grips with the knowledge that their husbands have been having affairs with other men. In some ways the experience is akin to finding out that a husband is having an affair with another woman. In other ways it is very different. Unique taboos are being broken and quite new ways of thinking are often called for. Also, the heterosexual affair is much more common. Wives, while typically not approving of such, are usually more mentally prepared – by the media and their own collective experience – for this assault on their marriage and feelings of self-worth. Few wives, however, are prepared for the double shock of having to deal with their husband's infidelity and bisexually at the same time. And, of late, they often fear the ramifications of AIDS.

On the positive side, dealing with an homosexual affair need not force a women to doubt her own abilities as a woman, since she knows there are no added feminine wiles or "techniques" that will help. It is not in her power to compete with her husband's male lover. She is, however, forced to confront her lack of ability to detect this major characteristic and need within someone she thought she knew intimately. She asks herself, "Why me?" And she, like her sister with a husband attracted to another woman, also has to decide what to do about it. Gochros addresses such issues.

More than the anecdotes of a therapist who has counselled couples with marital problems of all sorts, the book primarily (though not exclusively) offers the results of research. Correspondents and informants were sought from several cities across the United States.

The result is an in-depth study of 33 women and an additional 70 studied less intensively. They were older women and younger, those with children and those without, those deeply religious and others who were atheists. The book documents the feelings of women who stayed with their husbands and women who divorced or separated. Some of the women are quite bitter, others more philosophical.

The book describes couples who worked things out satisfactorily and others who were devastated by the experience. We meet couples to whom the revelation was seen as a "growth" experience and others to whom the event was cataclysmic, painful and hell. All provide grist from which Jean Gochros offers not only food for thought, but a better and clearer insight into the subject; one which allows a truer picture to emerge. Perhaps the greatest value will be for the involved readers who for the first time will be able to see that they are not alone and are offered insights into how they may deal with the situation. There are several different roads that can be traveled. There are options.

There is a need for this book. Bisexuality or extramarital sex and attraction of any sort is not a new phenomenon brought on by the flower children of the 60s or the yuppies of the 80s. It was written of in the Bible and is part of the religious and mystical lore of religions and cultures since time immemorial. And the practices will not go away. What remains current is the emotional price such behaviors extract and the need to have cogent ways to deal with them.

The book will be found helpful to men and women in the predicaments depicted, to the families and friends of such couples, and to those of the general population who are simply interested and trying to understand such conditions. The book will clear away myths and replace them with insight and information. Comparisons and contrasts are given to dealing with any high stress or grief situation. For some the book will offer hope.

Several underlying theses in the book are certainly controversial. On the one hand, the bisexuality discussed is not condemned outright. Neither is extramarital sex. Indeed, in many ways the author talks of how to preserve the relationship and come to terms with both the bisexuality and extramarital behavior. Sometimes incorpo-

rating both into a couple's marriage is seen not only as a way to save the marriage but even improve it. On the other hand, others will condemn the author for trying to save the marriage at a cost of personal integrity, let alone an affront to religious doctrine.

And "Why," argue some gay liberationists or feminists – each from their very different perspectives – "should either men or women, compromise?" Both groups of activists claim that neither needs the other and neither should give in. Either the husband or wife is seen as trying to impose unwarranted restrictions on the other. But leaving, for those involved, is not necessarily any easier than staying.

This brings up another point which the author makes quite strongly. The existing relationship and marriage can be filled with love, fairness, compassion, and understanding or be without these features. The revelation and its aftermath can be filled with growth and warmth or hate and anger. The crises may be of one long standing and chronic concern or may be episodic. And although the overall condition is very common, each couple's situation is always unique. The input of others can help, but the two individuals themselves must come to grips with their plight.

I think the book will be welcomed by the therapeutic community as well as the much wider population at large. Gochros offers hints on helping technique and perspective. But more importantly she offers a philosophical approach and set of caveats. Don't, she warns, regardless if you are male or female, be a male chauvinist expecting it is only the wife who has to change. And, she cautions, it is superficial to see this simply as a male-female matter or a heterosexual-homosexual conflict. The problems are those of any two mature people trying to meet their own changing needs as individuals while society changes around them. In this I heartily agree. She sees this phenomenon as part of a broader picture within "liberation ethics." The broad question remains: "How does a person satisfy his or her own individual needs that might be at odds with another's?"

"Crisis theory" holds that an acute relationship crisis will be relatively short lived; over in a few weeks or at most a few months. And it is only during the "acute crisis" that support is especially needed. This book documents, and my own clinical experience at-

tests, that crisis may persist and remain chronic and long lasting rather than be fleeting. The healing process may take months and even years and be accomplished as much from a therapist's assistance as the person's own efforts and developments in the surrounding world. In some cases, aspects of the crisis may persist life long. This book will help relieve many peoples' guilt in this arena.

Gochros ends her book with a plea that deserves emphasis here in the beginning. Basic to solving the problems recounted in this book, she calls for an end to bigotry and intolerance inherent in narrow views of sexual preferences, sex roles, marriage contracts, and just being different. I agree wholeheartedly. Such tolerance and understanding will go far to helping solve many relationship difficulties and other problems as well.

Enjoy the book. It has a great deal of human interest and it provides insight into the broad scope of marriage and human relationships in our changing times. It should, as the author hopes, shed light to help prevent future tragedies.

Milton Diamond, PhD

Acknowledgements

No book attains publication through the writer's efforts alone. First and foremost, I wish to acknowledge the editorial assistance of Bonnie Stone. Both her professional judgements and her faith in the book's merits were instrumental in helping this book find its way to The Haworth Press.

Thanks go to Suzanne Richmond-Crum of the University of Hawai, and Clifford Chang, Tony Natoli, Jeff Cornelius, and Dr. Will Butler of the Hawaii Department of Health's AIDS Antibody Clinic at Diamond Head Health Center. All were helpful as I struggled to translate the world of immunology and epidemiology into understandable English for the chapter on AIDS. My thanks also to Aurele Samuels and Dr. Dorothea Hays for insights from their own research, their friendship, and their encouragement.

Without the first draft editorial help of my husband, Harvey L. Gochros, as well as his patience, humor and encouragement, the book might never have progressed from first draft to second draft. Last but definitely not least, let me express my appreciation to Bill Cohen, Publisher, and Drs. Esther Rothblum and Ellen Cole of The Haworth Press, for their expertise, advice, enthusiasm, and support.

Chapter 1

Introduction to the Closet
Within a Closet

Sue Johnson is a tall, slender woman in her late 30s. She is neither beautiful nor attractive. "Nice looking" is the most apt description. Her husband Tim, an attorney, is a distinguished-looking man in his early 40s. Their 15 years of marriage have produced two children, 10 and 12. Their friends describe them as "the perfect American couple" and their marriage as "the personification of the American Dream."

Throughout most of their marriage, their sex life had been good. Not great, but good. Abruptly, about 4 years ago, it stopped. Tim became preoccupied, remote, and uninterested in sex. His doctor pronounced him in perfect health, yet he was having stomach trouble. He sought psychiatric help, but did not say why. Sue worried and wondered if she had done something wrong, but gave him time to work things out for himself.

Finally, Tim suggested some time out from the tension of work and child rearing. He booked a room at a posh hotel, and they had a weekend of fun, relaxation, intimacy, and romance. On Sunday they engaged in a bit of frivolous prebreakfast lovemaking. It was all very honeymoonish. Tim, however, did not want to get out of bed afterwards. He wanted to talk, and he was looking pale and tense. Sue steeled herself—for what, she did not know. Tim fingered the sheet, looking furtively at her several times before blurting out,

> I just paid my psychiatrist $50 for advice that I can't take! He told me not to tell you. But I *can't* not say anything—that would be too dishonest. There's a part of me that I've cut off

from myself and withheld from you. I can't keep on this way!
I have to tell you about it even if it means the end of our
marriage!

Sue sat numbly as he went on:

I love you! I always have. I always will! I want to always be
married to you. But . . . I'm bisexual. I have been since before
we met, but I guess I tried to pretend my feelings weren't
there. I can't pretend any longer. I have strong feelings for
other men!

Sue sat silently, lost in thought as Tim sat fidgeting, looking like
a man about to be executed. Finally she said, "I don't get it. What's
the big deal?"
She meant it. Actually, however, she was experiencing a typical
"stun" reaction. It was a while before her brain started functioning
well enough to ask pertinent questions, and after she asked them,
she went through considerable soul searching. Even now, 3 years
later, she's still doing it.
She doesn't know what the future holds. She has agreed that Tim
needs and should have a close intimate relationship with another
man. She doesn't know how she'll feel if that includes sex. In some
ways, she would just as soon not know. She is still grappling with
conflicting feelings. But in the 3 years since Tim's disclosure, their
marriage, which had always held warmth and laughter, has become
even freer, more close, and more loving. Their sexual relationship
has not only returned to normal, it has gone from "good" to
"great." She is still saying, albeit a bit nervously, "So he has some
homosexual feelings and needs. So what's the big deal?"

Mary and Bob McDermott are staunch Roman Catholics who
became friends while working together for a large realty company.
Mary saw Bob through a nearly fatal illness and was impressed with
the courage, humor, and kindness he displayed throughout his ordeal. When he was fully recovered, they started dating and fell in
love. They planned a huge church wedding involving all the relatives. Two days before the ceremony, Bob disclosed (1) that his

illness was not cured, as he had told her, but was simply in remission, and (2) that he had been homosexual before dating her.

He pledged love and fidelity, assured her she had nothing to worry about, and talked her out of either postponing the wedding or talking to their priest. She went through the ceremony in a stunned daze, feeling that she was committing a sin in the eyes of the church. She awoke after the wedding night to find Bob gone, and went into what is known as an acute crisis reaction:

> Pains shot through me. I was in a panic. I was sure he'd been dissatisfied and had gone to find a man. . . . I tried to jump out the window, but couldn't. I took the whole bottle of his pills in a suicide attempt, but I was sobbing so hard I threw them up. When he returned, he was hurt that I'd had so little trust, and furious that I'd taken his medicine when I knew he needed it for his health. He hadn't been with a man at all. He'd gone to buy me a present. I felt guilty and ashamed, and resolved never to get so out of control again.

Almost parenthetically, she added that "The rest of the honeymoon was a bit strained."

Despite its inauspicious beginning, the marriage for 2 years was a good one, until Bob began seeing other men. At first it was just occasionally. Then it became more frequent. Mary asked him to stop. She pleaded, cried, then stormed. Nothing worked. It was not infidelity, he told her, since it was with a man, not a woman. To give him a taste of his own medicine, she had a brief affair and told him about it. However, she felt guilty and Bob declared her actions immoral. The marriage deteriorated steadily. Finally, he told her he still loved her, but her demands for love were insatiable. He could not fill them.

They felt they could not divorce because of their Catholicism, but they did separate. Pledging her to secrecy, he told their friends that they had divorced because his illness had returned. In the eyes of others she was unfeeling and cruel, but she has never told anyone the truth. Despite her religious devoutness, she feels she cannot return to the church; she has sinned too much.

In the 5 years since their separation, she has found leadership skills and enjoyed unusual success in her business career. But she has almost totally isolated herself socially and has lost so much weight that her friends and relatives worry about her health. On the day I interviewed her, she was so clinically depressed that I took off my "researcher" hat and gave her an emergency referral to a therapist. Emotionally, she did not seem far from that first day when she'd swallowed the pills.

Since the start of the gay liberation movement in the late 1960s, as our society has become more accepting, more and more homosexually oriented men and women have begun to come out of their closets. What we may not realize, however, is how many kinds of closets exist or how restricting and painful they can be for their inhabitants.

One of those closets holds couples like the Johnsons and the Mc-Dermotts, where one of the partners — in this case, the husband — is gay or bisexual. A growing number of men and women have knowingly entered a gay/straight marriage with allowances made for extramarital sex. Such marriages seem to be working well. But when the homosexuality comes to light only after marriage (Mary fit into such a category emotionally, if not legally), the problems that ensue can reach crisis proportions.

There has been little written about this situation. Until recently, what little information existed dealt mainly with the problems of gay husbands. It either ignored the needs and feelings of wives or dismissed them in a paragraph suggesting that such wives are neurotic and unable to cope with the situation.

Nobody knows how many couples are in this situation. As early as 1948, Kinsey had reported that 10% (1 in 10) of married American men between the ages of 21 and 25, and 2% between the ages of 26 and 45 had had some amount of homosexual experience during marriage. Over 3% had had as much or more homosexual as heterosexual interest and experience.

Kinsey's study did not include Blacks. The 12% did not include men who had engaged in homosexual activity after divorce or the death of their wives. Many of those men had divorced because of their homosexuality. Moreover, Kinsey's study included hundreds of single men who had had sexual affairs with older married men not participating in the study. In considering these factors, Kinsey estimated the number of married men with some degree of homo-sexuality to be far higher than he could document (approaching 15% to 20%, judging by his figures). His study is still considered the most comprehensive and reliable one available.

More recent American and European studies of gay or bisexual men have reported anywhere from 10% to 54% who were at the time or who had been married, with the latter study reporting only on men who frequented public restrooms. The most frequent figure seems to be around 20%. Differing definitions of homosexuality and the fear of participating in studies prevents us from arriving at truly accurate figures. Some therapists and researchers, however, not only consider the 20% estimate far too low, they speculate that anywhere from 50% to "most" gay or bisexual men may marry in the course of their lifetimes.

A 1980 book, *Barry and Alice* by Kohn and Matusow, *Portrait of a Bisexual Marriage* (1980) gives the personal account of one such couple and the problems they faced. The authors had started a sup-port group by placing an ad in a Philadelphia newspaper. By the time their book came out, they had seen hundreds of such couples in that city alone. A Baltimore support group reports having served thousands in a 5-year span. Two current researchers have given "conservative" estimates of 2.6 million gay or bisexual American men who marry at some point in their lives.

Does that sound incredible? In the 70s it would have seemed so. Today, one study, several speeches and articles, counselees, and a sack full of mail later, I find such figures quite plausible. As one wife married to a gay husband said to me, "This may be the best-kept secret in America." In just the short time that has elapsed since I interviewed Tim and Sue, AIDS has made that secret an even more important and frightening one.

This book is about what happens to wives when they learn that their husbands are gay or bisexual. It is based partly on my own clinical experience as a therapist and primarily on an intensive study in which women gave their candid accounts of how such a revela-tion had affected their marriages and their lives.

It shares their immediate reactions and both the short-term and long-term effects on their marriages, their sex lives, and their mental health. It explores their attitudes toward homosexuality and how they compare their lives with those of women with heterosexual husbands. It includes the problems they faced, how they tried to cope with the situation, who they turned to for help, and how they rated the help they received.

It discusses the factors that played a part in their reactions, successes, and problems: their own personalities and backgrounds, their social and religious values, the reasons they had chosen their husbands, and their early marital and sexual relationships, their husbands' behaviors, and the various socio-economic conditions and societal attitudes that affected their adjustment. It will provide practical advice to others in this situation and to professionals, friends, and relatives who may have already tried to help someone or who may be in a helping role in the future.

The study wives were interviewed before either they or I could know that AIDS would have an impact on their own lives. Yet a book like this would be useless if it did not confront issues within the framework of new AIDS realities. Hence it will both update advice on sexual matters and include a special chapter on AIDS based on research, continuing information from wives, my present private practice, and my experiences in an AIDS antibody testing and counseling clinic. That chapter will provide information and practical advice on coping with the threat (or reality) of HIV (AIDS virus) infection. To prevent alarm, however, let me quickly reassure you that so far the incidence of AIDS in women because of infection by gay/bisexual husbands seems to be extremely low. Finally, the book will provide my own comments and suggestions as a researcher and therapist.

It will also discuss a theory that may make the women's reactions more understandable. If you have read *Passages* or *On Death and Dying*, you already know something about crisis theory. It was applicable to these situations in many ways. Kohn and Matusow (1980), in fact, labeled this a grief crisis comparable to the death of a loved one. My study, however, found some differences. Both similarities and differences will be important.

The confidentiality of those who participated in the study is protected by omitting or disguising identifying information. Interesting features of the study, however, were the similar themes, descriptions, and behaviors that emerged and how similar the people were to those I have seen in clinical practice.

Often words, phrases — even whole paragraphs — were so identical that had the interviews not been taped, the quoted excerpts would have been questioned as to authenticity. In an attempt to disguise one person, a description emerges that could inadvertently fit someone else. Indeed, when the study was reported on in several newspapers, one article contained a few vignettes. Not only did many not in the study feel that the vignettes fit them, one caller was sure that one vignette had been an account of his situation. Somehow the fictitious description of a family 8,000 miles away had exactly fit the description of the caller and his family, even down to a rare illness (*not* AIDS).

This is a book filled with sorrow and tears. People like Tim and Sue, still basking in the glow of what seems like an easy adjustment, may become uneasy as they learn that the path may not always stay so smooth. They should know ahead of time that it is also a book filled with the hope that comes from "happy endings."

The women in this book were all pioneers who had unwittingly traveled uncharted trails West with no wagonmaster. Neither they nor their husbands knew the terrain. They did not even know what dangers might lie ahead, much less how to avoid or overcome them. It is my hope and belief that through the wisdom gained from the trial-and-error successes and failures of earlier travelers, the Tims and Sues who follow will be able to map out easier paths.

Chapter 2

Why Such a Study
and Why This Book

GENESIS: WHEN THIS BOOK WAS CONCEIVED

The year was 1969.

The young man sitting across from me nervously twirled his fork in his plate of already cold spaghetti. His name was Don. He was tall, lanky, and nice looking without being actually handsome. Only 23, he'd already been married for 4 years. He was the star student in a graduate school of social work.

I was on the faculty of that school, supervising students as they learned to apply classroom theory to their real-life clinical practice. I also had a part-time private practice, and was one of the only therapists in town at that time doing sexual counseling.

"Can I get some advice on how to help a friend with a sexual problem?" Don had asked on the way out of his supervisory conference that morning. The "friend" ploy had been discussed so often in school, I doubted a student would use it. He'd sounded quite casual and more than willing to talk about it over lunch. I'd ruled out the possibility that his friend was fictitious. Yet here he was, embarrassedly dawdling over his food and reluctant to tell me exactly what the problem was.

"Well, Don," I finally said, "I figure sexual problems usually fall into one of two ballparks, heterosexual and homosexual. Maybe you can at least establish the ballpark for me?"

His suddenly pale face and slumping shoulders clarified the name of the ballpark and the person we were discussing. Haltingly, painfully, he told me the rest of the story. He had had homosexual experiences during high school. He had assumed they were part of the adolescent games many of his classmates played. When he fell in love with his childhood sweetheart and married her right after graduation, he was sure that he would no longer desire such kid stuff. Now he had the real thing! His expectations had been more than satisfied for the first 3 years. He told me — and it had always been plain to see — that he adored his wife.

For the past year, however, he had been growing less and less sexually interested in his wife and more and more sexually attracted to men.

"Am I gay?" he asked. "I love Carolyn too much to want to leave her or hurt her. And I believe in being faithful. But just last night it took every last ounce of will power to refuse a guy's advances. I don't know which way to go, but I can't keep on this way. I have to do something! I know I need help, but I don't know who else to turn to. Will you help me?"

In 1969, there were no therapists in town who would not have simply declared Don "sick" and tried to "cure" his homosexuality. Don was not asking for a cure, however. He simply wanted help in decision making. Although I usually disapprove of faculty counseling their own students, in this case there seemed no other way. I agreed, and we started counseling, first with Don alone and then with his wife.

Don made a decision and came to grips with his homosexuality quickly. He handled the "telling" sensitively, with utmost concern for Carolyn's feelings. She did not have the nervous breakdown he had feared. Instead, she handled it with what he termed "unbelievable strength and understanding." In fact, although she wept a bit, she told me she was relieved to find that the problem had not been her fault. I gave her what help I could, but she did not seem to need or want much.

Carolyn and Don stayed together long enough to provide each other with support and assistance in easing back to single life. They separated only when Carolyn, who had started dating again, told him he would have to move out: he was cramping her style. Don soon found a lover and moved away; they are still together. They started one of the first professional counseling agencies for gays in the country and have since earned great respect for their work. By now, over 20 years later, Carolyn is remarried.

Divorce is always painful. But this one had been less so than most. It was a true counseling success story!

Or was it?

In the pit of my stomach, I wasn't so sure. Considering the sense of loss Carolyn must have had, her relative lack of emotion (which Don said was atypical) did not have a good feel to it.

What I sensed was different from the usual pain of loss, yet was undefinable. Learning 2 years after the divorce that she was not doing as well as expected had not alleviated my uneasiness. Somewhere behind that facade of strength, I sensed internal emotional bleeding caused by things missed in therapy. I never lost that feeling. Although I did not realize it, and although it would take over 20 years to be born, it was at that point that this book was conceived.

I did not see another gay/straight couple until the late 70s, but with each of the next three such couples my concerns grew. With each, my co-therapist and I were able to help the husbands and have maintained contact with them over the years. We became increasingly worried, however, about our inability to provide adequate help for the wives.

Therapists today seldom judge success by whether they can save a marriage. Rather, they try to help people turn their marriages into a supportive, mutually satisfying framework for individual growth and fulfillment. If people begin to find that this will be impossible, then the goal is to help them turn divorce into a constructive, mutually supportive process that will send each partner off with renewed self-confidence, new coping skills, and hope for the future. My co-therapist and I have a pretty good track record on both counts. With gay/straight couples, however, we seemed unable to accomplish either task from the wife's perspective.

No matter how well we worked, something always seemed to go wrong. One of the first couples, for example, had started as a traditional marriage counseling case. It had quickly become apparent that each partner, individually, was heading toward divorce. Cliff had begun to face his homosexuality and disinterest in marriage. Janna had lost her own personality while trying to play the "good" wife. Through my careful and innovative strategies for Janna's personal growth, she was literally flowering before my eyes, picking up earlier career goals and becoming a personable, talented, and capable violinist on her way to fame and fortune.

Cliff reached his moment of truth a little ahead of Janna. He was terrified that her moralistic views would result in anger and vindictiveness, but he agreed that it was only fair to be honest about his reasons for wanting divorce.

The "disclosure" scene started off well. He handled it sensitively, and she responded not with anger, but with strength and understanding. There seemed to be no problem in using the homosexuality to reinforce what she had already begun to recognize — that she was not to blame for their problems and that divorce was not a failure but a mature recognition that the marriage could not meet their needs. Both partners agreed to "get the agony over with quickly." Janna suggested, typically, that they get their affairs in order and separate in a month.

And then it all exploded in one surrealistic moment. Cliff was so anxious and guilt ridden that his idea of "quickly" was not a month, not a week, but instantly. He wanted Janna to leave and he wanted her to do so that same morning. Essentially, he had dismissed her without notice.

Once he had voiced his wishes, nothing could soften Janna's sense of rejection. She was completely on her own, cut off from the support of family or friends. Born in upstate New York, the two had only recently come to town. They had no close friends. Counseling would simply not be enough to sustain her. There was nothing to do but provide temporary comforting, plaster on verbal bandaids, and see to it that Cliff got her back into the arms of a comforting mother as soon as humanly possible. I issued instructions for a therapist to be ready and waiting for her when she reached home.

Cliff soon found a lover and subsequently left for a successful acting career in New York City. Janna had promised to write me within the week, but did not do so. She did not respond to a note sent to her. A year or two later, Cliff reported hearing that she had immersed herself in church work, but did not seem happy. He had no other news. She would not talk to him. Eventually, however, she remarried, forgave him, and they ended up on friendly terms. What happened to her music, I don't know.

My co-therapist correctly pointed out that counselors are neither mindreaders nor magicians. We could not have foreseen such a tragic end to the counseling. Yet I was again left with a nagging feeling of having let Janna down, that there should have been more we could do to prevent or relieve such needless pain.

Even when two couples started out with the express desire to remain married despite the knowledge of homosexuality, things went wrong.*

The next situation was so complicated that only a few details can be given. A military psychiatrist referred Jim, an officer, his wife Abby, his civilian lover Tony, and Tony's wife, Marsha. The story was confusing and messy.

Marsha reportedly had attacked the two men with a knife and reported their liaison to Jim's commanding officer, thereby ruining his military career. Because he could not offer confidentiality, the psychiatrist did not dare see Jim. He did, however, offer consultation and help in obtaining psychiatric care for Marsha, whom he presumed was psychotic.

We met with three badly shaken people. Afraid for their safety and ours, they had refused to bring Marsha along. They could not understand her violent behavior, which had occurred when she found the two men in bed one day. They explained that she had known of the relationship for some time. Since Abby had been understanding about it, all four could have been friends. Was Marsha vindictive, psychotic, or both?

When I finally heard Marsha's version, her behavior became more understandable. It sounded like a crisis reaction to finding that both men had broken a promise to hold all their liaisons away from home. Tony, in fact, had broken several earlier promises. Finding

---

*Many people may wonder why we would even attempt to save the marriage and how we could possibly consider homosexuality compatible with marriage. There are, however, a growing number of therapists who see many viable possibilities both in and out of marriage. Whether two individuals could make such a marriage work, they say, would depend on how each person feels about homosexuality and monogamy, their reasons for marrying and staying married, and whether they could arrange a marriage contract that would be sexually and emotionally satisfying for both. Like any other marriage, the quality would depend on many issues, with sex being only one part of the total relationship. I'll explain this further in Chapter 4.

the men in her own house was the last straw. Locked out of her house, Marsha had indeed brandished a knife, but partly in an effort to cut through the screen door to get in. Not thinking clearly at that point, her behavior was potentially dangerous, but not deliberately so. Whether that was all there was to it, I was not sure. But the crisis was obviously over, Marsha had stabilized, and the immediate danger was over. The psychiatrist and I agreed that to send her for a psychiatric evaluation was not only needless, it would do more harm than good.

After a short evaluation period, we set up a contract with each couple to start marital counseling. All four expressed the basic prerequisites of love and concern for each other and the desire to stay married. We made no promises, but we were optimistic that the marriages could be saved. We suggested starting out by helping each couple establish fair contract terms, helping resolve the legal and economic emergencies Jim and Abby were facing, and helping each person sort out his or her individual feelings. We also suggested postponing work on the marital sexual relations, since it seemed unrealistic to expect good relationships under the strain they were feeling. Rather, we told them to start rebuilding the climate conducive to good sex through caressing and expression of affection, to try intercourse only if they felt like it, and to not worry about it if it failed. It could be dealt with later if necessary.

We set up contingency plans with them in case we had not finished counseling in 9 months, when I would be leaving for a year's stay in another state. But we did not expect such an event. We estimated about 6 months of work. Based on our earlier experiences, we assumed that if the men had not made a decision about their ability to sustain a marriage by the time the extraneous problems had been removed, they would do so quickly once we began to really deal with the marital sexual relations. We were now forewarned. There would be no more shockers. We foresaw no problems in helping the women should it prove impossible to save the marriages.

It was a good plan. It sounded good to the husbands. It sounded good to the wives. There was only one problem with it. It did not work.

Six months later we were still trying to untangle a snarled mess of problems and conflicts. Fair marriage contracts had not been established. The men had withdrawn from their wives, yet neither one wished to leave his marriage. Tony and Marsha were constantly battling. We could not determine the "unreasonable" party, nor could a friend of theirs who was asked to provide a "real-life" view. Instead of flowering, Abby's personal self-confidence and happiness was crumbling before my very eyes. Despite the fact that Jim was concerned and trying to be fair, she was looking more defeated every day.

When I finally realized that in her attempt to be "understanding," Abby had let her own needs and rights become increasingly disregarded, things suddenly moved with lightning speed. When she finally announced her very minimal expectations, Jim came to grips with the fact that he could not meet them.

With Marsha and Tony, some basic communication problems were finally pinpointed. We set up a traditional communication exercise that never fails. It failed.

Tony engaged in a cruel, taunting, and belittling verbal assault on Marsha that was out of character for the concerned, gentle person he usually was. It was so cruel that once again, we were all stunned.

When confronted privately with his unfairness, Tony began to face the fact that he could not juggle two love relationships and that he wanted only one — the one with Jim. Following an emergency late-night session and concerned for her welfare, he asked us to be present when he told Marsha. This time he was so sensitive and comforting and the scene was so moving and intimate that we finally left the room, feeling like intruders. The next day we proceeded to divorce counseling for both couples.

Unlike Janna and Cliff, there was no "dismissal" here. But neither were there constructive divorce processes. I was trying to help Abby start a new life for herself, but it was not moving very fast. Her friends had all been military wives. She no longer had them for support. She was loath to either confide in others or join a church group or organization. She was finding new skills and leadership qualities at work, but was underemployed. Although well educated, she did not have the credentials for a better-paying job, and Jim's need to start a new career had left them without the money for her to return to school. Jim was supportive and concerned, but his efforts to help and his true affection for her resulted in unintentional double messages that interfered with her ability to make an emotional separation.

Marsha and Tony soon resumed their battling, this time over how to manage the care of their children. We ended up giving them a plain, old-fashioned "Dutch Uncle" lecture, and told them to get their act together for the sake of their children. It's not our usual style, but it seemed to work.

By the time I had to leave, the two men were happy with their lives and delighted with the help they had received. The two women were bitter, feeling that their husbands had been "pushed" into homosexuality. I did not feel that Abby needed further therapy as much as she needed friends and a woman's support group to help her regain her self-confidence. I had a faculty friend who was willing to assist her in finding such a group. Abby saw her once and never returned. I never heard from Abby again. Eventually she left town, even asking Jim not to write because his support was impeding her progress.

Marsha was still in no shape to leave therapy. I left her in the hands of a psychologist. He agreed with me that most of the work had already been done, and he simply needed to tie up loose ends and be available as needed. When I returned a year later, however, Marsha was still in treatment. Despite the fact that she was a strong, intelligent, and capable businesswoman, she had become increasingly dependent upon the psychologist for help with even the most trivial decisions. The psychologist felt bewildered and helpless. The psychiatrist we had used as a consultant was just as baffled. We had all treated far more emotionally disturbed people. We had handled far messier divorce cases. What was wrong? Why weren't we more able to help? None of us knew.

When treatment failures occur, the reasons can usually be pinpointed either through self-exploration, consultation, or by examining the latest research and professional literature. In this situation, however, all were fruitless. Were the wives simply unable to accept their husbands' homosexuality? Were these particular couples unique? Was there something unique about gay/straight marriages that we had missed?

Self-exploration provided no real answers. There was no literature or research to read. The only two articles that had been published by 1977 were so obscure that I found them only through the help of a computer 2 years later. Even when located, they provided no real guidelines. And consultants? There was nobody with whom to consult. As far as we knew, we might be the only therapists in the world to have seen such couples.

We reasoned, however, that there must be others, and that they might be having similar struggles. We also reasoned that as the gay liberation movement gained momentum, more couples would surface and that more accurate information was needed quickly. By now I know that I was right on all three counts.

THE STUDY AND HOW IT GREW

The best way to obtain that information was through research. When my university provided the opportunity to do a study, I leaped at the chance. I wanted to get as much insight as possible into how such women had felt, what problems they had faced, and what had helped them. Common sense told me there would be a high divorce rate. I wanted to know both what it took to hold a marriage together following a disclosure of homosexuality, and what it took to ease the divorce process for a wife. Such a disclosure would be a crisis for many wives. I wanted to know if it would be so for all wives, how similar it was to other crises that people face, how severe it was, and what factors affected wives' reactions. Were there ingredients I had missed? If so, what were they?

I wanted as many kinds of people and situations as I could find. Thirty or so people is generally considered sufficient to provide in-depth insight and a variety of perspectives. One recognizes, of course, that the people seen in such a small sample may not be typical and that both their information and the researcher's interpretations will reflect some biases.*

Although many husbands, wives, and clinicians have reported experiences and feelings similar to the ones found in this study, there may be others whose experiences and feelings are quite different.

Such studies, however, have advantages. They can get more

---

*Further information about the research methods are given in the Appendix.

valuable and honest insights than can be obtained from the short questionnaires often sent in the mail. One is not limited by the questions or ideas one starts with. The people themselves suggest what is important to ask and know.

Originally, then, only 30 wives were sought. Indeed, I wondered if I'd even be able to find that many. I wanted people from different parts of the country, and although I wanted some from a gay-supportive city like San Francisco, I did not want to be overloaded with such a special group.

I started out with a "snowball" technique. I interviewed the one or two people I already knew, including Marsha. Every wife I saw was asked to suggest others. I sought referrals from social agencies, churches, and gay groups in Honolulu and Rochester, New York. I was given the names of a few people in San Francisco and Portland and arranged appointments with them en route to and from Rochester. This technique, however, brought in only a handful of people. I turned to the newspapers. Suddenly my "snowball" turned into an avalanche!

The first news release was buried on page 23 of a Honolulu newspaper. It was so small I combed through the paper twice before finding it. "No one will even see this," I wailed. That was a few minutes after the home deliveries. At that precise moment, the phone rang. It did not stop ringing for the next three days. By the time I reached Rochester, I needed only three more people.

In Rochester neither the suggested resources there nor the gay organization had any suggestions. Again I turned to the newspaper. A very skeptical reporter did a feature article, but warned me not to expect any response in such a conservative community. Neither of us was prepared for the deluge of responses that would again start within a few minutes of the home deliveries.

For the next 2 weeks I held two 4-hour interviews a day and 1-hour phone interviews in between. Feeling like the Sorcerer's Apprentice, I stopped the phone interviews and asked people to write. By the time I reached California, I was worn out. When my volunteers suggested other names, I put on mental earmuffs.

By the time I returned home, I found a pile of letters waiting for me not only from Rochester, but from all over California and such states as Florida, Iowa, and North Dakota. The article had been picked up by a paper in two states. It had also been sent to women by their former husbands. Letters often ran from 8 to 20 pages. Some women wrote twice. One military wife wrote from Europe and has continued a running correspondence.

The study had attracted interest in Honolulu. After each talk show, workshop, or interview with a reporter, the phone calls would begin:

> My God! I felt like my every thought and action was walking across the newspaper pages! Are you sure my wife wasn't in your study?
>
> "That was *Me* you described! My husband! Exactly! I can't believe it!"

I got calls from therapists:

> That's exactly what this wife said!
>
> That's exactly what's happening with my couple!
>
> That's exactly how I was feeling! No wonder I was so confused about what was going on!

The flood of responses had already told me what by now has been confirmed many times over. I had seen the merest tip of a gigantic iceberg. Not only had I found the 30 women I needed, I had ended up with information from 103. I could have gone on indefinitely. I had stopped at that number simply because I was no longer hearing anything new and lacked the time and financial resources to continue.

Found: A Missing Ingredient

More important, before I had even started an interview, I had found one of the "missing ingredients" I'd been seeking. Its name was "isolation." It was stressed by every woman contacted and was dramatically illustrated in the large and immediate response to the newspaper coverage, the extraordinary effort the women (and their husbands) gave to provide help, their enthusiastic identification with the project, and their insistence that I not let the study sit on a shelf to gather dust. It is one of four main themes that will be found throughout this book. Handmaiden to a sense of stigma, it was an ingredient to which I'd given a passing nod, without truly appreciating its impact.

Every letter and every interview contained and usually started and ended with a statement of isolation. It was a terrible sense of lonely uniqueness. Over and over again, I picked up the phone to hear a husky, fighting-back-the-tears voice whisper, "Thank God! I thought I was the only one!" Even women in San Francisco reported attending their first support group meeting, looking around at the others, and issuing that statement.

Over and over again I heard or read, "Thank God someone is finally paying attention to the wives! My husband is coming out of his closet. Now I'm the one in it!" "I came to help others avoid the terrible sense of isolation I felt." "I know now I'm not the only one, but I didn't know it when I needed to. If only this study had been done years ago!" "God bless you for doing this study!" From religious women I received so many "God bless you's" that I began to fight a messianic complex.

Over and over again women ended their interviews with an anxious, "Have I helped? Did anyone else feel the way I do? Oh, thank God! I thought I was the only one! Sometimes I thought I was going crazy!" Over and over again women who had never confided in anyone else paused on the way out of their interview to say, "I don't know if this helped you, but I feel like a ton of bricks is lifted from my shoulders."

Many women were so hungry to talk that the words flowed even before they'd crossed the threshold. One woman met me at a shopping center and started her interview before she'd even finished introducing herself. After 4 exhausting hours, many women were reluctant to leave.

Essentially, I felt I had made a contract with all of them. Most, in fact, made it very specific: "I'm here to help others. It's too late for me, I no longer need the help. If I participate, promise me you'll use this to help others. Promise me you'll publish your results."

Part of the promise everyone exacted was that if I did nothing else, I'd deliver this message to husbands, children, relatives, but especially to wives:

If you are in this situation, know that any and all of the feelings you may have had or will have in the future have been shared by others. Know that there are many others in your situation, and that you are in very good company.

You are not alone!

Chapter 3

Introducing the People
Who Live in This Closet

I am often asked who these people are: What kinds of backgrounds do they have? Are they religious? What type of woman marries such a man? What kind of marriage did they have before the disclosure of homosexuality? Often the questions take the form of a prediction game, which I call the "I bet" game:

> I bet you found women who married such men because they had such low self-esteem.
> I bet you found many women who "came out" themselves after the disclosure.
> I bet you found unattractive, passive, or masculine women.

Such assumptions were supported by two articles I'd read, characterizing wives of gay men as neurotic, and socially and sexually immature. One had been written by a therapist, based on her treatment of 12 wives of men undergoing "conversion" therapy. The other had been by a researcher whose study had focused on husbands but who had interviewed a few wives (much as I interviewed husbands) peripherally.

Although my own study was not designed to test such judgments, enough background material was obtained to allow for comment. Moreover, to see how disclosure affected the wives and the marriage, it is necessary to know something about wives' past backgrounds and personalities and about the predisclosure marital relationship. This chapter, then, forms the backdrop for the dramas to follow.

Socioeconomic Description

Into every study some statistics must fall. To keep them to a minimum, however, I'll ask you to imagine that you live in a neighborhood populated only by the couples from this study. Your neighborhood is composed mainly (80%) of white, Christian, upper-middle class to upper-class families in which both husbands and wives are college educated at the least and who are either professionals or in middle-level and high-level business positions.

The remaining 20% are mainly middle class to lower-middle class. The partners have graduated from high school and may have had some college or vocational training. The husbands are mainly skilled laborers or in lower-echelon business jobs, and the wives are mainly homemakers or in lower-paying, white-collar jobs. A few (about 2%) are far lower on the socioeconomic scale, with the husbands apt to be skilled laborers and the wives in factory work. An occasional wife may have had no more than an 8th grade education.

Occupations

The range of occupations, then, for both husbands and wives, is great. With many husbands and wives having or working on post-graduate degrees (education ranges from 8th grade to PhD), occupations range from factory worker to college professor. If you stroll down your neighborhood supermarket aisles, you will meet geologists, architects, artists, nuclear physicists, legal secretaries, attorneys, politicians, bankers, teachers, physicians, nurses, psychiatrists, social workers, psychologists, business administrators, engineers, chemists, realtors, and biologists. This will be true for both the husbands and wives.

You will meet a few steamfitters, plumbers, factory pieceworkers, salespeople, policemen, secretaries, clerical workers, and homemakers. You will meet military couples. You will also meet clergymen and their wives. In short, you will meet most of the people you meet in your actual neighborhood. It would not be surprising if you met your next-door neighbor, your closest friend, a family member, the couple who sits next to you in church, and/or your minister.

Religion

Despite the fact that 80% are Christian, you will meet people from every other major religion: Jews, Buddhists, Moslems, and Hindus. You will meet Presbyterians, Episcopalians, Methodists, Unitarians, and Lutherans. Moreover, here is a fact that may be surprising: although you will meet a few (9%) from "liberal" religious or nonreligious backgrounds, the majority (67% of the husbands and 54% of the wives) will be people who have been brought up in strict Catholic, Mormon, Baptist, Pentecostal, or other Fundamentalist families. Over half of those couples will still be strongly religious and often "pillars" of their churches, with more than a few ministers and their wives.

Does this suggest that religion breeds homosexuality? Absolutely not, although one would certainly think so from those figures. It's impossible to know just what they mean. They may be just a fluke of circumstances, although they seem to run true in the men and couples that have shown up for therapy or support groups since the study. They may simply represent American society: certainly, the representation of the larger religious categories (Protestant, Catholic, and Jewish, as opposed to the denominations within those categories) was consistent with that of the general population in the areas I visited. Perhaps the majority of Americans *do* come from such strict backgrounds, although it seems unlikely. The most plausible explanation is that people tied to churches with especially strong sanctions against homosexuality felt exceptionally isolated and hence participated in the study partly to "give" and partly to "get" information and/or help.

Race and Ethnic Backgrounds

Again, this group of people presented a paradox in that on the one hand it seemed homogeneous, on the other hand a heterogeneous mixture. In continuing your neighborhood supermarket walk, you will find mostly white, but an occasional black and Asian couple. You will find Americans with such ethnic backgrounds (and often strong cultural identification) as English, Scotch-Irish, German, Polish, Russian, Italian, Scandinavian, Japanese, Chinese, Filipino, and Hawaiian. You will meet Chicanos. You will also meet people born in such European countries as Germany or Holland who had come to the United States during or following World War II. In short, despite the predominance of white faces you will encounter, you will also see a microcosm of American "melting pot" society.

Length of Marriage

When interviewed, the couples had been married anywhere from 1 to 35 years, with an average of 8 years. Approximately 60% had been divorced or separated anywhere from 1 month to 6 years, with the average 3 years. Because of the difficulty in defining a "disclosure" date, a truly accurate account of how much time had elapsed before and after the disclosure was impossible to obtain. It seemed, however, that the number of years before disclosure had ranged from 1 to 20 years, with an average of 11 years.

The amount of time that had elapsed since disclosure ranged from 1 week to 27 years, with an average of 5 or 6 years. Divorcees had stayed together anywhere from a few months to over 10 years after disclosure; most had separated within 5 years. Still-married wives had learned of the homosexuality anywhere from 1 week to 27 years earlier.

Children

The number of children the couples had ranged from 0 to 5. That children were important to them is suggested by the fact that the average was 2, with only one couple deliberately childless. Their children ranged in age from 6 months to over 21 years, with most under 16. A few couples were too recently married for children, or included wives who were pregnant or unable to conceive and in the process of trying to adopt a child.

Physical Appearance

In their book *The New Couple*, Nahas and Turley note that women attracted to homosexual men are often unfairly stereotyped as too obese or otherwise unattractive to find a heterosexual partner. My study supported their findings that such a stereotype was unfounded. As a group, the women in the study (and those who come to me for counseling) appeared no different from those who might be found in any other group.

A few were exceptionally attractive. None were exceptionally homely. One had extreme strabismus caused by blindness. Although this might have been expected to impair sexual attractiveness, it had not interfered with the woman's ability to find sexual partners. Some were slender and petite, others tall and stately, and still others mildly overweight. A few had been slightly embarrassed by their overweight during adolescence, whereas for others it had been no social barrier. Some, in their 50s, appeared matronly. Wedding photographs they showed me suggested that if anything, most had been quite attractive when young.

This was also true for five wives who were extremely obese. For one, obesity had been a serious problem throughout life. The others, however, had put on their weight during the period surrounding disclosure. This will be further discussed as a way of coping with the stress of that period.

The same lack of distinguishability was true for those husbands who were interviewed or described by others. I assessed one man, and one wife described her husband as appearing "slightly effeminate" upon introduction only. For the others, there seemed nothing to identify them as anything other than heterosexual men.

Intelligence and Personality

In contrast to the expectations noted earlier, the most striking feature of this group was that the women (and those husbands who were seen) seemed almost without exception highly intelligent, well educated, well read, articulate, assertive, and thoughtful. For the most part, they also seemed personable and self-confident. Most of those with only high school educations showed the same personal attributes. The only two who seemed more "average" came from distinctly lower socioeconomic milieus and mainly lacked the sophisticated self-assurance and vocabulary of the others. I might note, however, that following a speech on this study, a clinician reported having just received a request for help from a wife who described herself as retarded.* The level of intelligence in such couples, then, obviously covers as wide a range as can be found throughout society.

Asked to rate themselves on personality traits (differentiated from temporary feelings created by the marital situation), 80% rated themselves as above average in intelligence and self-confidence, and only 3% rated themselves as below average. Over 70% considered themselves above average in assertiveness and only 12% labeled themselves below average; 61% felt they were more and 24% less outgoing than others. Several rated themselves as exceptionally high on all those qualities. One wife had trouble in making the assessment, since she felt that prior to disclosure she had felt low in all qualities but considered herself high in all at the time I interviewed her.

Premarital Attitudes and Knowledge About Homosexuality

Over 65% of the wives knew "very little" about homosexuality prior to marriage or the disclosure of homosexuality; 7% knew little about it at marriage but had known "a lot" by the time of disclosure; 9% had "some" knowledge by the time disclosure occurred; and only 3% knew "absolutely nothing." Most wives had felt "neutral" about it before disclosure. The next largest group felt "slightly negative." The next was equally divided between "moderately negative" or "moderately positive," and the smallest number was equally divided between "very negative" and "very positive."

Heterosexuality of the Wives

Again, these wives did not appear to fit the expectations cited earlier. They were asked to rate themselves on the Kinsey Scale at three different points of time: (1) when they were married, (2) when

---

*This self-label should not be equated with lack of self-esteem. People with impaired intellectual functioning are often encouraged to thus identify themselves when calling for professional help, to alert the "helper" to the potential need for providing added patience, clarity, and perhaps assistance in getting to the office.

they learned of their husbands' homosexuality (i.e., the "disclosure" point), and (3) at the time of the study.

The Kinsey Scale is a 7-point scale with 0 representing exclusive heterosexuality, 3 representing absolute bisexuality (i.e., 50-50), and 6 representing exclusive homosexuality. A few wives went from 0-1-0 or 0-0-1 in their self-ratings on the basis of an occasional fantasy or dream. Two of those wives had one or two homosexual experiences following disclosure, and did not rule out the possibility of one in the future. Nevertheless, they considered themselves heterosexual. One wife was living in a lesbian relationship when interviewed. She was still legally married to her husband and had occasional sexual relationships with him. She considered herself primarily but not exclusively lesbian. With that exception, 97% of the wives rated themselves as exclusively or almost exclusively heterosexual.

Marital History

Again, expectations that most of the women had had a long history of marriages to gay men did not seem to fit this group. Very few had had previous marriages: only one had been married more than once. No previous marriage had been to a gay or bisexual husband. When interviewed, most divorced wives were still single. A few, however, had either married or were living with a heterosexual man. Unless they had been divorced only recently, most of the others were having occasional heterosexual affairs.

Expectations at Marriage

Almost all wives had married with the expectation that the marriage would be strictly monogamous. A few had allowed for the possibility that either partner might have an occasional heterosexual extramarital experience.

A few wives had known of their husbands' premarital homosexual experience. They either assumed that it had been part of adolescent experimentation or were told that the homosexuality no longer existed.

WIVES' LIFE HISTORIES

Most wives considered themselves products of traditional middle-class, upwardly mobile families with traditional values. Many had departed from tradition enough to have entered or planned careers before marriage, to have had premarital sex, or to have become more liberal religiously and politically than their parents had been. Most wives described good relationships with their parents, sisters and brothers, and peers. A few had not, and considered themselves "rebels." Nan provided a typical statement from a "traditional" woman:

> I was raised on Moon, June, and Croon. I believed in saving my sexuality for marriage. I believed in work, thriftiness, making money, and in the sanctity of marriage. I believed women found their fulfillment in serving their husbands and having children, whether or not they had educations or worked. I believed in nice houses, two children, a dog, and a white picket fence. In short, I believed in "The American Dream."

Even those who considered themselves rebels maintained some aspects of "the American Dream" (quoted here because so many women referred to it). However, they were more apt to recount experiences like those of Fran:

> I was the family "kook," doing things that were good for my own growth, but that the family did not understand. They just never knew what to do with me. They still don't. I stopped counting on them for emotional support by the time I was 10 years old.

Again contrary to expectations, only a few had had poor relationships with their parents and only a few had come from broken (or even unhappy) homes. Of those, three women departed from the norm dramatically in child or adolescent experiences. Their stories were each unique, with the only commonality the quality of an intensely complex novel.

Harriet's story, for example, could have been written by Lilian

Hellman. Harriet was born in Nazi Occupied Poland. Her mother had died when she was very little. She was protected from some of the horrors of war by being brought up in a Catholic convent. She had a good relationship with her father, whom she saw frequently, and considered her life in the convent happy. Her only remembered "horror" was that of witnessing a rape by a German soldier and being told by the nuns, when she tried to ask about it, to wipe it out of her mind and never mention it to anyone.

Harriet's father died when she was in early adolescence. At the end of the war, she was placed in a Russian labor camp. She was released after a year, when relatives who had emigrated to the United States sent for her. She arrived in upstate New York at the age of 16, spent a brief and unhappy time with her relatives, and then worked her way through higher education. She met her husband while she was in medical school and married him shortly after graduation.

Laura's story might have been written by Tennessee Williams. Laura's parents were part of the impoverished aristocracy of the Old South. Though they eventually divorced, they remained on good terms and Laura had a good relationship with each of them. She was sent not to college, but to finishing school, and "came out" as a debutante.

When she was 17, her mother "married her off" to a wealthy older man with the promise that he would take care of her financially and "be good to her" in exchange for her performance of "wifely duties." "Wifely duties," of course, included sex. When she complained to her mother and minister that she was simply being "used" and that she was unhappy, she was given sympathy but told that God expected her to serve her husband faithfully.

Over their protests, she divorced as soon as she was legally of age to do so, and promptly fell in love with and married a "bronzed Adonis" who swept her off her feet in a whirlwind storybook romance. He too was part of Southern aristocracy. Together they made mad passionate love and danced their way through Europe, with the rich and famous as their friends. She was too starstruck to realize how irresponsible he was. She worked, and he drank up most of the money she made. Becoming increasingly jealous and paranoiac about the men she met at work, he finally threatened her with a knife, accusing her of infidelity. She left him immediately. Although still in love with each other, he was too proud to reach out to her, and she had been taught that a lady never makes overtures to a man. Whether counseling might have solved their problems she does not know. As a "lady," she would not have presumed to suggest it.

A few years later, she had a sexual liaison with her employer, a kind and thoughtful man who had helped her through the aftermath of divorce, and who had become a good friend. When it resulted in pregnancy, the two agreed to marry. Although the sexual experience had not been a good one, Laura assumed that the problem was a temporary one. This would not be the storybook romance of her adolescence, she knew. But it would be a stable marriage based on affection. She entered her third marriage determined that she would be a good wife and mother and that this would be the traditional "till death do us part" marriage.

In contrast to Laura's tale of southern aristocracy, Iris's story seemed to have flowed from the pen of James Baldwin. Iris grew up in the black ghettos of Chicago's South Side. Her mother was the barely literate daughter of Alabama sharecroppers. Her father, however, was a well-educated teacher who, like most well-educated blacks at that time, was both underemployed and underpaid. He was determined, however, that his children would climb out of the ghetto and reach their potential.

Iris's father read her bedtime stories every night. They were not, however, stories of Peter Rabbit: they were tales from Greek mythology and Shakespeare. Her nursery rhymes were by Longfellow and Keats. By the time she was 10, she was imbued with the same thirst for knowledge and the same dreams that her father had.

Unfortunately, the combination of poverty, discrimination, and disparate personalities eventually took their toll on her parents. Both became increasingly emotionally disturbed. The mother began to suspect infidelity, and whether or not she was correct, she began to hallucinate. The father, despite his insistence that his children receive a good education, sent them all out to work at the age of 12. The marital relationship became marked by violence, with the children cowering under the bedclothes at night, listening to the sounds of abuse.

The parents divorced when Iris, at the age of 13, tried to intervene in a fight and was inadvertently punched by the father. Her mother was eventually placed in the State Hospital. Iris married at an early age to get away from her unhappy family, only to discover that her husband was both an alcoholic and a gambler. She stayed with him only long enough to earn enough money to support herself and then began saving money toward the education she both needed and wanted.

She met her husband through her sister, several years later. He, too, had grown up in the ghetto. He had been reared by strict and punitive grandparents who threw him out when he was 13. On the streets with neither money nor education, he had survived by granting sexual favors to men in exchange for money, food, lodging, and what little affection they were willing to provide.

When old enough, he had joined the Marines and started to renew his education. By the time Iris met him he too had begun college. He had become a "born-again" Christian, sure that God had saved him from his homosexual past. The two first became good friends and then fell in love. He was the kindest, most personable, most affectionate man she had ever known. When he asked her to marry him, she started the happiest period of her life. When I interviewed Iris, she had been married for 2 years. For the most part, they had been extremely happy. Then a week before my interview with her, her husband told her that in panic over an argument they had had, he had just had a homosexual liaison.

These stories are related not because they are typical, but because they (1) are more interesting than the "typical" stories I heard and (2) demonstrate the wide range of backgrounds and the seemingly innate strength some women seemed to have had even before marriage. The following descriptions, however, will more accurately describe the courtships and early marriages of the group as a whole.

Courtship and Marriage

Again, there seemed great variation with little to distinguish this group from any other group of middle-class, mainly college-educated women. Aside from the vignettes already given, a few had married childhood sweethearts after high school graduation; most had married college classmates after graduation from college. A few had met their husbands at work. Two high school teachers had married former students, one leaving an unhappy marriage to do so. One had met and married her husband while attending a school for the blind. Several couples met on blind dates or were introduced by friends. Many courtships evolved from friendships.

What qualities or attributes of the men had led to marriage? "Lack of sexism," clearly specified in some way as "different" from "other men" was one of the most common characteristics named. Fran's description, for instance, was similar to many others':

> He was not playing the big sex game that I found I couldn't break through with other men. We were friends as well as lovers. He was interested in me as a person, not as a sex object. Most men wanted sex first and then intimacy or maybe no intimacy at all. He wanted intimacy first. Sex was never an issue. It just gradually grew as our intimacy grew, very naturally.

Karen added another typical statement:

> He treated me as an intellectual equal in a way that few men do with women.

Such qualities as caring, sensitivity, kindness, loving, thoughtfulness, and gentleness were mentioned even more often. They usually accompanied "nonsexism," with a statement that these men were higher in such qualities than "most" men. Many women stated that those qualities were combined with "strength."

Women often mentioned such qualities as interesting, exciting, adventurous, a good sense of humor, and fun. Several included intelligence, creativity, and charm. Some named looks and physical attraction. Three women described many of these qualities but actually had married because of pregnancy. One had done so with considerable conflict. The other two, because of religious values, had seen no other option.

Several women could not label their reason for marriage and described what might be termed a "senior syndrome": they had reached graduation, everyone was marrying, it was "the thing to do." They had a good relationship with a man who shared their values; marriage seemed a logical conclusion. In their words,

> It was the expected step for fulfillment of the American Dream.

Aside from those who married because of pregnancy, only one woman, Gloria, listed a single reason such as sex or first chance:

> As an overprotected blind person in a strong Fundamentalist setting, I had had no opportunity for sex or even a decent relationship with boys. I was 19 and I was having the adolescent rebellion most kids have at 16. I was sexually "hot." I wanted sex, but I didn't want to go to Hell. When a sighted Christian (and a minister to boot) asked me to marry him, I grabbed the chance. It never occurred to me that he was marrying to be socially acceptable to the Church, just as I was marrying to have socially acceptable sex. We each told ourselves that we loved the other, but we really didn't.

The others had selected their husband because of specific qualities, as the best of several opportunities in potential mates.

Premarital Social and Sexual Experiences

Most women described good relationships with peers, although some had been rather shy during adolescence. As a group, the women tended to consider themselves sexually naive at marriage, mainly as a result of religious proscriptions against premarital sex and lack of adequate sex education. Many, if not most, had married long before premarital sex had become socially acceptable.

Nevertheless, some had had sexual experiences with others prior to meeting their husbands. Those experiences had ranged from "horrible" to "fantastic." Some had had their first sexual experience with their husbands prior to marriage. Of these, Laura was the only one to have found that experience unsatisfying, and she had married because of pregnancy.

Predisclosure Marriage

Marriages will be described here up to a point that could be called a "predisclosure buildup." Given the wide variations in number of years before disclosure and the highly individual variations, comparisons are difficult. Six overlapping kinds of marriages, however, can be defined:

1. The American Dream

These marriages were characterized by companionship, shared interests, clear and empathic communication patterns, good sexual relationships, and the general continuation of all the qualities in the husband that had attracted the wife in the first place. Dorothy gave a typical "American Dream" description:

> We had the American Dream! We had a big wedding, big, close families, a nice house, and a beautiful baby. Everything was perfect. I considered myself very fortunate. We had a good sex life, but we were best friends and playmates as well as lovers. We were very close. Sometimes we could sit up all night, just talking. I felt above a lot of our friends and neighbors, who all seemed to be having marital problems.

2. "American Dream, But . . ."

These marriages had most of the components of the earlier category, but either started going downhill gradually and almost imperceptibly or had a mild "but" attached. As Fran told me,

> . . . But I began to feel there was something missing. A sense of intimacy, I think. We could talk about everything in the world except about ourselves. And sex—he was superb mechanically, but sometimes I felt I was making love to a machine.

Sometimes the "buts" were purely about sex. Some wives described the sex as good but infrequent, others as loving but lackluster, with the wife nonorgasmic or the husband having erectile problems. The wife generally blamed herself or was blamed by the husband for what still seemed to be mild problems. Laura, for example, stated,

> I knew he had a problem from our premarital experience, and I certainly knew I'd satisfied other men. Still, I blamed myself. Homosexuality never occurred to me. I just thought I was doing something wrong. He told me nothing was wrong, I was just oversexed and he had more important things on his mind. But sex was our only problem. Otherwise our marriage was perfect.

Over half the marriages were described as fitting into one of these two categories.

3. Mixed, Up and Down

These marriages were characterized by "ups" that were very good and "downs" that were very bad, or that were very good in some respects, very bad in others. For example,

> We had ups and downs from the beginning. We'd married because of pregnancy, but our love quickly became very strong. Our sex was just okay at first, but then became great. But as the kids got older, he'd yell at them, and about every 6 months we'd have terrible fights about them, not about ourselves.

4. What Can I Say?

Descriptions of these marriages typically started with "What can I say?" and ended with a shrug of the shoulders and a laugh. They were characterized by poor communication, some bickering, and poor sexual relationships. Yet they were not really "bad" marriages, and the wives were so caught up in child care and work routines that they did not think of themselves as either happy or unhappy. As Nan put it,

What can I say? We fulfilled the American Dream in many
ways, and I was not unhappy, really. It was a good life, I
suppose, and I really don't have much to complain about. It
was just that I always felt an undercurrent of resentment and
criticism. I never could really put my finger on it. When it
came to sex, we were like spoiled children. We needed more
affection. We craved it. But we didn't know how to reach out
for it, and we stood in our respective corners and sucked our
thumbs. We were both at fault. And he called me frigid. I
resented it, but I began to believe it. I don't know what to say.

5. Horrendous

The milder end of the "horrendous" category was composed of
marriages that had once been "American Dreams." The change in
these marriages could not be described as a "predisclosure
buildup." Such a buildup period was usually of relatively short
duration, was moderate, and usually culminated in a voluntary disclosure.

A "horrendous" change, however, was a complete and baffling
behavior change that continued as long as the wife tolerated it. Although it possibly represented the beginning of homosexual activity, the husband appeared to have no intention of revealing his secret unless forced to do so and usually evaded direct questions or
lied in confrontations. The marriages became marked by verbal violence, an abrupt end to a formerly good sexual relationship, and
almost flagrant infidelity. Connie's description was typical:

I don't know what happened. The first 5 years were super, and
then things suddenly went downhill. We'd had fantastic sex.
Suddenly if I asked for sex more than every 3 months, he'd
accuse me of being a nymphomaniac. I knew that was non-
sense, so I thought something was wrong with me personally.
I adored him. I'd molded myself to fit his needs. I was liberal,
he was a John Bircher. So we agreed to not talk politics. I was
open to people. He didn't like that, so I stayed home, minded
my own business, and was there when he needed me. But he
stopped needing me. He began instructing me what to say and
not say at parties. I began to feel stupid, to lose self-esteem,

and to put on weight. First I suspected another woman, then homosexuality. But I couldn't prove anything. So I just concentrated on bringing up the children and dismissed my own ideas.

A few wives formed the last category, marriages that were horrendous from the moment of their inception. Gloria, the 19-year-old blind bride, for example, had the worst marriage in the group. Her description started,

> By 7:00 a.m. the first day, I knew I'd made a dreadful mistake. I'd taken the rest of my life and put it in the garbage can.

From there it was a downhill plunge.

Her husband, George, could not fulfill the heterosexual expectations of his wife or church. Sexual relations ended when George's desire for a pregnancy was achieved. By the time their infant was a month old, however, the major goal in Gloria's life had stopped being sex and had become one of survival. Gloria could not fulfill George's expectations of a housekeeper or mother. The result was wife beating, Gloria's eventual frightened and frustrated child abuse, and occasional self-defensive husband battering. When the child was finally placed in a foster home, both parents returned to school. As each became more educated and sensitized to gay and women's issues, and as George took another job and moved away from his ministerial duties, he became more sensitive to her needs. The marriage became better, then, as he moved toward disclosure. It almost achieved a semblance of happiness. But it remained more of a Hollywood melodrama than a marriage.

Only a few marriages fit into either of the "horrendous" categories. All but one of them represented a distinctly different socioeconomic and cultural milieu from the rest of the group and were held together purely by strict religious proscriptions against divorce and the wives' economic dependence on the husbands. All the husbands were described as having always been or having become stereotypic male chauvinists who chanted a similar refrain: "Don't ask questions! I do what I want and I go where I please. No woman tells me what to do!"

Two husbands had not admitted homosexuality by the time of the study, and one had done so only a week or two before the interview. All "horrendous" situations presented extreme examples of the issue to be discussed in Chapter 5: i.e., the difficulty in defining homosexuality and "disclosure" of homosexuality.

CONCLUSIONS

The existing literature, and as will be seen more in future chapters, the assumptions made by others, had suggested that women who marry gay or bisexual men differ from other women in having had poor family and peer relationships, low self-esteem and assertiveness, unattractiveness, latent lesbianism or asexuality, and a history of many marriages to gay men who could not possibly meet any of their needs.

If there was any "different" profile suggested by the study, however, it was one of a well-educated professional woman in a high socioeconomic status, who had had good family and peer relationships, who held at least "average" interest in heterosexuality, who was well able to attract heterosexual men, who rated herself (and appeared) highly self-confident and assertive, and whose predisclosure marital history had been that of one sustained and highly satisfying marriage. The only other noted group characteristic seemed to be an emphasis on nonsexism in choice of mate and a self-rated sexual naiveté at marriage. How "different" that naiveté was from that of other newlyweds, particularly in the era in which most of these women had married, is questionable. In a seeming paradox, there was also a wide range and high degree of diversity in both characteristics and experiences.

In short, although the expectations fit some women (as they might for any group of women), they appeared to be purely unwarranted stereotypes for the group as a whole. In general, there seemed little to distinguish this group from any other group of mainly, but not entirely, college-educated women.

Chapter 4

Emerging Perspectives
on Sexual Orientation

While the purpose of this book is not to discuss homosexuality itself, we can hardly consider the possibility of homosexuality within heterosexual marriage without a basic frame of reference. This chapter will first answer the questions I am asked most frequently about homosexuality and will then explore various perspectives on sexual orientation and its implications for marriage.

QUESTIONS AND ANSWERS

Q. *What is homosexuality?*

A. That sounds like a question with a simple, clear-cut, and obvious answer: homosexuality is being sexually attracted to members of one's own sex. The question is far from simple and clear-cut, however, for it has to do with the fact that (1) thoughts, feelings, and emotions are not behaviors; (2) thoughts, feelings, emotions, and behaviors can and do change frequently; (3) people can have contradictory feelings at the same time; and (4) feelings, emotions, and behaviors — even sexual ones — are not dictated purely by biology, but are highly affected by cultural and religious beliefs and social mores.

For example, many — perhaps most or even all — people are occasionally "turned on" by someone other than their own spouse: either a known person, a movie hero or heroine, or just some fantasied sex object. Does that sensation alone brand them as "unfaithful?" Many people have a warm, intimate, and loving relationship with someone of the opposite sex and may derive considerable sensual pleasure from backrubs, hugs, or caresses. Feelings may border on the erotic, but are never translated into actual sexual desire or action. Is that relationship to be considered a sexual relationship?

Some people are chocolate cake lovers and others are apple pie lovers. Do they go around calling themselves Chocolate Cakes and Apple Pies? Are they so labeled by others? Are their lives defined and ruled by their food preferences? Does preferring one automatically rule out enjoying the other? Of course not.

A ridiculous analogy? Perhaps, yet it points up the ridiculous logic often used when the issue is sexual orientation. For that matter, the analogy between food and sex turns out not to be so ridiculous after all, when we realize how culturally bound our definitions of morality are. One Polynesian culture, for example, felt that it was not immoral to be seen having intercourse, but that to be seen eating by the opposite sex was highly immoral. Since dining took place in a communal hall, women ate at one table and men at another, sitting back to back so that they would not see each other.

A continual problem, then, is how to define and measure homosexuality. Is it a sexual thought? An emotional feeling? A physiological response? A behavioral act? A lifestyle? Kinsey estimated that 37% (2 out of 5) white American males reach orgasm through at least one homosexual experience between adolescence and old age and that almost 50% have either overt experiences or fantasy or erotic reactions to another male at some point in their lives after the age of 16. Yet only 8% of those men become exclusively homosexual. More recent studies vary, some considering his figures too high, others too low, but they generally corroborate his findings that about 10% to 15% of the total population (around 25 million men and women in today's society) are bisexual: that is, they exhibit some combination of heterosexual and homosexual desire and activity. We'll discuss this further as it applies to marriage, but for now, let's go on to two other common pertinent questions.

Q. *What causes homosexuality?*

A. Clinicians and researchers have expended considerable time and money over the years trying to learn what causes homosexuality. Explanations come and go, regain popularity as some new piece of research revives interest in a discarded theory, only to be discarded again. There are explanations of hormonal imbalance, of chemical imbalance, of heredity and "different" gene structures. There are psychological explanations of poor parental modeling by an overly strong mother and a weak, shadowy father; of poor parental modeling by an overly strong father and a weak, shadowy mother; of deliberate behavioral "teaching" and "learning" through seduction and initiation into homosexuality by some unscrupulous "teacher"; of nondeliberate teaching and learning through the unconscious modeling of an ideal, caring, and ethical father or father figure who unconsciously acts as a model not by his homosexual behavior, but simply by being a person children want to emulate.

The truth is that despite all the research and all the explanations, nobody yet really knows what makes some people homosexual. For that matter, there is no clear explanation for what makes some people heterosexual. Possibly the most that can be safely said is that like other animals, human beings are born with the biological capacity to reproduce themselves, with enough biological urges or instincts and enough sensual gratification from the act of mating to ensure that it will take place.

Unlike other animals, however, human sexual urges and responses are not totally tied to the biological reproductive cycle and process. Men and women sexually attract and respond to each other whether or not the woman is in a fertile period. Sexual responses and behaviors are not purely instinctive. They are highly affected by emotion and intellect, varying considerably according to individual personalities and cultural mores. They often change from one locale and generation to another. They are frequently "sensual" in nature, providing physiological sensations to the right kind of "touch," for example, no matter who or what does the touching.

I do have my own hunch, based on my reading of research and history. That hunch is that human beings are all born with the capacity for bisexuality, but that we were taught not to pay attention to the homosexual side of that bisexuality because of the needs of earlier civilization. For example, biblical and prebiblical societies had limited technology and knowledge. They lacked the technology to see mothers safely through pregnancy and children through infancy. They needed many pregnancies to ensure societal survival.

But they often believed that men had only a limited supply of sperm and that if sperm were used up in such frivolities as masturbation or homosexual behavior, there would not be enough left to make the necessary babies. Hence rules against such behaviors found their way into social, political, and religious proscriptions.

Of course, each society has had its own variations, and modifications have appeared over time, but the society from which most Americans spring has largely held to those rules, despite the fact that we now need to decrease rather than increase our population and that both our knowledge and our technology is far more advanced.

I suspect that had we all been left to our own devices in earlier civilizations, we would all show some degree of bisexuality. The marvel may not be that so many have "learned" homosexuality, but that so many have done so well at "unlearning" it and that some people — for some reason or combination of reasons — are less easily molded. Perhaps the startling changes in societal needs, knowledge, and technology in the past century are simply leading us to the reclaiming of our natural bisexual capacity.

For now, that's simply an idea to ponder. A question of more immediate concern to people, however, follows.

Q. *Can a person's homosexuality be "cured" or "unlearned"?*
A. Sexual response comes from some combination of biological, intellectual, and emotional processes. We know that fact. We do not know the combination. Just as "explanations" for homosexuality have come and gone through the years, so have "cures." Some claims for cures come from religion. Some come from psychotherapy aimed at overcoming "diseased" psychodynamics of parent-child relationships. Others come from psychotherapy aimed at modifying specific behavioral responses through specific "learning" techniques that "train" people to respond positively to heterosexual stimuli, negatively to homosexual stimuli. Some therapists use a combination of techniques.

The results, based on research, have been neither satisfying nor conclusive. No matter what the technique, it seems to be a case of "sometimes the magic works, sometimes it doesn't." Some so-called cures last a lifetime, some for many years, some for only a short time. Many of the men in this study had supposedly been cured before marriage or vainly sought cures after marriage. Michael Ross, in a recent book *The Married Homosexual Man*, has cited convincing evidence that marriage itself does not cure homosexuality.

Perhaps the most we can say at this point is that when heterosexual expression has been hampered by anxiety, anger, misinformation, fear, and negative experiences, much can be done to erase those problems and enhance heterosexual expression. One important question raised by many therapists is not "How can we eliminate homosexuality?" but "Do we want to? Would it not be better to devote our attention to helping people enhance their sexual repertoire according to their own needs and abilities?"

NEW PERSPECTIVES ON HOMOSEXUALITY

We have taken a look at some specific questions and issues. Can homosexuality possibly be compatible with heterosexual marriage? Research focused on this issue is barely beginning. Out of the wealth of general literature and research on homosexuality, however, it seems to me that there are three major — often overlapping — perspectives that have emerged in somewhat historical fashion and that affect the issue of whether homosexuality and heterosexual marriage are compatible. Each perspective represents many writers and researchers and variations. I have oversimplified them and put them into categories that I will call Group A, Group B, and Group C.

Group A

Those who belong to Group A see heterosexuality and homosexuality as dichotomous, bipolar, and mutually exclusive: that is, they see the two sexual orientations at opposite sides of a pole, with the presence of one eliminating the possibility of the other. This is a black–white perspective. According to this view, one can no more be both homosexual and heterosexual than one can be "a little bit pregnant." One either *is* gay or *isn't*.

Group A people have a negative view of homosexuality. From a religious stance they consider it immoral; from a psychological perspective they consider it "abnormal" (that is, sick, pathological, unhealthy) — a disease to be cured either spiritually or through some kind of psychological therapy. Often, heterosexual marriage is seen as a curative step or as proof that a cure has been achieved. Anita Bryant and Jerry Falwell would be prime examples of the religious branch of Group A. Many Freudian therapists constitute the clinician's branch. (Some of Freud's followers may not realize, however, that in a now-famous letter to a distraught mother, Freud revealed his own uncertainty as to whether or not homosexuality should be considered a sickness.)

Group B

Kinsey was the originator and prime example of the Group B perspective. As was seen in the statistics cited earlier, he found that homosexuality and heterosexuality were neither bipolar nor mutually exclusive. He saw them as ranging along a continuum and devised what is known as the Kinsey Scale. Although the scale has limitations and new researchers are attempting modifications, it remains the standard by which "degrees of homosexuality" are measured.

The Kinsey Scale is a 7-point scale with "exclusive heterosexuality" at one end (0), absolute bisexuality in the middle (3), and "exclusive homosexuality" at the other end (6). Individuals are rated along this scale in the following way:

0 Exclusively heterosexual

1 Predominantly heterosexual, incidentally homosexual

2 Predominantly heterosexual, more than incidentally homosexual

3 Equally heterosexual and homosexual

4 Predominantly homosexual, more than incidentally heterosexual

5 Predominantly homosexual, incidentally heterosexual

6 Exclusively homosexual

A man who identifies himself as a "Kinsey 1," for example, would presumably have had no more than one or possibly a few homosexual experiences, fantasies, or erotic arousals, few homosexual friends, and his sexual experiences would be apt to be more out of curiosity than arousal. A Kinsey 2, however, would have more than a few. Sexual experiences would be based on some degree of sexual arousal, although not as deeply as felt in heterosexual experiences.

Kinsey's findings suggest that for at least 3 years between the ages of 16 and 55, 1 out of 4 white American men are "Kinsey 2s," 1 out of 6 are "Kinsey 3s," 1 out of 8 are "Kinsey 4s," 1 out of 10 are "Kinsey 5s," and 1 out of 13 "Kinsey 6s." Only 1 out of 26 are "Kinsey 6s" throughout their entire lives.

Of course, these are approximate figures that have been subjected to criticism. One problem in Kinsey's scale is that it does not really differentiate between such "psychic" responses as "love" versus "erotic feelings," and a "once in a lifetime" experience and "more than a few." Kinsey himself noted that his categories overlap and are ill defined. Moreover, in assessing an individual at any given point, his scale does not show changes over time. We only know from his other findings (corroborated by clinical experience) that such changes occur and that whereas some people are aware of homosexual responses in their earliest adolescence or preadolescence, others become aware of them late in life, sometimes only after a divorce or a spouse's death. I myself know men who discovered homosexual impulses only in their 60s or 70s.

No matter what its faults, Kinsey's data clearly showed that although lifelong exclusive homosexuality is relatively uncommon, some degree — a considerable degree — of homosexuality over the course of a lifetime, is not. Similarly, there is no way of knowing whether Kinsey's data on young married men who had had homosexual experiences within the preceding 5 years included simple premarital adolescent experimentation ("Kinsey 1" behavior). Kinsey's various studies, however, showed clearly that many married — supposedly "heterosexual" — men have homosexual experiences and fantasies before marriage, during marriage, and after marriage, falling somewhere between 0 and 6 on the Kinsey Scale at any given point.

One other feature of a Group B perspective, based on Kinsey's findings, is that homosexuality is seen less negatively. There are two branches within Group B. One is the "less negative" branch. Clinicians are more apt to view homosexuality as a "variant" behavior rather than a "pathological" one, to assess a person's mental health individually, and to try to "cure" the homosexuality only at the patient's request and if the homosexuality does appear to be harmful. Nevertheless, this attitude is little more than a softening of the Group A perspective and really depicts the "overlap" between Group A and Group B.

The real difference of a Group B perspective lies in the "positive" branch, in which homosexuality is truly seen as simply variant behavior. Not only is mental health judged individually, the homosexuality itself is never a criterion for making such a judgment. In fact, the presence of heterosexuality is sometimes judged a symptom of poor adjustment, for it is in this branch that the militant gay stance arises, bringing with it an ironic political alliance with Group A.

Dr. Fred Klein, in his book *The Bisexual Option*, points out the irony in a situation analogous to that of the clash between white supremists and black militants. Just as white supremists and black militants both argue that one drop of black blood in one's history renders a person "black," he notes, so the Moral Majority and gay militants both argue that one "drop" of homosexuality renders a person "homosexual."

Neither group, then, accepts the idea of "bisexuality," whether that bisexuality falls at the "Kinsey 3" midpoint or somewhere else between 0 and 6 on the Kinsey Scale. One group argues that the presence of any homosexuality indicates pathological inability to form satisfying heterosexual relationships, the other that the presence of any heterosexuality indicates either political cowardice or pathological denial of one's "true" homosexuality.

Group C

The newest group, Group C, with Dr. Klein as its originator, starts where Kinsey stopped and is still evolving. Pointing out the deficiencies in the Kinsey Scale, researchers and clinicians in this group, to varying degrees, are apt to have both a positive view of homosexuality and an even more positive view of bisexuality (although few consider a truly 50-50 split possible or even "good"). To some extent, they are trying to improve the Kinsey Scale.

Some in this group, however, raise the question, "Unless there is an immediate practical need for such an assessment, why bother? Why not do away with all labels and categories? They really don't mean anything. Often even self-labels have more to do with political pressure or our society's need to pigeonhole people into nice neat little categories than they do with reality. Why not simply declare people sexual and help them enhance their sexual repertoire according to their needs and wishes?" One recent study, in fact, found that individual degree of "sexuality" was more important than degree of "homosexuality" in dictating the sexual behavior of bisexual men. Those who were more heterosexually active were also more homosexually active; those who were less sexual homosexually were also less sexual heterosexually.

In general, Group C people see bisexuality as covering a broad range of behaviors and relationships that are subject to many changes over time, with many possible combinations and permutations. One person may be exclusively homosexual for awhile, then exclusively heterosexual. Another may have concurrent homosexual and heterosexual relationships. The same pattern may represent emotional "health" for one person, may be a symptom of emotional "illness" for another, and may be completely irrelevant in assessing the mental health of a third.

ATTITUDES TOWARD GAY/STRAIGHT MARRIAGE

As might be expected, the ironic alliance of Group A and Group B in attitudes toward bisexuality leads to the same alliance in attitudes toward gay/straight marriages and particularly toward straight wives in such marriages. Members of both groups are likely to take the stance that homosexuality, no matter what the degree, is simply not compatible with heterosexual marriage. Group B writers would say that men who marry despite some degree of homosexuality do so because of social pressure and inability to come to grips with their homosexuality; writers in both groups would say that women who knowingly or inadvertently marry such men do so for some neurotic reason.

For example, Myra Hatterer, a Group A clinician (1976, p. 275-8) reported on a group of wives of husbands in treatment to cure their homosexuality:

> The women felt inadequate in . . . their gender and erotic identifications; they demonstrated sexual repression, passive–aggressive personality traits, and retarded psychosexual and social development. . . . The wife's need to maintain the neurotic contract of the marriage undermines her husband's treatment.

Brian Miller, a Group B clinician and researcher (1979, pp. 544-52) discussing the reactions of wives and children to a disclosure of homosexuality, wrote:

> Wives tended to be the least accepting. . . . This . . . is explainable by reference to the homosexual denial system. . . . Wives—for economic, ego, and social reasons—tend to deny numerous clues indicating their husband's homosexuality. . . . When this elaborate denial facade is exposed, the wife's confrontation with her own self-deception as well as her husband's deceit is frequently devastating.

The two authors, representing totally opposite views of homosexuality, had arrived at essentially the same views of the wife.

A Group C perspective, however, is more apt to consider such marriages as potentially viable, depending on the reason for the marriage and the ability to lead an unconventional lifestyle. Group C writers find no evidence that when freed from stigmatization, such marriages are more "neurotic" than any others or that the essential ingredients for a satisfying relationship are different from those of a heterosexual relationship.

There seems to be some historical evidence that homosexuality can be compatible with heterosexual marriage, for not all societies have translated their early need for reproduction into the antihomosexual stance that American society has. Dr. Erwin Haeberle (1977) notes that in ancient Greece, where homosexual love was exalted, extramarital homosexual love relationships were common but did not interfere with marriage. Similarly, in feudal Japan, the quintessentially masculine Samurai frequently had homosexual relationships without interfering with the relationships with their wives.

That's not to say that those societies should be our models — they were the epitome of male chauvinist societies, and today's wife would hardly wish to trade places with the wives of ancient Greece or Japan. It does suggest, however, that having homosexual experiences does not prevent men from sexual functioning in heterosexual marriages.

More modern-day equivalents can be found. When the first three couples I interviewed all turned out to have been in the Peace Corps (in three related although different cultures), I was fascinated by the coincidence and asked a (gay) friend and former Peace Corps volunteer if he could offer an explanation.

He told me that in all three cultures (which he knew well), single young men and women slept in segregated dormitories and that when married men had to work at considerable distance from their villages, they too slept on floors in dormitories. With the close physical contact came frequent — albeit accidentally initiated — homosexual acts. Although such acts were never discussed, neither were they considered anything unusual or improper. The next day single men simply went back to their girlfriends, married men to their wives.

The only ones to be disturbed were the American Peace Corps volunteers, who often had their first homosexual experience in this situation, who were guilt ridden and devastated at the realization that they could be homosexually aroused, and who then were apt to have heterosexual erectile difficulties that they ascribed to homosexuality. Many marriages disintegrated in the Peace Corps, he said, and a number of suicides occurred simply from the stress of Peace Corps living. But some disintegrations were aided, he felt, by the difference in cultural assumptions about heterosexuality and homosexuality.

It would seem logical that reactions to a disclosure of a husband's homosexuality would be affected by the perspective not only of both partners but also of their peer and professional reference groups. As we shall see, that is exactly what happened.

I should note at this point that from now on, I shall use such words as "homosexual" (or "gay") and "bisexual" as if they were synonomous. It seems safe to assume that most of the men in this study were bisexual to some degree, falling somewhere between 0 and 6 on the Kinsey Scale. Nevertheless, a few men could be presumed Kinsey 6s. To continually differentiate will become cumbersome. Since it was the homosexuality, not the heterosexuality that was the issue, unless I specify to the contrary or the context itself makes a clear differentiation, please bear in mind that the terms "homosexual" and "bisexual" will be used as "catchalls": I will be referring solely to the husband's actual homosexual feelings or behaviors, no matter where he might fit on the Kinsey Scale.

Chapter 5

Coming Out:
Disclosures and Reactions

This chapter will explore the various ways in which the wives had learned of the homosexuality ("disclosure"), the types of disclosure found, and the reactions each had produced. Before continuing, however, a closer look at the term "disclosure" is necessary.

DISCLOSURE: EVENT OR PROCESS?

When the study was designed, the research questions related mainly to how wives had reacted to the disclosure of homosexuality, whether or not it was a crisis, and how they had adjusted. The basic interest was in issues such as (1) What was the situation like as a whole? What was it like to live with a man who was more or less homosexually oriented? (2) Did *knowing* about it change things? If there were marital problems, did they stem from the homosexuality itself or the *knowledge* of the homosexuality? Did disclosure help or hurt? (3) Could a wife accept and adjust to the homosexuality?

What was not realized, however, was that at times consciously and at times unconsciously, the total approach to the situation had been based on the same assumptions that other writers seem to have used. In some cases, they may have seemed logical assumptions, but they were in fact, simplistic, misleading, and often simply inaccurate.

It had been assumed, for instance, that disclosure would be a single *event* that would clearly reveal the fact of the husband's homosexuality, the degree of his homosexuality, and what it would mean for the future. It had been assumed that one could evaluate the total situation, the effect of disclosure, and the wife's ability to accept homosexuality simply by specifying the disclosure date and examining the situation before and after. It had also been assumed that if a crisis was found, it would be relatively short lived (usually a few months, but at most under 5 years), with a clear-cut beginning, middle, and end.

Moreover, even though such notions had been intellectually rejected, the planning had nevertheless been based on the idea that not only is homosexuality easy to identify, it is also simple to differentiate between homosexuality and bisexuality. Finally, it had been assumed that the immediate reaction would depend mainly on the wife's ability to accept homosexuality or bisexuality and that subsequent events would be based on her reaction to that one single disclosure and how well she had adjusted to it. I am now convinced that failure to go beyond such assumptions had resulted in serious misinterpretations of wives' reactions by many husbands, counselors, and the researchers quoted in Chapter 3.

For some women, some of those assumptions were correct. For many, however, disclosure was less an event than a process of growing awareness, punctuated by specific events often separated by long periods of time. For many, there were two or more separate disclosures. Each one differed in nature and hence resulted in different reactions and consequences. The total process might take just a few months for one wife, over 20 years for another.

An analogy can be drawn with the realization that one had built a house in a geological fault area. The knowledge could come about in many ways, either gradually or suddenly, with only one "event" or many. Each tremor or quake might differ in intensity and nature, with its own life cycle and effects. No single event necessarily demonstrated the total effect of living in such a region. Unless or until the occupant moved away or died, neither the final consequences nor the time it took to reach them could be determined.

Whereas faults and quakes held common elements, each area, house, and set of inhabitants differed. For a few women, by the time an "official" disclosure had taken place, the marital house had crumbled and the health of its inhabitants had been shattered. Disclosure was purely a formality: a way of obtaining emotional closure by confirming that the damage had been related to seismic activity.

Problems of "labeling" complicated the process. Just what is homosexuality? Is it a behavior or a lifestyle? Is it a static condition or a changing one? If a behavior, how many behaviors does it take to indicate homosexuality? Such issues were real problems for most wives and often the husbands themselves, both before and after an initial disclosure or disclosure-like event.

Sometimes even an official disclosure by the husband occurred in a "cognitive vacuum." It held so little meaning for the wife, or was so far removed in time from its real consequences, that it was hardly considered a disclosure. Several women were unable to decide whether disclosure was the point at which some event had focused attention on *possible* homosexuality, the point at which the homosexuality had been officially confirmed, or the point at which a subsequent event had given an earlier disclosure meaning.

Although the word "disclosure" will continue to be used for lack of a better term, it should be interpreted loosely not as "the" event, but as one of many, to be viewed within its particular context at its particular time. Initial disclosures often held the most impact and often were indeed crisis situations. Most wives emphasized, however, that it was less the fact of disclosure that was important than the actual content of that disclosure and the context in which it occurred. This will be further discussed later, but in view of the problems just stated, it seems appropriate to describe the clues to homosexuality when one had *not* been told that it existed, and the various ways in which an official or a sharp disclosure took place.

Clues to Homosexual Interest or Activity

The few women who actually began to suspect homosexuality described a beginning pre-awareness period of having "funny, vague feelings," "a sense of something going on, without being able to define it." As Nan, a 40-year-old businesswoman put it,

> . . . I really couldn't pinpoint what was wrong. Just a feeling of resentment toward me . . . toward women in general . . . over-solicitousness with male students who lived with us. Not seductiveness, he has far too much integrity for such a thing. Just over-solicitousness, depression when they left . . . it just seemed he was overreacting. . . . I never could put my finger on it.

Only three women reported child molestation on the part of their husbands. Elizabeth, one of those three, described "gut feelings" that led to suspicion of homosexuality:

> . . . I don't know, just being uneasy in certain situations, finding myself *watching*, yet not knowing why. Like, he had a habit of touching. At first young boys, but later girls and women too. A mixed bag. And nothing really wrong, just a stance he'd assume so his elbow would touch a person. Nothing I could put my finger on, but when you see this happen over and over again, you start making connections.

"Funny feelings" became more focused as a wife began to realize that social life was becoming centered around male, unmarried, and sometimes homosexual friends rather than heterosexual couples. Still, awareness generally remained at a low level. If defined at all, it flickered in and out of consciousness with passing thoughts that were instantly dismissed as bigoted, stereotyping, and irrational.

Sometimes awareness grew in sudden flashes of insight. An incident, remark, or bit of information in a class or book might trigger thought about some past incident or behavior. Karen, for example, when reading an article about police entrapment, suddenly remembered what she had thought was mail from the police department about an unpaid traffic ticket. Her husband's defensiveness had seemed strange, but had been quickly forgotten. Years later, the article made her wonder about it again. Hallie, who was particularly unsophisticated regarding homosexuality, reported a similar incident:

> . . . I was reading in this magazine about how some gays shave their body hair. Then I remembered my husband did that once. He said he had a rash and he didn't want sex for awhile. I couldn't see a rash. But I didn't want sex then, anyhow. I was upset about the affairs he was having with *women!* So homosexuality never occurred to me till that article. Then I remembered about how he called out his cousin's name in his sleep, and how upset he was when his cousin moved away, and it started me thinking.

Unless or until such thoughts were supported by other evidence, they were usually dismissed as disloyal, ridiculous, and crazy.

Perception grew sharper with unexplained absences, late nights at the office, secrecy about outside activities, or late-night partying with "the boys." Occasionally, the discovery of gay pornography or a specific event held the impact of a disclosure without eliminating all doubt. Connie, for example, had grown increasingly suspicious. When her husband lied about having had guests in the house while she was out of town and then brought a new "friend" to dinner and she could "sense the electricity between them," she confronted her husband. He told her she was crazy, always jumping to conclusions.

Such events usually led to a confrontation that resulted in an official disclosure. If the confrontation was met with evasiveness, half-truths, or outright denials and anger, as they had with Connie, the wife reported feeling shame, guilt, and "craziness." A few wives withdrew for fear of making the situation worse, but by then there was usually so much tension between them and so much suspicion that the wife took stronger steps to learn the truth.

Sexual problems might be expected to provide clues, but usually did not. Problems were often attributed to the settling in of middle marriage, a difficult pregnancy, or the aftermath of surgery, or most often, the wife's inhibitions and sexual incompetence. The wife's requests for marital or sexual counseling were usually turned down or given a one-shot try to help "her" with "her" problems. The tendency for both partners to blame the wife was discussed earlier.

These clues, of course, were reported by those women who had indeed had some suspicion. Most, however, reported no suspicion at all prior to an initial disclosure, some only "a little," and only about 10% had become highly suspicious.

How Could a Wife Not Know?

Given some seemingly obvious clues, the question arises why it took some wives so long to pinpoint their suspicions or to confront their husbands. As noted earlier, most of the literature had stressed the "denial" and "self-deception" of wives. Many men interested in the study asked about it. One man reported that he had "told" a friend about his own homosexuality when she was "ready to know." She had known all along, he stated. She asked about it when she was "ready to hear." Other men (never women) asked, "If a wife wondered, why didn't she just ask? Wasn't her unwillingness to ask an expression of homophobia* and a denial of the homosexuality?" Because the issue of "self-deception" affected the wives' self-esteem so deeply, it merits special attention.

When the wives were asked about it, a few agreed that they had deceived themselves and a few were uncertain. An overwhelming majority, however, emphatically disagreed. Those few who agreed (and interestingly enough, they were the only ones who could be called truly homophobic) ascribed their self-deception to their own "neurosis." It was hard to evaluate their assessment. One or two gave ample evidence that it had been accurate, one or two did not, and two letter writers simply volunteered the opinion without saying why.

Laura, who had been taught that a "lady" avoids confrontations at all cost, gave one of the few examples of true denial. Walking into her study during a party, she found her husband engaged in a homosexual act. Unnoticed and in shock, she both literally and figuratively shut the door on the scene and wiped it out of her mind. For years she continued to blame herself for their marital/sexual problems. Her husband's increasing alcoholism and emotional deterioration finally forced her to face reality and leave what had become an untenable marriage. She has never confronted her husband with her knowledge of the homosexuality. As will be seen, both partners' inability to discuss the issue led to a particularly tragic situation.

Laura presented the example of harmful inability to face reality. Denial, however, was not always harmful. For Gloria, the blind and battered young bride, a brief period of denial was perhaps the most useful, appropriate reaction possible. Despite her handicap and with minimal help, she had managed to put herself through through college, gain a Master's degree and then her PhD. While finishing the PhD, she failed to "hear" her husband's increasingly strong hints. One night, while studying for her comprehensive exams, she threatened to lock her husband out if he went "out with the boys," even

---

*The word "homophobia" has come to mean irrational fear of homosexuality and prejudice or bigotry toward homosexuals.

though she had still not truly perceived the homosexuality. She presented the picture of a woman trying desperately to stave off the wolf of one more crisis at the door until she had finished coping with the one at hand.

Despite those few examples, by far the most common response to the idea of "denial" was outright rejection of such an idea. Even those who expressed uncertainty felt that they had faced the homosexuality as well as circumstances would allow. Most women noted that in retrospect, there had been clues that they had failed to recognize. To have assumed at the time that they were symptoms of homosexuality, however, would have been entirely inappropriate, the wives declared. They expressed annoyance and even anger about what many women termed "Monday morning quarterbacking." To the extent that it was possible to make an accurate determination, the wives' own assessments seemed honest, thoughtful, reasonable, and to show a high degree of insight into their own behaviors both before and after an initial disclosure.

It is important to realize that reported clues to homosexuality did not occur in a vacuum, but within the context of a total relationship. Sometimes they were so subtle that they appeared obvious only in retrospect and had been obscured by an unusually positive marital relationship. Sometimes more obvious clues were lost in the intricacies of a chronically poor or rapidly deteriorating marriage, with verbal or physical violence of more immediate concern. Often such factors as severe illness or a handicapped child's needs diverted attention.

Sometimes it was impossible to tell whether suspected infidelity was homosexual or heterosexual. Whether deliberately or inadvertently, the husbands usually let the suspicion of heterosexual infidelity stand. Several husbands had gone to considerable effort to hide their homosexual activity. Others, whether deliberately or not, paved the way for disclosure by bringing home books on homosexuality, discussing the topic, supporting gay causes, etc. Either way, they were often genuinely amazed (and sometimes never believed) that their wives had not recognized the homosexuality. Yet such so-called "clues" were entirely appropriate for the husband's profession, a class he was taking, the couple's social/political milieu, or even just the increased public curiosity about homosexuality following the rise of the gay liberation movement.

One might suspect that like children (or even adults) with a guilty secret, the husbands imagined that their secret was written across their foreheads like a scarlet letter and that their wives could read their minds. Such a notion is understandable, but it is the magical thinking of childhood. Women may have achieved considerable intuitive skill over the years, but they are not mind readers.

Even when the wives' suspicions had focused on homosexuality, the question raised by some exclusively gay men — "If the women were wondering, why didn't they just ask their husbands?" — seems incredibly naive, especially when such men were likely to have just finished discussing how difficult "coming out" had been for them and how they had suffered from the reactions of homophobic heterosexual men. Surely it could not be so difficult to understand the fear and risk involved for a wife to ask her husband without being very sure of the answer.

Heterosexual men in today's society simply do not take kindly to being asked if they are homosexual. If a wife was wrong, she risked truly hurting a man she loved through stereotyping or guilt by association. She risked punishing him for behavior and values she admired. She risked ruining a good marriage. If the marital relationship was poor, with the husband "macho" and homophobic, she risked making the situation worse. A few women were truly afraid of violence if they proved to be wrong.

Some religious women were so unknowledgeable about sex and homosexuality that the thought never occurred to them. It is important to remember here that many of these wives had married — and the problem had cropped up — long before the sexual revolution and gay liberation movement had provided information that now seems basic. Moreover, neither knowledge about sex or homosexuality, nor of a husband's past homosexual activity proved helpful in detecting subsequent secretive activity. Those most knowledgeable knew that homosexual experimentation in adolescence is reasonably common and hence attached little importance to it. Often a husband's therapist had told him that the homosexuality had been cured. Often such a cure seemed verified by the couple's satisfactory sexual relationship both before and after marriage. Although wives whose husbands had revealed earlier experiences were more sensitized to the possibilities, they also worried that they might be overreacting and that questioning their husbands might incur guilt or anger and cut off communication. To the factors that had confused them earlier was now added guilt about rewarding honesty with suspicion and doubt.

Finally, some wives like Connie *did* "ask" and received less than honest answers. Some wives sought professional help once they pinpointed their concerns. As will be seen in Chapter 8, such guidance was seldom helpful and in three cases was so harmful that it served as a further deterrent to confrontation.

In short, except for a few cases, there seemed little to warrant the blanket assumptions of denial found in the literature or suggested by people who asked about the study. This will be discussed further in the concluding chapter, after we've seen how this issue continued to plague wives following disclosure.

How an Official Disclosure Occurred

Official disclosures might occur in a number of ways. Given in the order usually (but not always) from least stressful to most stressful, they are as follows:

1. The husband voluntarily told his wife.
2. The husband told when pressured by the wife's questions.
3. The wife discovered incriminating evidence like a love note or gay pornography, confronted her husband, and he then revealed homosexual interest or activity.
4. The husband told when forced to because of an arrest, job dismissal, or venereal disease.
5. The wife was told by another person, sometimes the husband's lover, and the husband, either sensing the situation or pressured by the lover, then "voluntarily" told her.
6. The wife was told by or in the presence of another person, usually a professional, with the husband admitting homosexuality after years of denying it. One variation was that a wife received confirmation of her suspicions, but the husband never admitted anything. Either way, such a disclosure sometimes relieved the wife's tension, rather than adding to it.
7. The wife discovered the husband in a homosexual act.

TYPES OF DISCLOSURES, IMMEDIATE REACTIONS, AND FACTORS LEADING TO THOSE REACTIONS

With all these ways of learning about the homosexuality, then, it seems obvious that it's simply not enough to ask how a wife reacted to disclosure. Many factors other than the homosexuality itself were important. Reactions to any given disclosure depended on (1) the past context from which it had stemmed, (2) its content and immediate context, (3) what occurred next, and (4) what other stresses and/or stress-relieving supports were present. Of course, individual personalities and attitudes toward homosexuality were also important. Those factors will be discussed, but it is my opinion that they seemed to play far less a role in immediate reactions than the factors listed above. So let's take a closer look at those factors.

A reminder might be in order at this point. Only the wife's viewpoint is being presented. So if a factor is said to be "the degree of the husband's concern for the wife" or "the quality of the marriage," remember that this really refers to how the wife *perceived* the husband or the quality of marriage.

Context

Context refers to the past and present nature of the marriage and the way a disclosure was seen as either potentially or actually changing that nature. "Nature" refers to such factors as predisclosure "style" and "quality."

For example, was the style that of a traditional sex-role stereotypic marriage with the wife dependent on the husband for emotional, social, and sexual gratification? To what extent was the wife economically self-sufficient? What were the power relationships between the two partners? What values were held about homosexuality, monogamy, fidelity, or divorce?

Definition of the word "quality" was based on both verbal and nonverbal communication patterns. Was the husband seen as honest and supportive or withdrawn, critical, and dishonest? How affectionate was the husband toward the wife? How committed did she think he was to her? How satisfying did she think the sexual relationship was for both of them? What was the quantity and quality of the recreational time they spent together?

The immediate context of the disclosure included the way it had come about and the attitudes and feelings the husband displayed. For example, had the disclosure been voluntary or forced? Was the husband showing understanding and concern for the wife's feelings? Or was he blaming her for the homosexuality? The surrounding context included such factors as the wife's vulnerability because of other stressful situations and both the access to and use of a stress-relieving support system. For example, a transitional point of marriage like childbirth or even marriage itself, as in Mary McDermott's case, the rearing of a handicapped child, the death of a parent, or the problems of Peace Corps living added to the wife's vulnerability and stress. Were there friends, relatives, or professionals the couple could turn to for help? Did the couple do so? And were those people truly helpful?

"What came next" went hand in hand with the content of a disclosure. It included the degree to which the husband's behavior and attitudes maintained, improved, or decreased the wife's estimate of the quality of her marriage or her own self-esteem and happiness.

Content

The content of any given disclosure contained the husband's statement or the wife's perception of the degree and nature of his homosexual interest or activity. For example, was his homosexual expression limited to fantasy? Was he having uninvolved sex or an intense love relationship? How frequent was his activity and how much did it interfere with the marital relationship?

Content also included the stated and perceived degree of emotional/sexual commitment to the wife and the degree to which the marital contract had been violated. For example, did the husband want to stay married or did he want a divorce? Had he told her as soon as he had come to grips with his own feelings? Had he carried on clandestine activity for years with guiltless breaking of the marriage contract? Had he known about the homosexuality at marriage without ever intending to be either honest or sexually faithful?

If the disclosure was a second or later one, content might include a change in status like a rise in the frequency of sexual activity, a change from uninvolved sex to a love relationship, or a request to bring a lover into the marriage. It might include a change in the commitment to the wife, ranging from a partial withdrawal to a request for divorce. It might include a betrayal of an already rene-gotiated sexual contract. "What came next" was dependent partly on the wife's own personality and behaviors. But from her point of view, what was important was the degree of commitment to and concern for her, and the kind of emotional support she received.

All of these factors affected not only the wife's specific reaction to a disclosure, but the marriage, the wife's self-esteem, her general happiness, her sexual satisfaction, and her general functioning and mental health. No one factor dictated her reactions, but rather how the various factors fit together to form a constellation. The factors were constantly interwoven, with any given factor sometimes pro-ducing paradoxical results. For example, two wives might have seen their predisclosure marriage and the sexual relationship as high in quality. That perception might serve to decrease stress with wife A but add to shock and increase stress with wife B.

I can't stress the complexity and interweaving of factors enough, because I keep running into descriptions and interpretations of wives' reactions based on the assumption that all disclosures are the same and that the wife's reactions stem simply from her attitudes about homosexuality. The inaccuracy of such an idea will be dem-onstrated in the following examples of the various types of constel-lations and we will see how reactions could be predicted by the constellation, rather than by the wives' personalities or beliefs.

TYPES OF DISCLOSURE AND THE IMMEDIATE REACTIONS THEY PRODUCED

The types of disclosure have been labeled according to the kinds of constellations formed by the combination of factors. They ranged along a continuum from "positive" (relatively speaking, that is) to "very negative." There was considerable overlapping, however, so that a particular example may not fit its label in every respect.

Positive Disclosures

A particular disclosure was considered positive if it was voluntarily given, arising within the context of a good marriage, if the content was of fantasy or infrequent and recent homosexual activity, and if there was expressed and perceived concern for, empathy with, and commitment to the wife. There were some variations. What would ordinarily be a very negative disclosure, for instance, might have been put into the positive realm because of the husband's renewed commitment to the wife or because the disclosure spelled potential improvement in the marital relationship. Most positive disclosures were initial ones, but occasionally a later one might remain positive or even be more positive than the earlier one had been.

Occasionally, a positive disclosure was so mild that the reaction was what I call a "cognitive blank." It simply held no meaning for the wife, and she did not know how to react to it. It was like being told a story or joke and not being sure one had understood the punch line. Sue Johnson, for example, with her "I don't get it, what's the big deal?" reaction was a good example of the cognitive blank:

> I could see he was distressed, but I couldn't see what all the fuss was about. He hadn't done anything, he didn't seem to be planning anything to hurt the marriage, and I couldn't understand either his need to tell or why he was so frightened about telling me.

Jessie's husband had told her about being vaguely aware of interest in other men during adolescence, experiencing an upsurge of attraction, and wondering how she would feel if he had an occasional experience. She had been "surprised but not shocked," understanding, and willing to let him try it out if he needed to. "It wasn't denial or martyrdom," she told me, "it was naiveté. I simply had no conception of how it might affect our sex life or marriage." In such cases, immediate stress was so minimal that it held only the slight apprehension expressed by the typical statement, "If others get so upset and he's so frightened, what's wrong with me that I'm not? Is there something I don't know?"

Sometimes an initial disclosure was either deliberately or unintentionally placed in such a context that it was diluted or almost obliterated by other stimuli. Cathy and Bill, after 12 years of an "American Dream" marriage, were on their way home from a party with a gay friend:

> He was telling me how great I was, how much he loved me, how he could even tell me he was gay and I wouldn't be upset. Somewhere he threw in a small "Because I am, you know." But he was very drunk, we were both laughing, and I really thought he was just drunk and babbling. I honestly didn't think he was gay or even that he thought he was. I bet he's even forgotten about it. It didn't come up again for 2 years. He'd been upset. I'd thought it was about business. He said he needed to get away for a vacation. He was going to visit our gay friend who'd moved to San Francisco. That's when I realized, without being told, that he was going to try out the gay life.

In both types of cognitive-blank situations, the first event was hardly perceived as a disclosure and was forgotten unless or until subsequent events or a new disclosure gave it meaning. As Jessie told me,

> Even though I told him he could try it out if he really wanted to, he didn't. We had a really good marriage and nothing changed one way or another. He never mentioned it again for 20 years, and I forgot all about it.

A more common form of positive disclosure, however, followed a predisclosure buildup of tension and was either the first disclosure or the followup to the cognitive-blank situation. It was usually based on guilt about fantasy, secretive homosexual activity, or a "close encounter" that forced the husband to recognize and deal with his desires. Whether the buildup was gradual or sudden, it was usually marked by some degree of marital friction, the husband's withdrawal and irritability, and often both partners' depression. Depending on how much the wife had been blamed or blamed herself, she often suffered loss of self-esteem during this period. Some women half expected the husband's request for a "serious talk" to be the announcement of "another woman" and a request for a divorce.

Occasionally, it was the wife who brought things to a head. Brenda's husband, for instance, started to tell her and lost his nerve. Suddenly making the connection between his anxiety and the books on homosexuality that she'd thought were for his psychology class, she herself helped him voice his concerns. A few disclosures had no buildup at all and came as a complete surprise.

The content of a positive disclosure might reveal pure fantasy or simply a desire for closer nonsexual relationships with men. The husband might be asking for a cure or revealing fantasies and promising not to act on them. Most often, he was asking for a change in the sexual contract to allow for homosexual activity.

No matter what the variations, *all* positive disclosures were accompanied by the husband's own guilt and anxiety, concern for the wife's feelings, at least a reasonable amount of empathy for them, and distress over causing her pain. They included reassurance that she was not at fault, that she was sexually attractive, that he had always loved her, still did, and wanted to stay married to her if she was willing. Usually, they showed evidence of advance planning and sensitivity to "timing."

Immediate Reactions

The most typical immediate reactions to such disclosures were mild shock or "stun" reactions in which the wife saw the situation as a "challenge" or "opportunity" that offered a possible explanation for and solution to a problem. Arlie, a very unconventional young woman, came home from a short trip, for example, to find,

> . . . a wall between us, not like anything we'd ever had before. I thought he was having an affair with my best friend. For a month I was miserable! When he told me finally that it was a *man*, I was almost relieved—and maybe even a bit titillated. Even when he brought a lover home! It seemed like an adventure! I thought we'd be a new kind of family. It was exciting! I never thought we'd be a 'picket fence' type of couple!

Fran, on the other hand, was a more conventional woman. Her husband had merely talked about adolescent experiences, a recent "close encounter," and the desire for a contract that allowed them each to have occasional extramarital experiences while away at business conventions. She viewed the disclosure as a "breakthrough in communication and another chance at the intimacy I'd begun to feel was lacking in our marriage."

Intellectual functioning, however, was almost always impaired. Wives set up instinctive priorities. Just enough questions were asked to determine that they had done nothing wrong and that the love and commitment were still intact. Then attention was mainly focused on maintaining (or feigning) enough calm to help relieve the husband's often severe stress.

This might take the form of a deliberate "nonreaction" designed to reassure the husband. It often included getting back to normal routine and conversation as quickly as possible or retiring to sort out in private the myriad of conflicting emotions that had already begun to descend.

Mild shock was helpful to the extent that it prevented impulsive decisions and allowed time for "processing" the situation. It was harmful to the extent that it delayed obtaining pertinent information and coming to grips with feelings. Both stunned and deliberate "nonreactions" also came back to haunt many wives whose husbands misinterpreted their seeming calm as "not minding" or "denial."

Several variations occurred. Some women, for example, were too stunned to cry. Others could not control tears, even though they did not necessarily feel too distressed. Such tears were often the flooding of emotion that is typical in a crisis or simply a release of tension. As will be seen, however, misinterpretation of a wife's emotional expressions also became a future problem.

Usually, a positive disclosure resulted in an immediate positive effect on both individuals and the marriage. The partners recommitted themselves. The wife, empathic with the fear that had delayed disclosure, considered the revelation proof of basic honesty and trust. The husband's guilt and anxiety abated. If there had been a predisclosure buildup, the wife too experienced relief and renewed self-esteem. Although there were exceptions, the release of tension and improvement in communication usually led to immediate improvement of the sexual relationship.

Over half of the disclosures could be labeled positive. No matter what the variations, Brenda's summary was so typical that it was repeated by others almost word for word:

> Actually, I was kind of proud of the way I handled it. I was stunned, in shock, yet not really shocked in a negative sense. I felt I was pretty cool and calm, all things considered. I didn't have hysterics. I was handling something with relative ease that would have made many women fall apart. I was understanding and flexible, and willing to change our contract to meet his needs. I wasn't denying the homosexuality and I wasn't being a martyr. I wasn't even all that threatened, although I was a bit anxious. I simply loved him and wanted him to be happy. And even though I had conflicted feelings, I didn't want to add to the excessive guilt he already had. Only . . .

What came after the "only" was also typical. It showed the start of a rapid transition to a confused "interim" period, which, depending on what followed, could last from a few weeks to over 10 years:

> Only . . . sometimes I wondered if I was stupid to be so understanding. Maybe I was just being a sucker! I kept going from high to low every 2 minutes, and the more I thought about it, the more confused I got."

Reactions to a positive disclosure ran the gamut from little or no stress and shock to fairly severe stress and shock, depending upon the situation. A stressful situation like an arrest might still be relatively "positive" because of the husband's commitment to the wife. Conversely, what would ordinarily have been a positive disclosure might become a negative one because of poor timing and a husband's insensitivity to the wife's feelings. Mary McDermott's prenuptial disclosure experience was an extreme example. While her experience was not quite so extreme, 21-year-old Lisa was hurt, bewildered, and frightened when 2 days after the birth of their baby, her husband confessed that he had just had a homosexual liaison.

Negative Disclosures

Disclosures were considered "negative" to the extent that they revealed a strong betrayal of trust, occurred within the context of a poor marriage and spelled no chance of improving it, were second or third disclosures that violated the terms of an already renegotiated contract, or withdrew commitment to the wife and marriage. They were also considered negative to the extent that they were forced rather than volunteered, showed past or present lack of empathy or concern for a wife's feelings, needs, and rights, blamed the wife, or showed unconcerned, deliberate deceit for years or even the entire marriage.

At the more positive end of the continuum, the disclosure might be positive in all but one respect: the husband felt he could not maintain a heterosexual relationship and was hence asking for a divorce, despite the fact that he truly loved and was concerned about the wife. In such cases, the wife saw the disclosure as a loss or threat of loss. She felt more anxiety and grief than anger, and was apt to go through a "grief crisis" similar to what people go through at the death of a loved one.

When the content of the disclosure and the husband's behavior and attitudes seemed to show lack of caring and guiltless deceit, however, the wife viewed the disclosure as one of betrayal. She was apt to voice a sense of having been "used." Although she too felt a sense of loss, hurt and anger were her predominant emotions. Her immediate shock was especially acute and often led to the kind of bizarre behavior—or "crisis reaction"—that my own client, Marsha, had shown. If there was one single factor that determined the wife's reaction to a given disclosure, it was that perception of the husband's "caring" versus his "not caring."

Although a sense of threat, loss, and betrayal were the major attributes of negative constellations, there was so much overlapping that only extremes were clear-cut. The following is an example of a negative disclosure tempered by the husband's ongoing commitment to the wife, his ability to tolerate her anger, and the couple's immediate access to a support system.

Winnie had known prior to marriage of a single homosexual experience. The marital contract held an explicit promise not only of fidelity, but of honesty should the desire for homosexual contact reappear. After a 12 year "American Dream" marriage, she

> was telling him about this woman at work who had not known of her husband's 2-year affair. I couldn't believe she'd had no clues. I told him I'd stake my life on knowing where he was. He said, "I wouldn't do that if I were you." I said, "WHAT? ARE YOU TRYING TO TELL ME SOMETHING?" He said "Yes." I told him not to say another word. I ran upstairs and called my support group co-therapist.* I talked to her till I felt I could handle what I thought was going to be the announcement of an affair. Then he told me he'd been homosexually active for the past ten years, starting when I got pregnant. *Ten Years!* AAGH! TERROR! SHOCK! RAGE! FURY! [laughing] I stormed, ranted and raved! . . . He kept pleading with me to not leave, to deal with it, etc. I kept yelling at him to leave me alone, I didn't want to hear any more! . . . I paced, he paced behind me. [Laughing] WHEW! What a SCENE! I really wanted a divorce, but—thank God—I agreed to marriage counseling.

The next examples depict extremely negative constellations. Karen had had a "mixed, up and down" marriage. The "ups" had included good sex and Joe's tremendous support for her return to school. The "downs" had been increasingly frequent fights about Joe's impatience with the children. During the "predisclosure buildup," marital counseling had not helped, but Karen was pleased when Joe announced his decision to join a married men's support group.

Then one night, following a phone call, Joe informed her that he had a venereal disease and that it had come from a man. Despite her

---

*This couple belonged to a popular peer counseling and support group that helps people solve everyday problems. It is not therapy, but some members become trained in marital counseling.

acute shock and anger, Karen also felt sorry for Joe. She attributed their problems to the fear and stress he must have felt. She was willing to change the contract to meet his needs.

But as they talked about the situation, she realized that there was no room in Joe's life for her. He wanted to stay married, but out of convenience, not love. He did not want sex with her. The support group he had joined was a gay support group. He had always known he was gay. He had encouraged her return to school so that she would be able to support herself when he himself became financially able to leave her. "Gayness I could accept," she told me. "But he had planned all this from the start. There was no doubt. I had been used. I'd been *had!*"

Harriet's marriage had been marked by her husband's frequent business trips and his lack of sexual interest in her. After 2 years without sex, disclosure was a two-event process with each disclosure one of extreme betrayal:

> One day he was hospitalized with some mysterious illness. Next day I got a call from the Health Department, saying John had V. D. and had named *me* as the source. I thought they were nuts. But our family doctor confirmed it. He specified homosexual contact, but I was in such shock, I don't think I really heard it. Later, John convinced me it had come from a bar girl. But who cared? That wasn't the real issue. I filed for divorce the next day. When he threatened suicide, I said "Go ahead." But then he appealed to my guilt. He told me "God forgives, why can't you?" He reminded me how I'd been upset at having only one parent, and asked if I was willing to deprive our son of his father. He promised fidelity. So I agreed to stay 2 years till our son finished high school. But . . . I was pretty unhappy.
>
> A few months later he brought home a business friend for dinner. I didn't think much about it. Then one day, I was putting things away after he'd left for a business trip, and a packet of letters caught my eye. It was a bunch of love letters from that man. Later, my son said he'd seen my husband kissing the man while I was fixing them dinner. But he'd been afraid to tell me.

Harriet went into an acute crisis reaction and planned (literally) to kill her husband. Luckily, she was not functioning well enough to figure out how to get his rifle past airport security. So she flew to where he was staying, confronted him, and when told "It serves you right for snooping" and that he had been homosexually active prior to and throughout their marriage, she simply threatened him with murder if he ever returned and flew home again. Equally angry at herself ("He couldn't have done this to me if I hadn't let him"), she made the first of two suicide attempts 2 days later.

Aileen provides an example of a change from a positive initial disclosure, within the context of an "American Dream" marriage, to a negative second disclosure, within the surrounding context of other stressful situations:

> After the first disclosure, we'd made a recommitment to each other. Our sex got better again, we were free from tension, our marriage was even better than before. Then he went on a business trip. When he got back, suddenly things changed again. He seemed to resent finding me there when he got back. He began dressing strangely. Our friends thought he was having a mid-life crisis. Then my father died. When I came back from the funeral, he told me he'd fallen in love with some man and wanted a divorce immediately. Our agreement had been that nobody would be brought home. He showed me pictures he'd taken with that man in *our* bed!

> He told me he'd known before the first confrontation that he was going to leave me. He didn't see why I was upset, since I was well educated and had a good job . . . Actually, my job folded that same week, when the place where I work went out of business. I felt like I'd lost my father, my lover and best friend, and my job, all at the same time! It was horrible! I was in absolute shock! I still can't believe it!

When no "official" disclosure took place, wives reacted to specific rejections and disclosure-type events until a final crisis was reached. For example, Connie, whose confrontations had been met with her husband's denial, finally resorted to confirming her suspicions "unscrupulously" through their best–gay–friend. Both the effort and the confirmation were actually stress relieving and positive steps.

These, then, were a few samples of the kinds of disclosure that occurred and the wives' immediate reactions. It was how the husband dealt with the homosexuality and the kind of disclosure that determined a wife's immediate reactions. An extremely complex network of interweaving factors other than homosexuality itself was involved. If any single conclusion could be formed, it seemed to be that when an initial or later disclosure combined a sense of the husband's honesty, sensitivity, concern for and commitment to the wife, most wives' immediate reactions were relatively positive and understanding.

Chapter 6

Crisis:
Coping with and Recovering from

Most people have probably used the term "crisis" often in their lives to describe a sudden calamity that may be as major as a tornado or as minor as an adolescent discovering a pimple while dressing for the Junior Prom. Kübler-Ross has made famous the five stages of coping with dying (denial, bargaining, depression, anger, and acceptance). To understand wives' varying reactions and the extreme behaviors I have already called "crisis reactions," however, it is necessary to go beyond the popular concept of crisis as a "calamity."

From the moment of birth to death, people continually face a series of "problems" and "tasks" (obtaining food, climbing stairs, crossing streets, passing tests, making friends, planning budgets, etc.). Both formally and informally, they learn and build a large repertoire of skills and strategies that help them cope with both old and new problems. Any new situation can create some stress. If it is so new that a person has developed few or no coping skills, however, it can create a period of extreme stress with feelings of disequilibrium and helplessness, even in normal individuals and families. It is this situation that we call a crisis.

Some crises are simply stages of life common to most or all people yet new to the person going through them. Marriage, childbirth, and menopause are common examples. Others are specific calamities like a job layoff, a car accident, a major fire, a fatal illness, or the death of a loved one. Still others are long-term processes like the breakup of a marriage. Each type of crisis has its own characteristics and life cycle, and each produces common reactions. Yet people still bring their own unique reactions to the situation, based on their past experiences, personalities, and ways of coping with new situations. For example, losing a job is depressing to most people. Yet one person may view it simply as a defeat, whereas another may also see it as an opportunity. Some situations are so prolonged that they really cannot be called "a crisis," yet they contain the potential for many kinds of crisis within them. Adolescence is the prime example. Naomi Golan, a leading authority on crisis, calls such circumstances "crisis-prone" situations.

Golan (1978) also provides an excellent description of the "life cycles" of crises in general and how people react to them. She sees crisis as a total sequence of events with five overlapping phases:

1. A hazardous event or series of events with cumulative effect, which more or less disrupts people's equilibrium and puts them into the next phase.

2. Vulnerable state. This is the internal reaction to the hazardous event(s), both at the time and later. Individual reactions may vary according to individual personalities, past experiences and sets of coping skills, the kind of event, and the amount of information and help available.

For example, if the event is (or is seen as) a threat to one's integrity, individual functioning, or basic survival needs, anxiety and fear will be the most predominant reactions. If it is (or is perceived as) a loss of a person or an ability, grief and depression may be the major reactions. If it is (or is seen as) a challenge or an opportunity, the person may feel slight or moderate anxiety mixed with hope and excitement. Of course this is oversimplified. People usually have a mixture of perceptions and emotions, and depending on the situation, may feel also shame, guilt, anger, and confusion.

During this time, people go through a series of coping stages that again overlap considerably. First they try to use the skills and strategies they have always used to solve problems. If these do not work, tension increases and new emergency trial-and-error (sometimes called "groping") measures are tried. If these too fail to solve, decrease, or redefine the problem in an acceptable way, tension and stress rise to a peak, and the person becomes increasingly disorganized. Depression, anger, confusion, a sense of helplessness, loss of hope, and often behavioral regression increases. The stage is set for

3. The precipitating factor or "last straw." Often people cope well with a first "hazardous event." They may even handle a series of such events with relative equanimity. There is only so much stress, however, that a person's "system" can take. Some final event — perhaps a major one, but often some triviality such as a cross word or a ruined dinner — overloads that system, raises stress to an untenable degree, and sends the person into the state of acute disequilibrium popularly termed "falling apart." A "last straw" may coincide with the "hazardous event" (for instance, a heart attack may be followed quickly by a death). Whether it occurs at the same time or is simply the final blow in a series of problems, that "falling apart" point is called the

4. "Active" or "acute" crisis state. The person's feelings and behaviors are called *crisis reactions.* During this period people also go through overlapping phases of adjustment or "coping." The first may be psychological and physical turmoil. Confusion may lead to aimless activity. There may be dramatic and frequent mood changes, sleep and appetite disturbances, physical symptoms. People may become so immobilized that they cannot function at all either mentally or physically. Their random "groping" behaviors may become increasingly harmful rather than helpful.

They may be unable to perform their daily work, child care or other tasks, or their reactions to people may seem bizarre and crazy. They may, in fact, become extremely dangerous to themselves or others. For example, they may drive recklessly, lash out at their children, commit suicide, or kill someone.

It is important here to realize two facts: such seemingly crazy behavior is not because the person is mentally ill. It is a natural reaction to excessive stress. One person may have less capacity to handle stress than another and hence may hit "overload" more quickly and recover more slowly. Nevertheless, "overload" produces similar reactions in everyone, with the severity of symptoms more related to the details of the situation than they are to the ordinary emotional stability of the individual.

At the same time, the fact that crisis behavior is "natural" does not make it any less serious. I often hear people say, "Oh, don't worry about John. He's depressed, but he wouldn't kill himself. He's not crazy. If you had the things happen to you that happened to him, you'd be depressed too." That may be true, but no matter what the cause, acute depression is acute depression. If a person sees no hope, suicide may be seen as the only solution, and no matter what the cause, "dead" is "dead."

This, of course, brings us to "solutions," i.e., recovery from crisis. Most crisis theorists believe that the human system simply cannot maintain such stress for very long, and by the end of 4 to 6 weeks people have begun to gradually remobilize, adjust, and develop new solutions. Those solutions may be helpful (functional) or harmful (dysfunctional). The ultimate harmful solution, of course, is suicide. Often, however, it is at this point that the person, who is still feeling pretty helpless, is most willing and able to seek or accept help from others. At any rate, as pain and anxiety begin to subside, the person gradually enters a

5. Reintegration phase. The process of recovery from acute crisis is essentially a more effective continuation of the end of the previous phase. Except for the ultimate solution of suicide, some kind of reequilibrium must be regained. Depending on how functional or dysfunctional the solutions are, the person will end up emotionally back to normal, worse off, or better off than he or she was before that first hazardous event. For example, we often speak of people who have been "emotionally scarred for life" or someone who is "back to his or her old self." We often speak of some tragedy as "a blessing in disguise."

This reintegrative period also consists of several overlapping steps or stages. First the person may try to cope intellectually, filling in gaps in information and understanding through reading, talking to others in or expert about the situation. Next the person may come to grips with emotions, first accepting such feelings as grief or anger and then releasing them through words, tears, and other behaviors. Finally, new—usually more helpful—strategies are found. This too is a point where people are often more willing and able to accept and use help from others. For example, it may be the point where someone seeks professional help. People already in therapy gradually develop new coping behaviors and new resources, becoming stronger and less dependent upon the therapist.

The factors affecting both the process itself and the eventual outcome include individual personalities and styles, social and cultural

backgrounds and beliefs, community resources, economic resources, and the influence of family, friends, caregivers, and professional counselors. Dysfunctional solutions may include such defense mechanisms as excessive denial, withdrawal, and lashing out
at others. Many "strange" behaviors may occur. They have in
common two problems: (1) though they may temporarily reduce
pain, they do not really provide effective solutions, and they tend to
create more problems than they solve; (2) they lower, rather than
raise the person's self-esteem. Functional solutions, however, produce a sense of "mastery" and increase self-esteem.

Different types of crisis may follow different courses, each with
its own personality of identifiable stages and life cycles. For example, the death of a loved one is usually either a relatively short
process or a very sudden event. Although the active crisis state that
ensues following death may be very painful, people are usually able
to regain their equilibrium and begin rebuilding their lives relatively
quickly.

Divorce, on the other hand, seldom happens suddenly and is usually the culmination of a lengthy and conflict-filled process. There
may be considerable information, many companions, and social/
economic support to help one recover from a community crisis like
a flood. For still another type of crisis (incest), isolation, stigma,
and lack of information may make for a far longer and emotionally
more devastating process.

Generally, a crisis is described as an emotional roller-coaster dip.
How deep and wide that dip may be depends on the individual circumstances. The stages and steps I have described may seem or-
derly on paper, but in real life they are not. There is continual overlapping and interweaving, with one stage containing elements of
others and some degree of turmoil continuing long after a person
has presumably "reintegrated."

CRISIS INTERVENTION

Professionally helping people through crisis is usually called
"crisis intervention," and it may be aimed at either preventing or
resolving a crisis. Generally, it is believed that brief counseling—

often no more than a month or two—when a crisis first starts is far more helpful than long-term therapy after the acute crisis has been resolved. Partly that's because emotional resources are usually more intact at the beginning. Although individuals may be worse off emotionally as they head into acute crisis, they are also more willing to accept help. By the time they have recovered from acute crisis, however, they are more apt to have already become locked into dysfunctional solutions, to have depleted their emotional, economic, and social resources, and to be facing a far more complicated situation. Moreover, having slightly eased the pain with the help of "bandaids," they are understandably fearful of tearing off those bandaids, and often resist efforts to provide more adequate long-term help.

In helping, counselors face the need to work calmly but quickly. They do not waste time taking long histories, delving into people's childhoods or even the long-term history of a marriage, unless there is some good reason to do so. They simply obtain pertinent background history of the crisis at hand, get a general impression of the present situation, and set up priorities for what needs to be done. They try to provide realistic hope for the future, relieve panic, assess the immediate danger of violence, and if necessary, take emergency steps to prevent it. They provide needed information and assess and utilize other resources (friends, doctors, relatives, support groups, etc.).

They also assess the degree of immobilization: people in an acute crisis state may need far more "advice" and help than they would ordinarily. Intensive effort may be given to provide that help. The goal, however, is to help people remobilize and recognize and utilize their own strength and independence as quickly as possible, for their sense of helplessness becomes increasingly self-defeating.

Of course, prevention is always better than cure. Once a situation is known to be "crisis-prone," professionals often try to take preventive steps. For example, many a postpartum depression has been avoided now that professionals provide more information about infancy prior to childbirth and help new parents obtain peer support and relief from fatigue after childbirth.

In short, the most fundamental aspects of crisis theory and crisis intervention are that

1. Crisis behavior is not based on "sickness" or pathology. Rather, it is a natural response to extreme stress, caused by ventures into the unknown without the help that accurate information from past experience provides.
2. People facing a crisis are generally capable individuals who simply need more than ordinary help when facing unusual (for them) problems.
3. The more successfully people master one crisis — that is, the more they develop functional "crisis-coping skills" — the more ability they have to master future crises.
4. People's precrisis emotional state may be "sick" or "healthy." If past experiences (or past crises that have not been mastered successfully) interfere with the ability to cope with the present crisis, then they may need to be discussed. Unless there is reason to believe they are relevant, however, they are presumed irrelevant.

IS THIS A CRISIS SITUATION?

There is no question that all but a few of the 103 wives in this group had undergone all five components of crisis at least once and often more than once. Those who had not were still in the "vulnerable state" that follows "hazardous events": i.e., they were in the "interim period" that followed the initial reaction to an initial disclosure.

The basic vocabulary of crisis literature and its subjects was the basic vocabulary of the wives. Words like "shock," "overwhelmed," "dazed," "stunned," and "disbelief" were used repeatedly. The same was true of described emotions, behaviors, and intellectual functioning:

> I cried standing up, sitting down and lying in bed.
> I felt rage wash over me in waves.
> I was terrified! My whole world seemed to be falling apart.

Almost all women described one or more periods of confusion, many becoming more disoriented with each successive traumatic experience or disclosure:

All my beliefs about the way the world operated seemed to be going down the drain. I couldn't make sense out of anything!

I was almost 9 months pregnant. When he left the house after we'd had a fight, I began drinking and wandering around, sorta dazed. I went into the nursery we'd set up. Next thing I knew it was morning, and I was lying in the baby's crib, curled up in a fetal position.

I wandered around the city disoriented, in a fog. Then I just sat on the beach. I don't know what I thought.

The only issues, then, are how many crises the women had undergone, how severe the stress had become, and how to compare this kind of crisis with the description of crisis already given.

Two wives did not relate the homosexuality to their marital problems and hence labeled the specific issue as a mild crisis. A few wives had avoided an acute crisis state. Terri, for example, had gone through a series of potential "precipitating factors" or "last straw" events with relative ease and considered each disclosure a "mini-crisis." We'll see later why she had so much easier a time than the others.

Several wives had reintegrated from a first crisis, and two (including Sue Johnson) had experienced so little stress that they considered the situation as "nothing more than one of life's little problems." Nevertheless, they could all be considered in a vulnerable "interim" period. Judging by the others' experiences, only time will tell whether a happy adjustment remains stable and whether or not those still in a state of turmoil will suffer more crises before a final reintegration takes place.

CATEGORIES OF CRISIS

Given the wide variation in experiences, outcomes, and life spans found, it is impossible to define the situation by sticking it into a category and giving it a simple label like "grief crisis," "divorce crisis," or "infidelity crisis." It would more aptly fit into what Golan has called a "crisis-prone situation" in which no full five-stage crisis, one crisis, or many crises might occur.

Neither divorce, grief, nor infidelity occurred with everyone. For one wife, a simple term "grief crisis" and "grief reaction" might be appropriate. Janice, for instance, had had an American Dream marriage for 5 years. After a brief predisclosure buildup, her husband told her he had a gay lover. Although he was distressed at causing her pain, he had no intention of giving up the lover. He saw no reason to leave the marriage, but he also saw no reason to discuss or do anything to perk up their own deteriorating sexual relationship. Janice sought professional help, but when her husband refused to participate in counseling and did not seem to care whether or not she divorced him, she divorced. The whole process took a little over a month. She had been divorced only a few months when I saw her. Although her wounds had obviously not completely healed, she was well into the process of starting a new life for herself and was looking forward confidently to a happy future.

For wives like Karen, who had undergone an extreme breach of trust, the situation might be termed a "betrayal" rather than a "grief" crisis. Although the reactions were more complicated, the stress more severe, and the recovery slower, it was still a one-time limited crisis with an easily identifiable beginning, middle, and end.

With most wives, however, the situation was less easily defined. Whereas a grief crisis might result from a decision to divorce, it was only the final one in a series of crises and might be more or less severe than earlier ones had been. A few wives had forestalled an "acute" stage of crisis or had gone through the total sequence of stages with only a minor "rollercoaster dip." Moreover, as with adolescence, one can hardly label a 20-year period a crisis.

STAGES OF CRISIS

Identifying the stages of adjustment in such a situation, then, becomes an unwieldy task. Each separate crisis was a microcosm of the whole and had its own individual life cycle. Taken as a whole, however, the crisis-prone situation could be viewed as having three overlapping periods: (1) the beginning stage, (2) the interim stage, and (3) the reintegration stage.

The Beginning Stage

The beginning stage included the predisclosure buildup and/or the immediate reaction to an initial disclosure. It produced reactions that ranged from little or no stress to acute crisis.

The Interim Stage

The interim stage often began within minutes of the initial disclosure and lasted until either the couple had successfully coped with all possible crisis-producing events or until the wife had begun her reintegration following divorce. In some cases, however, the wife was in a vulnerable interim period even though she had not yet defined or confirmed the homosexuality. Moreover, whether or not she felt stress, she was actually in a "vulnerable" position following an initial disclosure. Reactions ranged from little or no stress to acute crisis during this period. There might be many dormant periods, but as with volcanoes, there were times when emotions bubbled underneath a seemingly calm surface and either "last straw" events or new and negative disclosures created both minor and major eruptions. In short, it was this period, rather than the initial disclosure period, that was most "acute-crisis" prone.

Reintegration Period

The reintegration stage started with a transitional phase in which the wife came to grips with her feelings and began to make some final plan for her future. Following divorce, full reintegration seemed to take about 3 years, but in a few cases had not occurred after 5.

STAGES AND STYLES OF ADJUSTMENT

Within the broad phases of crisis, the women went through all the stages of adjustment described by Golan. Those stages, however, were individually determined by each individual disclosure and the priorities that were perceived or dictated by the circumstances of the moment. For any given woman at any given point, a particular disclosure might be a hazardous event, a "last-straw" precipitating factor leading to acute crisis, or the end of an acute crisis and the beginning of reintegration.

Often neither "disclosure" nor "homosexuality" per se was the issue. Rather, a specific rejection by the husband or an actual request for divorce was what dictated the wife's specific reaction. Although there is no doubt that wives' general descriptions of their feelings and behaviors at different times generally corresponded with patterns described by Golan, there were some possible differences — perhaps more in degree than in kind.

For example, the description of crisis as a "rollercoaster dip" certainly fit this situation. Many women used the term "rollercoaster" spontaneously, and many were well acquainted with crisis theory. When they described the rollercoaster effect, however, they were not simply talking about one "dip," they were describing a giant rollercoaster ride in which they went up and down emotionally from one dip to another several times a day, week to week, or month to month.

For example, it took Arlie only 1 month to recognize that her "new type of family" had become disastrous instead of "exciting" and to leave it. Two excerpts from our interview follow:

> Q. I'm trying to get an idea of sequence here. . . . Immediately after learning of the bisexuality, how did you feel?
>
> A. Well, it's very funny. One moment I'd absolutely freak out over being such an aware, forward thinking woman, . . . very much ahead of my times, . . . and then I would bottom out and feel like an absolute fool and a gutless wonder. So it was a roller coaster.
>
> Q. Did you change gradually or suddenly? For example, could you say this month I felt mainly this way and that month I felt mainly that way?
>
> A. This day, this way, that day, that way. Sorry, it'd be nice if they [my feelings] would only change by the month. At that point it was daily. Then maybe every other day. Now it's almost 2 years since the divorce. I've gotten it down to weekly or biweekly.

Brenda, still in a "basically happy but struggling" marriage 6 years after disclosure, described several full-length crises. Three years after disclosure, for example, she had been

> . . . on a roller coaster—some days very positive, some days very negative. Some days, "gonna make it, it's gonna be all right," other days, "Why are we bothering?" Up and down.

Asked how she was feeling at the present time, she said

> It depends on which day you ask me. I'm really worrying about the answers I give you. They're true for today. But tomorrow they might be entirely different. I really surprised myself today. I'm feeling really good. I haven't shed a tear. But if we'd held this interview yesterday, I would have cried the whole 4 hours.

Aileen, describing her recovery from the loss of her job and her father and her husband's betrayal of trust and request for divorce, put it this way:

> Hey, you're talking about crisis theory, aren't you? Well, I know all about it. I'd read Kübler-Ross and *Passages* and the stages of crisis, and the mixed emotions and all that stuff—I went through them all. But what the books really *don't* prepare you for—what I didn't expect—was going through *all* of them: love, hate, embarrassment, confusion, guilt, self-hate, self-love, and so on. I didn't expect to have them all at once. I didn't expect to go through every stage of crisis and every phase of adjustment every day or sometimes every morning or even in the course of 2 hours. And I didn't expect it to go on that way for so long! It was horrible!

COPING STRATEGIES

Both in individual crises and in the total long-term process, then, there was a 'somewhat' linear progression from one stage of adjustment to another. Yet as each new disclosure produced a new crisis or if it took years for an official disclosure to take place and the wife could react only to a series of rejections, emotional changes and both functional and dysfunctional coping strategies occurred chaotically, every which way: in linear fashion, circularly, cyclically, and simultaneously. They were essentially trial-and-error "groping" behaviors throughout the interim period and were highly individualized. The same behavior might be functional and helpful for one person or at one point, dysfunctional and harmful for another person or at another point. It might start out as a planned, rational, and seemingly functional step, yet later prove to have been dysfunctional on the basis of results that had accrued.

Avoidance

At any given point, a wife might try to avoid painful or excessive stimuli. This might mean a "stun" or "shock" reaction that decreased or even stopped intellectual functioning. When it meant refusing to face reality, it could be called dysfunctional "denial."

Laura's shutting the door on both the sight and the memory of her husband's homosexual activity was one extreme example. Grace faced the disclosure of homosexual desire realistically and helped her husband obtain counseling. When he later converted his fantasies into sexual behavior, however, she tried to "deny" it. Asked what she meant by that term, she said, laughing,

> Well, he was pretty blatant about it, and I was willing to believe some pretty lame excuses for coming home late so often. I mean, like – how many flats can a man have in a month? Most cars only have four tires. His seemed to have ten.

Some women (although in contrast with the stories I'd heard, very few) tried to completely separate the heterosexual and homosexual worlds by asking that all evidence of homosexuality be kept completely out of their awareness. They did not even want to hear the word mentioned.

As we saw with Gloria, however, denial was not always negative. In her case, facing the reality of homosexuality at the point her husband was finally trying to discuss it would have actually interfered with her development of new skills and resources for improving the quality of her life. She was instinctively wise in postponing the discussion for a few weeks. Partial avoidance was often useful and necessary. Instead of shutting out all evidence of homosexuality, most women simply asked that they be spared the pain of "pouring salt onto wounds." They did not want detailed accounts of homosexual fantasies or relationships. Although they wanted honesty, they did not want to be told of extramarital sexuality unless they asked or unless it was of import for the marital relationship. Many wanted extramarital activity so "discreet" that they would not be embarrassed or that children would be neither embarrassed nor upset. Sometimes this meant asking that sexual activity be limited to out-of-town "conference" affairs.

Sometimes avoidance meant shutting out either negative or positive feelings, ascribing all of the husband's behaviors to homosexuality and avoiding recognition of either more basic positives or negatives in the marriage. Sometimes it meant simply stemming the flow of contradictory and confusing thoughts and perceptions. It might take the form of refusing to read about homosexuality and bisexuality, or refusing to see a counselor, to meet the gay community, or to join an available support group.

Whether or not avoidance was functional or dysfunctional depended on the degree, the form it took, the context in which it occurred, and the reason for its use. Trying to decide whether a given coping strategy was realistic or inappropriate was a highly perplexing issue for the wives. Often avoidance was simply a point at which they ended up "trying not to think about it any more, in order to stay sane." Many women distanced themselves, viewing themselves as actors in a Theater of the Absurd, and using Black Humor to see them through. Fran's comment was typical:

> I kept thinking what a good soap opera this would make. I've written a hundred books in my mind. Once I told my husband it was too bad I wasn't lesbian, then we could double date.

Confronting the Issue

While some kind and degree of avoidance was always part of the scene, generally these wives dealt with life cognitively. Trying to make a rational assessment and a cost-benefit analysis of whether to stay in the marriage and what sexual contract to make and to assess their own options, feelings, and wishes was generally their first, interim, final, and major way of dealing with the problem. Filling in the intellectual gap, which put them into the "interim" phase, usually began within minutes of even a strong shock reaction.

Most women read everything they could find on homosexuality, partly trying to understand it better and partly trying to find guidelines for the situation they were facing. They talked (or tried to talk) with their husbands and asked questions both about homosexuality in general and about the husband's own feelings. They carried on interminable internal debates, trying to sort out issues, options, and feelings. They often sought professional help or help from the homosexual community, and some women made arduous attempts to find a support group. One woman, Ruth, increased her understanding in a unique way — sexually:

> When he first told me, I couldn't understand why it was so different with a man. I said to him, "Well, let's have sex now and you show me what it's like." And it was so rough, so physical — he's just not into the loving form of gayness — I do not have the strength to be a match for it, nor did I enjoy it. So then I understood that it really *was* different, and it really *was* a need I couldn't fill — and didn't want to.

Increasing Options

Several women returned to school or speeded up their education. Some women found that anxiety interfered with concentration in studying, but others found it a catalyst. Cheryl, for instance, reported that she finished her dissertation in the shortest time on record at her university. Several women sought work for the first time or changed jobs. Such actions were either part of a long-range plan to divorce, a protection in case the husband should ever ask for divorce, or simply a way of enhancing autonomy and emotional gratification.

DEGREE OF STRESS

Despite the fact that a few wives never experienced more than minor stress, despite the fact that disclosure did not always create high stress and often relieved it, the crisis-prone nature of the total situation was evident in the high degree of stress that most women experienced sooner or later. That stress showed itself in intellectual and emotional deterioration, out-of-character dysfunctional behavior, and stress-related physiological response.

Dysfunctional Behavior

More than half the wives reported one or more periods of over-sleeping or inability to sleep, excessive drinking and eating (or, conversely, loss of appetite), taking tranquilizers, or a combination of "gulping down booze and drugs." Although such behavior was usually the first to go as reintegration started, the excessive weight gain of five women remained. Their self-destructive behavior was of more concern to them than the homosexuality had been. One wife, of normal weight at marriage, gained 50 pounds in the year prior to divorce and 100 more in the year after.

Most women described one or more periods of serious impairment in work, child care and housework, and social functioning. Aileen, for example, was afraid to look for a new teaching job following her divorce for fear of crying during interviews. By the time she had recovered from her summer of depressed immobility, school vacancies had been filled. Arlie, on the other hand, went through 20 job interviews while still in acute crisis. "The way I looked," she told me, "I needn't have bothered." Other women described functioning, but—as Marcie put it, "so taut that if anyone looked at me cross eyed, I rushed away weeping." One more wife came close to child abuse, and other mothers were parented by their children following divorce.

Sexual Functioning

Women handled their feelings about sexuality in a variety of ways. Again, it was often difficult to determine what was a functional strategy and what was dysfunctional. Masturbation was used to handle some tension, but often led to guilt feelings, particularly with highly religious women who considered masturbation immoral.

Several women tried to seduce their husbands and to increase their sexual attractiveness by losing weight, changing hair styles, etc. Some agreed to sexual techniques they had been unwilling to try before. Whether this was functional or not depended on the behavior, the reason for the flexibility, and the result. For example, oral sex might be a way for one couple to see that both partners' needs were satisfied, with the wife increasing her sexual options and pleasure as a result. For another wife, the same behavior might simply be an interim "groping" (so to speak) behavior, with the wife resentful at feeling coerced into a behavior she did not want or enjoy.

Flexibility around the sexual contract was the most common initial behavior planned to increase options. For some women, however, it was again an interim, desperate grabbing at straws. For still others it was a functional reintegrative step. Again, what started as a planned, functional coping behavior often proved in the end to have been dysfunctional.

Three women, for example, allowed their husband's lover into the marriage without any sense of coercion. For Terri it proved a happy arrangement, dissolving only when her husband, seeing that his lover's increasing dissatisfaction with "second place" status was beginning to create problems, broke off the extramarital relationship entirely. For Brenda, the arrangement had mixed effects. For Arlie, it quickly proved disastrous.

Many wives—particularly right after a positive disclosure—found that the freedom from guilt and the chance to explore new options in lovemaking eased tension and increased sexual satisfaction for both partners. But many also reported one or more periods in which performance anxiety interfered with sexual functioning. They worried that their husbands were going through the motions of

making love while "really making love to a man." Cindy, an unusually attractive and "feminine" young woman, suddenly became
ashamed of her own body.

Some wives worried about venereal disease. I might note here
that AIDS had not yet hit the headlines. In couples I have counseled
since the study, concern about AIDS has neither destroyed the mari-
tal/sexual relationship nor has it been the primary counseling issue.
Nevertheless, it has certainly added tension, limited the sexual
"technique" options, decreased frequency of intercourse, and contributed to sexual dysfunction on the part of both partners, even
though a husband may never have been promiscuous or may have
reduced or even stopped all homosexual activity.

Any erectile problem became anxiety provoking for husbands
and wives alike. Wives worried about whether the cause was their
own incompetence or lack of desirability, the aging process, anxiety, or homosexuality. Some became overly sexually demanding
out of the need for reassurance. Others were afraid to ask for sex for
fear of increasing the anxiety. Several suffered a decrease in sexual
desire because both their own and their husband's anxiety had made
lovemaking so stressful.

Determining and assessing their own sexual options outside the
marriage created more stress. Some wives were simply immobilized by their conflict over whether or not to have an affair. Several
engaged in dysfunctional extramarital sex either to confirm their
own adequacy, out of anger, as a desperate attempt to please a
husband who was encouraging such activity, or for a combination
of the above reasons.

For example, several highly religious and conservative women
suddenly became "promiscuous" (their own term), flitting indis-
criminately from bed to bed. Mary, you may remember, had an
affair and told her husband about it purely in order to lash back and
as a desperate device to make him stop his own affairs. Abby and
Marsha, my own former clients, had gone along with their husbands' suggestion of a foursome. Their reaction? "We tried it, but
we definitely did NOT like it!"

Cathy was one of those who went along with anything her husband suggested, purely out of helplessness, confusion, and guilt
about not being "liberated." You may remember that for her, the

initial disclosure was a drunken, half joking one that she did not take seriously. It took on meaning only when her husband decided he needed some "rest" — in San Francisco. Although she did not confront him, she left him a note saying that she realized what was happening but did not want to add to his present strain and would wait until he was ready to talk it over with her. He never replied.

From then on, each disclosure became increasingly negative. Soon after he returned, he stayed out all night twice without calling home. The first time, she was frantic with worry. They did talk about the homosexuality, but he was sure it would never happen again. The next time, she was simply enraged. Filled with remorse, her husband became more realistic in his discussion and asked for a weekend "getaway" trip twice a year. For some time it seemed a satisfactory solution to both.

Then her husband, described as "always planning thoughtful little surprises for her," gave her a surprise Christmas present of a vacation at a ski resort. Partly, she realized, he was replacing his "getaway" trip by sending her away. Yet she was touched that he also wanted her to have fun at such a time. They arranged a "bon voyage" supper at an intimate restaurant. Halfway through their intimate supper, he blurted out that his getaway trips were not enough and that he was desperately unhappy. "What do you want?" she asked. His reply was "a divorce." Then he put her on the plane, in a state of shock. When she returned home, she reported,

> . . . I asked if we couldn't explore a contract that would be more satisfying to him. We entered a series of renegotiations. I felt trapped into agreeing with anything. If I ever objected to the number of nights out or anything he did, he just said, "Well, you were the one who wanted to stay married." When I asked for marriage counseling, he refused, saying he wasn't going to spend all that money just so someone could tell him they should divorce.
>
> He kept urging me to have extramarital affairs. I knew it was partly to relieve his own guilt, but also I knew he was trying to be fair. One night we were in a bar. He noticed this man flirting with me. He pushed me toward the guy, told me

to have fun, and left. I felt utterly abandoned! He turned out to be a really nice guy, and we did end up having an affair. But each time we were together I felt dirty, and I showered to get the dirt off just like rape victims do. See, I didn't think it was immoral, but I wasn't doing it out of my own need. I was just still desperately doing anything he [my husband] wanted me to, not thinking for myself. And that's just not like me! I'm usually pretty assertive!

Such behaviors served to create far more stress than they alleviated.

PHYSIOLOGICAL STRESS RESPONSE

Q. Right after disclosure, did you experience any physical symptoms?

A. No. Did other women?

Q. Well, some people I've talked to did, others didn't. Some women mentioned things like eating too much or too little, or headaches, stomach ailments like nausea or diarrhea, trouble sleeping, things like that. But other women had no problems at all. I guess you were one of those?

A. Oh, well, *those* things, sure. Almost all of them. But nothing serious. I thought you meant *real* problems. The real problems—the serious stuff—came later.

That conversation was typical for women who had had positive initial disclosures. Mild physiological stress-related symptoms attributed to the situation were so much a part of the scene that in comparison with what was to follow, they were shrugged off as inconsequential and all but forgotten.

Following an initial negative disclosure, symptoms were far more severe. Winnie, for example, after the revelation that her husband had been homosexually active for 10 years of marriage, suffered a first-time gall bladder attack severe enough to require emergency surgery. As situations deteriorated, physical symptoms increased. Several women described all the symptoms of an acute anxiety attack (i.e., "butterflies in the stomach," chest pain, rubbery legs, a sense of impending death, and often hyperventilation). A few women developed ulcers. One woman had the symptoms (but not the actuality) of a brain tumor.

Sometimes a planned and functional coping strategy produced enough interim stress to create physical problems: Gloria, despite her blindness and with minimal help from anyone, had put herself through graduate and postgraduate education. She was exhilarated when she successfully defended her doctoral dissertation. Her body, however, was less enthusiastic. A few hours after the defense she collapsed with a ruptured spleen, so near death that she was given last rites.

A few women required psychiatric care with hospitalization. More often, they had outpatient psychotherapy with a psychiatrist, psychologist, or social worker. Most women felt they should have had therapy or should have had it sooner than they did. In fact, part of the agreement I had made with all women was that in return for their help, they would be entitled to 4 hours of free counseling from me or help in obtaining a therapist in their own area. Several women who had not had previous counseling took advantage of that offer.

THE EFFECT ON SELF-ESTEEM
AND GENERAL HAPPINESS

"Self-esteem? What Self-esteem?"

I wanted to kill myself. I mean it! That's not kidding or a figure of speech, I just didn't want to live any more!

The most dramatic portrayal of crisis was the interim assault on self-esteem and general happiness. The difficulties in delineating the disclosure point made for some problems in separating pre- and post-disclosure effects. Often self-esteem and happiness rose immediately as a suspicious wife lost her sense of "craziness" and/or the marital relationship improved following an initial disclosure. It then fell sharply as a new disclosure and future events removed the optimism. Sometimes it worked the other way around. Wives in a "horrendous" marriage and unable to confirm their strong suspicions of homosexuality were apt to be at their lowest point immediately before disclosure.

While self-esteem and happiness tended to rise and fall together, self-esteem did not always fall as sharply and was usually quicker to return. Women attributed this to the fact that they did not expect themselves to be "men," and hence suffered less loss of self-esteem than they might have if their competition had been female. Moreover, many felt that they had handled the situation as well as they could, and any decision following a period of indecision immediately restored some self-esteem.

Self-esteem, then, seemed more related to women's individual values regarding monogamy and homosexuality, to the degree of stigma and blame they had received, and to their ability or inability to make a decision. Depression (which was used as the measure of happiness or unhappiness) seemed more related to the sense of rejection and loss. A decision to divorce, for instance, might restore self-esteem but increase depression.

Self-Esteem

No matter what the relationship between the two variables, self-esteem fell so low during the interim period that when asked about the effect of their situation cn their self-esteem, many women laughed and said, "Self-esteem? What self-esteem?" All but a few reported one or more periods of feeling stupid, "like a big fool," irrational, sick, crazy, bitchy, nasty, unlovable, unneeded, unwanted, ugly, and incompetent. Those who had engaged in dysfunctional sex added evil and immoral to the epithets they had given themselves.

Depression

Almost all wives became moderately to seriously depressed. Almost 50% of the wives were assessed as having been a high suicide risk at some point or another. In fact, 10 out of 15 such wives in the group of 33 studied most intensively had made one or more serious suicide attempts or gestures. Only 6 of those 33 had suffered little or no depression. The percentages in the 70 other wives seemed to be roughly the same. I make a distinction only because with the original 33, I was able to supplement verbal accounts with written questionnaires and scales to actually measure depression. Also, a few letter writers simply did not provide the information and since I prefer to err on the side of understatement rather than overstatement, I did not count them as depressed. The assessment of degree of depression was based on:

1. Such symptoms of general depression as stated depression, sleep and appetite disturbances, suicidal thoughts, immobilization, withdrawal, deliberate social isolation, my own clinical observations during interviews, and, where possible, reports from others.
2. Expressed loss of hope and intent to die.
3. Suicidal thought that was more than just a passing thought or intellectual game: it involved serious plotting of strategies arising from loss of hope and was sufficiently out of character to precipitate a decision to obtain professional help, to divorce, or both.
4. A high degree of danger associated with a specific behavior, whether or not suicide was actually planned.
5. Depression scale scores for those who were seen.

The other side of the suicide coin, of course, is homicidal potential. This will be discussed later. For now, it is sufficient to note that although wives usually directed violence at themselves, the potential for violence toward the husband or someone else was certainly there.

Neither suicidal nor homicidal thoughts or behaviors appeared directly related to either the disclosure of homosexuality or the homosexuality itself. Rather, they were precipitated by a "last straw" act or statement that personified and often magnified a long accumulation of rejections and betrayals, an "ultimate" rejection and loss scene, or they were planned actions arising from despair when after all their efforts, the marriage seemed unsavable.

I can't stress that point enough! Such figures are both dramatic and alarming. Since most women felt that often neither their husbands, friends, nor therapists realized just how depressed they were, they are figures that need to be known. Unfortunately, they are also figures that can make the situation worse rather than better, if a husband or therapist mistakenly interprets them to mean that wives cannot cope with learning about homosexuality and should not be told.

Several husbands, seen either as part of the study or in counseling, had delayed telling their wives because of the fear that the wives would not only throw them out but would kill themselves. Like Jim, most had expressed amazement at the "strength and understanding" their wives had shown. Harriet and Mary were the only wives who appeared to have reacted violently to disclosure itself. One was reacting not to the admission or fact of homosexuality, but to an extreme betrayal of trust. The other was the result of an ill-timed and highly insensitive disclosure. Similarly, only one wife I have seen in counseling has had such an extreme reaction to disclosure, and she too had been faced with a negative, albeit voluntary, disclosure. One might suggest that had the husbands not been so convinced of their wives' inability to face the news and had they been more honest at the beginning, there might not have been so many "negative" disclosures and reactions.

The only difference between a suicide "gesture" and a suicide "attempt" was that "gestures" were impulsive actions, whereas "attempts" were well planned. Both were serious, and both came when a wife felt completely powerless. Often the act itself released enough tension to allow her to recognize anger, ease the sense of "powerlessness," see a more constructive way of coping with her feelings, and regain hope for her future. No gesture or attempt appeared manipulative. The wives neither threatened nor told what they had done. They simply returned home and/or began putting their new plan to work.* Often this meant starting divorce proceedings, at which point three husbands threatened suicide.

---

*A recent client of mine, however, provided one exception. Following a negative disclosure, she had become severely depressed. By the end of one interview, her depression had lifted considerably. Later, however, her husband refused to communicate with her and told her his relationship with their family physician was none of her business. She immediately swallowed all the tranquilizers given her by an emergency room physician, told her husband what she had done, and then called me. How one feels about such an action depends, I suppose, on one's point of view. This was clearly a hurt, angry, manipulative, and guilt-provoking gesture with no intent to end in death. Yet it was an improvement on her formerly serious suicidal planning and was mainly a desperate effort, using the only means she felt she had, to force her husband to pay attention to her feelings.

Connie, whose suspicions of homosexuality in an increasingly "horrendous" marriage had still not been confirmed, went through one last effort to save her marriage, only to receive a humiliating rejection. She asked her husband, "Why are you doing this to me?" and was told "Because I don't love you any more." The next night he took off his wedding ring, telling her there was no point in wearing it, since he no longer loved her. She told me

> The night he took his ring off, I wanted to kill myself. I mean it! That's not just kidding or a figure of speech, I just didn't want to live any more.

Often, behaviors were so dangerous that even in a gamble with death, survival was probably due more to luck than to any unconscious stacking of the cards. Some women sped down highways looking for, with one wife finding, an accident. Two wives aimed their car at a bridge (one taking her mentally handicapped child with her) and changed their minds almost at the point of impact. Gloria deliberately upped her already dangerous dosage and combination of drugs and liquor.

Harriet had been released from psychiatric care following her first suicide attempt, but remained far more depressed than the psychiatrist realized. A physician herself, she deliberately ignored what she knew were the symptoms of a bleeding ulcer until she collapsed and was taken unconscious to a hospital, clinically dying. Had her own doctor been unavailable or a shade less empathic and quick thinking in persuading her to permit surgery, she probably would not have survived.

THE REINTEGRATIVE PERIOD

Discussion of reintegration is again complicated by the fact that there were often several crises with several reintegrative periods. The sequence of steps in a final reintegration was determined by what had been attempted earlier. Thus for one woman, seeking professional help might have been the first coping strategy, and turning to friends might have been the final reintegrative step. For another woman, the steps may have been reversed. The same could be said of turning to the homosexual community, telling children or parents, reading about homosexuality, accepting or refusing an open sexual contract, and other measures.

No matter what the sequence, the steps for women who were still married included:

1. *Making a final decision to stay married or to divorce, based on choice rather than fear or confusion.* A decision to stay married usually meant continued affection between the partners. Occasionally, however, it was merely the best option for the moment and was actually part of a long-term plan to divorce when conditions (usually financial) were right.

For example, Winnie, despite her hurt and anger at her husband's disclosure of long-standing infidelity, agreed to marriage counseling. Gradually—almost in spite of herself—she began to forgive him. At first she softened only to the extent that she was willing to go with him on their traditional weekly bicycle ride. She would not talk to him. She called it "parallel play." When he was hurt in an automobile accident, however, she began to reexamine her priorities.

> I began to get back in touch with basics, to let myself remember how much I loved him and to think about how sad life would be without him. Sure, trust is just as important as love. But I began to hear the fear that had caused that breach of trust, to hear the pain he had been feeling, and to recognize the courage it had taken to tell me at all, when he obviously could have gone on fooling me for the next 10 years if he had chosen to.

Hallie, on the other hand, in a horrendous marriage with a man who still had not admitted homosexuality, decided that as long as she'd stuck it out this far, she'd wait for 2 more years until retirement pay. Doris had decided that no matter what the problems, she needed her husband's help with the care of a mildly handicapped child. She told me, partly tongue in cheek,

> We're not all that young. I figure that when Bobby is old enough to care for himself, if my husband hasn't already died a natural death, I'll divorce. In the meantime, we don't really have a marriage, but now we help each other when we need to,

and we each assume responsibility for making our own happiness instead of blaming each other for our unhappiness. I was a real mess for years. But now I enjoy life, and when the marriage ends officially, one way or another, it'll be even better.

"Assuming responsibility for one's own happiness" was part of the second step in reintegration:

2. *Turning to new resources for help and developing new relationships, skills, and autonomy in seeking emotional gratification.* Doris, for instance, finally broke her self-imposed social isolation and insisted that her husband provide more help with their child. Previously a stereotypically traditional and subservient wife, she entered college, joined the women's movement, started a small business that brought her "exciting new experiences and new and interesting friends — both male and female — from all over the state."

3. *Defining and asserting one's own needs and rights, despite the risk that the husband might then wish divorce.* This might include obtaining extramarital sexual satisfaction in a functional, self-esteem-raising way, rather than out of anger, panic, or confusion. As Nan told me,

> I finally had my first affair a week ago. It happened naturally, I didn't plan it. Maybe I'm just ready for it now, when I wasn't earlier. It was wonderful! Knowing I could give and receive sexual pleasure, having him actually delight in my body, feeling turned on and knowing I was turning him on — Look at me! I'm 45 and I'm giggling like a schoolgirl!

Sometimes the enhanced self-esteem provided by such an affair enabled a wife to stay in a good marriage. Other times it enabled a woman to leave a poor marriage. For some women, asserting one's needs and rights meant halting a frantic effort to be "liberated" and asserting the right to maintain or return to traditional sexual values.

4. *Experiencing acceptance, release, and management of emotion.* During the beginning and interim periods, a flooding of emotions sometimes accompanied acute crises. Periodically a "spillover" occurred as tension was released in spurts of tears or anger,

with the emotions diffuse and undefined. If the husband was able to meet such reactions with empathic problem solving, emotions were released at low levels.

Generally, however, this did not happen. Hence the emotions were quickly bottled up and left to fester. In what seemed to be a transitional phase between the end of a final acute crisis and the beginning of final reintegration, weeks, months, or years of accumulated unexpressed anger often came out unexpectedly and explosively.

Twelve women reported such reactions happening either all at once or in a series of reactions to minor incidents. Milder behavior included hitting pillows, hitting the husband with a pillow (". . . with all my might! Thank goodness it wasn't a baseball bat!"), shouting, throwing ashtrays, and "standing in a corner, hitting the wall and howling in grief, rage and frustration." A popular book, *Loving Someone Gay*, read to gain understanding, was thrown out of windows and smashed against walls. Sometimes women would overreact to some unrelated frustration: one wife became furious when she had to wait in a hospital emergency room to have a broken arm treated and then became doubly frustrated when she could not explain that this was simply a "last straw."

Dorothy was still in a relatively happy marriage despite the fact that the initial disclosure, 10 years earlier, had resulted from an arrest. She had never confided in anyone, but considered her husband understanding and helpful whenever she had a "spillover" of emotion. Worried about being "disloyal," she did not definitely decide to participate in the study until she had asked him for permission, and was pleasantly surprised to have him actively encourage her to come for the interview. After it was over, she remarked that she had been surprised to hear the anger in her voice and words — she had not realized how much anger she held. Then she laughed. "But I think I'm getting more assertive. When I was getting ready to come over here," she said,

> my husband suddenly got scared. He asked me what I was planning to say, and then said "I want you to talk to that woman, but you're not going to tell her *everything*, are you?" I just put my hands on my hips and said "It's *my* interview,

and I'm going to say whatever I feel like saying, and I'm *not* going to tell *you* what I said."

A few weeks later, she called to take me up on the free counseling session all local wives had been offered in return for their participation in the study. The night before, her husband had been 5 minutes late in meeting her and she had suddenly felt "waves of rage wash over me." Overwhelmed and frightened by her overreaction and feeling too foolish to explain to her mystified husband, she had gone straight to bed.

Sometimes anger became projected onto on a husband's lover. Nan reported,

> One day, when I was feeling really down, my husband came to meet me on my coffee break, and just sat with me in the park. It was the first sensitive thing he'd done in months. I was really touched. Then suddenly he said it was time to go. I looked up, saw his lover at the far end of the park, and realized that my husband had really come to meet *him*, not me. I raced over and started screaming at him, really irrational. For weeks, every time I saw him, I saw red! Literally. I thought, "Smash!" "Kill!"

One wife reported standing calmly washing dishes as her husband prepared to go out, and suddenly "seeing" a glass "fly across the room and shatter against the wall, just missing him." Another time, she smashed a wine glass over his head while they were driving.

Another wife, trapped financially and religiously into a "horrendous" marriage, tried to seduce and even rape her husband. After a fourteenth and "final" sexual rejection, she told me, she hysterically lunged at him trying to bite off his penis ("He rolled over quick, thank God"). A few women required being told of such extremes before they dared admit their own behavior. Aileen, upon hearing the story, burst out laughing and said,

> Good for her! Well, I didn't try that, but rumor has it that I cracked a rib or two. He came home drunk one night, made one of his new horrible filthy cracks to me, and I let him have it! Me! I never hit anyone in my life! I always wondered how

boxers could punch people. Well [laughing], I found out it was relatively easy!

Such extremes emanated only from wives who had felt unusually mistreated. Usually, both the feelings and the behaviors were so frightening to the women that psychiatric help was sought immediately, but the release of anger had already paved the way for more constructive coping devices. The majority of wives maintained a more moderate level of anger that could be released without assigning excessive blame. Nevertheless, both divorced women and women still in reasonably happy but struggling marriages expressed frustration at not knowing how to handle anger:

> I wouldn't ever suggest that a husband be deliberately cruel — that'd be terrible! But sometimes I envy women whose husbands are just plain bastards. This way, there's no one to blame. It's not his fault, it's not my fault. I'm left with all this anger and no place to put it.

Many women did handle it during reintegration by becoming politically active, particularly in the gay rights movement or the women's movement. Many utilized writing ability in the form of diaries, poetry, or even planning or starting books or articles. Many cited and displayed the use of humor as a reintegrative device.

Following divorce, reintegrative steps were similar to those already cited but were often prefaced by a period of depression, mourning, and cathartic crying. This period was followed by developing new friendships, particularly with women. Eventually, most women formed new and satisfying emotional and sexual relationships with other men. While such relationships aided self-esteem, a return of self-esteem was not based purely on relationships with men. Whether or not they remarried, they were considerably more independent and autonomous than they had been in their former marriage.

Occasionally, reintegration started with a close brush with death that marked a transition point as sharp as that of the common movie scene in which the doctor looks up from the patient's bedside and dramatically announces, "The fever has lifted! The crisis is over!"

For example, when we last left Harriet, who had threatened her husband with murder, tried to kill herself, and then deliberately ignored a bleeding ulcer, she had been taken unconscious to the hospital. She continued her tale with the tears streaming down her face, in a Don't-stop-me-or-I-won't-get-through-this monotone:

> When I came to, a team of doctors was standing over me. My own doctor was there. He told me I was losing blood fast, and if they didn't operate immediately, I would die. I refused to sign the papers. I told him "I don't care. What do I have to live for? Just because I got adjusted to my life doesn't mean I like it." I remember he looked at me a long time. Then he came over and whispered in my ear, "Remember, if you die, you have no other relatives here. Your son will go to your husband." I sat up and said GIVE ME THE PAPERS!

At that last sentence, she began to chuckle. She had recovered, she told me, in record time. While still in the hospital, she had begun to plan more realistically for her son's care in the event that anything unintentional should happen to her, asked a gay colleague to help her understand more about homosexuality, read the literature he had suggested, and decided that both her son and her husband had the right to a father–son relationship no matter what her own grievances may be. By the time she returned home, she had made plans to renew old friendships and seek new ones. When interviewed, she was in a happy marriage-like relationship with a man, but was so enjoying the freedom that separate dwellings provided, she was still debating about whether to legalize the marriage.

For others, the road to recovery was long, painful, and tortuous. For Gloria, both blindness and religious proscriptions against divorce complicated the process. After she obtained her Ph.D. the marriage improved, but it was never truly happy. Both partners skirted the edges of disclosure until a gay friend helped them deal with the homosexuality directly:

> Our gay friend finally forced my husband to admit to me that he was "exclusively homosexual" — a "Kinsey 6." I was finally forced to face that fact. We made an "intelligent" decision to divorce, and our other friends, who did not know about the homosexuality, thought we were really "cool." Some friends in California offered to let me stay with them temporarily till I could start a new life, but I said no. I thought I was

pretty cool, too. Only when the divorce papers came, that's when it hit! I was in acute crisis!

Our gay friend suddenly offered to drive me to California if I could leave with him immediately. My husband practically pushed me and our son into the car. Although I hated him for it at the time, it was probably the kindest thing he ever did for me. . . . But when we reached California, I found my friends had never expected me to come. They had no room for me and offered no help. So there we were, one sighted "physical" child and one blind "emotional" child, both feeling rejected and alone in a strange city. It was like falling into an abyss — I've never felt so alone.

We wandered around the city for 2 years, my son acting as seeing eye dog and trying his best to be helpful. Poor thing — I was in too much pain myself to hear his. Finally, feeling both suicidal and homicidal, I sought psychiatric help. The psychiatrist I'd seen before had been forced on me by the church and was both punitive and useless. This time it was *my* choice, and my psychiatrist saved my life! My child and I literally grew up together, and now we have a marvelous relationship. I have good friends and two satisfying jobs. I finally found a church sect I'm happy with. So now, finally, my life is wonderful!

THE FINAL OUTCOME: THE PROMISE OF HAPPY ENDINGS

The women I interviewed were all in different stages of the total process. For those who had gone past the turmoil of the interim and beginning reintegration periods, the major theme, as with Harriet and Gloria, was that of a "happy ending" for the wives, no matter what the outcome had been for the marriage.

Self-Esteem

In a written questionnaire, asked how the disclosure of homosexuality had affected their *current* self-esteem, approximately 48% of all wives said "positively," 27% said "mixed" (positive in some ways, negative in others), 12% said "no effect" and 12% said "negatively.

General Happiness

When it came to "general happiness," women were more uncertain; 57% cited a "mixed" effect, 24% a "positive" effect. Still, 15% said "no effect," and only 3% said "negatively."

Sexual and Marital Satisfaction

As one would expect, the areas of sexual and marital satisfaction received the worst marks. A "positive" sexual effect was given by 36%, a "negative" one by 33%; 12% said "no effect," and 18% said "mixed." When it came to the current effect on marital happiness, 57% said "negative," 15% said "positive," 15% said "no effect," and 12% said "mixed." (Percentages are approximate.)

Sometimes a "positive" answer reflected a new sexual or marital relationship. It's important to remember here that these answers also reflect the stage women were in at the time of the interview. Except for "marital satisfaction," almost all "negative" and "mixed" reactions came from women who were either still in the confused "interim" period with a struggling marriage or who had been divorced less than 3 years. The same could be said of their scores on scales measuring self-esteem, depression, and sexual satisfaction. Those for whom long-term effects could truly be measured had either reached or surpassed the level of satisfaction they had had prior to the beginning of the pre-disclosure buildup. Those farther along in the reintegrative stage had already begun to show movement toward that end. With only one or two exceptions, only those still in the confused interim stage or the still turbulent beginning reintegrative stage scored low in self-esteem and high in depression. Although caution should be used in interpreting such scores, since they were based on women's memories of how they had felt at certain points and may not be entirely accurate, "current" scores were consistent with verbal and written discussion, and "past" (memory) scores were consistent with how women said they had felt at those times.

Of course, these figures represent the effect on the wives' feelings. The effect on the marriage itself will be discussed in the next chapter. For now, though, let's go on to give those "happy ending" statistics some meaning.

The interview tended to temper the one-word questionnaire reactions. Women who had summarized with "positive" responses felt free to include some "negatives" when elaborating during the interview. Women who had given a "negative" or "mixed" reaction felt free to include some "positives."

No matter how "negative" or "mixed" they might have been, all women stated that they had surpassed predisclosure or even pre-situational levels of autonomy or independence and assertiveness and in so doing, had increased their self-esteem. Women in still-happy marriages cited in especially glowing terms the increased communication, intimacy and affection, sexual satisfaction, and combination of freedom and commitment — in short, "joy" — that disclosure had brought to their lives. Terri, who had escaped an "acute crisis" state and considered disclosure a "mini-crisis," told me,

> I can honestly say that if I died tomorrow — and I certainly don't want to — I could stand before God with no regrets for my life. There's been nothing I've wanted to do and haven't done, and nothing I've done that I haven't wanted to. Well, [laughing], I haven't gone to Europe yet, I guess I'd still like to do that.

While Terri gave the most totally positive assessment (I'll talk more about her in the next chapter), with very few exceptions, most of the following "positives" were cited by every woman (whether still married or divorced) in the group:

> I'm a better person for this experience. I've found strengths and skills I never knew I had, and might never have known.
>
> Before, my self-esteem was based on my relationship to my husband or some other man. Now it's true self-esteem, based on my own abilities and attitudes and my relationships with many people.
>
> I know that whatever happens to me in the future, I'll be able to handle it.
>
> I've grown and matured. I have more compassion for people. I'm less bigoted. I've made wonderful new friends, both gay and straight, that ordinarily I would never have allowed myself to meet.

I've discovered my sexuality and found sexual and emotional happiness I never thought possible.

I've learned to be more careful about the contracts I make, not only with my husband, but also with other people, to make sure they're meeting both our needs and are not oppressive to either one of us, and to be more flexible.

I've become more assertive, more able to take responsibility for my own life and happiness, without basing my every thought and action on what others think. I expect my husband (or other people) to "help" me be happy, but I don't expect him (them) to just hand me happiness as if it were a commodity that can be "given" to someone.

I've discovered new ways of relating to men, and a new approach to life.

I enjoy women more.

I'm having fun. I'm enjoying my life. I don't envy people, they envy me. I'm looking forward to the future.

A few women were still in the midst of the confused interim period or just recently out of the postdivorce depression. They were still making cautious, tentative attempts at socialization, and although one had recently had her first "date," they had not yet established new sexual relationships with men. One or two of those women were still pretty bitter — either about their husbands or men in general. Yet even they stated most of the above positives. Whether or not they seemed headed for happier marriages or divorce, or expressed fears about the future, sexual frustration, or confusion about themselves and others, almost all appeared to have achieved some degree of positive reintegration and to be on the road to the happy ending that others had already reached.

In fact, three wives wrote or called several weeks after the interview to report that they had obtained high-paying and prestigious jobs and entered into a new and satisfying relationship with a man and that their "recovery" was now "complete." The only wife who remained severely depressed 5 years after divorce was Mary McDermott, who had been subjected to unusual rejection and isolation because of her promise to maintain the lie that she had divorced because of her husband's illness. She was given an emergency referral for therapy and wrote a few weeks later to say that she was already feeling better.

"Happy endings" were not "Hollywood" endings. There were financial problems for divorced wives and problems in working out children's relationships with both parents. One couple had agreed that their son would be happier and better off with his father. The wife sorely missed the mother–child relationship. All wives who had had good marriages, and especially those who maintained good relationships with their former husbands, expressed some "whistling in the dark" and sadness at the felt loss. Some spoke wistfully of fantasies that some day, when sex was no longer a concern, they would reunite with their husbands and grow old together.

No matter how "reintegrated" they were, pain had diminished but had not disappeared. Almost all women wept during the interview. In fact, I learned quickly not to start an interview without a full box of tissues on hand. Lamenting our failure to buy stock in Kleenex corporation the day before I started the study became a standard joke. Whether or not they cried, almost all women — even some who had been divorced for 10 years — expressed surprise at how vivid their memories and how strong their feelings still were.

Chapter 7

The Problems Wives Faced

What problems led to the extreme stress of the interim period? They fell into three categories: economic, intrapsychic, and interpersonal. Within the last two fell five interweaving problem areas: stigma, isolation, confusion, and cognitive dissonance (the disparity between old perceptions or beliefs and new realities).

ECONOMIC PROBLEMS

Wives faced the same economic problems found in any strife-ridden marriage where divorce is either considered or actualized. Even well-educated and professional women seldom earned enough for economic sufficiency. Those who had no jobs or work skills felt trapped in the marriage. If divorce did occur, there were the usual problems of financing double housing and child care. Both partners (and sometimes children) usually required therapy. Often there was an added fear—particularly acute and realistic for military couples—that the husband would lose his job if the homosexuality became known. In one case, reputed child molestation did result in loss of a job.

INTRAPSYCHIC PROBLEMS

Intrapsychic and interpersonal problems overlapped considerably and were almost inseparable. The intrapsychic problems, however, started almost simultaneously with the initial reaction to disclosure or even simply predisclosure perception of homosexuality. Wives went through several identity and integrity crises, starting with the internal questions "How did I get in this situation?", "What does it say about me?", "What will my future decisions say about me?". Almost all women felt several simultaneous or almost simultaneous emotions and perceptions that completely contradicted each other.

Sexual Identity and Integrity Crises

On the one hand, most wives suffered less conflict than they might had their competition been female. They could not, they reasoned, be men. Hence they were not at fault, and, as supportive husbands assured them, a need that they could not possibly fulfill did not detract from their own self-worth, femininity, and sexual desirability. On the other hand, they felt rejected and punished for the very fact that they were women. At the same time, they felt guilty about — and rejected for — their traits of intelligence, assertiveness, and competence at work. They wondered if they had driven their husbands to homosexuality because of such "masculine" traits, because they were not pretty enough, because they had gained weight, or because they were not competent enough in bed.

They worried that perhaps unconsciously they had chosen such a husband out of some neurosis. They worried that perhaps unconsciously they were asexual or even "latent lesbians." Any period in which they had had orgasmic difficulty or had not wanted intercourse when their husbands did heightened such fears.

Two wives reported that being given mannish haircuts also increased such a concern. Brenda was inadvertently given such a haircut by her husband, who was simply inept with a scissors. Her "butch" appearance created some anxiety, but the fact that her very pregnant stomach not only gave her a comical look but also announced her heterosexuality to the world, allowed her to take it in stride and treat it with humor. The second wife, however, had quite a different reaction.

Arlie, the young nonconformist, had accepted her husband's lover into the marriage for what she thought would be "an exciting new lifestyle." It turned into a month of horror. Her husband had always delighted in her assertiveness and nonconformity. Now he and his lover frequently told her that she thought like a man, acted like a man, and was probably a lesbian. An attractive, stylishly dressed young woman, she had gone to a party in a high-fashion outfit and was told by a gay man that her attire was "real macho."

Her husband's lover, a professional hairdresser, gave her and her husband free service. One day she arrived at the beauty salon late for a picnic and still in office garb. After her haircut, she accepted his offer to lend her what he called "appropriate picnic clothes." She took one look at herself in the mirror, saw a butch haircut and mannish clothes, said "Oh my God, it's true!" and went into an acute crisis reaction.

At that point she decided she was in danger of losing her whole identity and having a nervous breakdown. She immediately closed off communication with the circle of gay friends they had accumulated, and started divorce proceedings. The seemingly bizarre and distorted stories she told of cruel and humiliating baiting by her husband and his friends were confirmed by the spontaneous description from a friend who had witnessed some of the scenes. The friend, in fact, had added to Arlie's own story by describing the incident in which a "very sexy, high fashion" outfit had been labeled "macho."

While this was an extreme example, wives' fears were often reinforced rather than alleviated by others' tendency to blame them for their husbands' homosexuality. Professionals, trusted friends, liberals and conservatives, parents—sometimes even the husbands themselves—often told them, "Well, if you had stayed home more . . . ," "if you weren't so assertive. . . . ," "if you dressed more sexy . . . ," "if you weren't frigid . . . ," "if you weren't so oversexed . . ." and so on. Several wives stated that one of the first questions asked them by their therapists was "Do you think you're attracted to gay men?"

Several wives expressed fear of being labeled a "fag hag" (a woman who associates with homosexual men because she is afraid of heterosexual men). Terri was given such a label by the homosexual community at the same time she was perceived as a sexual threat by other wives. Two women in new marriages reported that whenever their new husbands became angry with them, they would say "Don't make me into a queer like you did your first husband." Another wife in a new relationship started a new business. When her first client happened to be gay, her new partner said "What is it about you that attracts them?"

Mental Health Crises

Women familiar with mental health literature — especially those in the mental health professions — worried about "neurosis" versus "mental health." Was it healthier and a sign of self-esteem to leave the marriage or to stay with it? Was refusal to renegotiate the sexual contract "assertive" or was it only "rigid?" Was willingness to do so "flexible" or only "passive?" Was it more "masochistic" to stay or leave? Was it healthier to tell others or not tell? To ask questions or not ask questions? To have their own sexual affair or not to? No matter what the issue, there were often at least two contradictory, equally persuasive ways of assessing any option they considered.

Moral Crises

Religious women faced severe dilemmas around moral integrity. They took their marriage vows of "forsaking all others," "in sickness and in health," and "till death do us part" very literally. This did not necessarily prevent them from accepting their husbands' extramarital activity. Not only did it make it more difficult for them to consider extramarital sex an option for themselves, however, it increased their sense of guilt if they did engage in dysfunctional sexual escapades.

For women tied to a Fundamentalist church with rigid proscriptions against divorce and a strong belief in female subservience to men, the dilemmas were especially acute. They felt they could neither divorce nor protest their husbands' actions. Yet the homosexuality was sinful in the eyes of the Church. Often both partners desperately needed the Church, but unless the husband wanted to "convert" (i.e., to exclusive heterosexuality), they felt they could not actively belong. Occasionally, both partners handled the situation by depersonalizing each homosexual thought or act ("It was just a behavior or a symptom. It wasn't really part of the *person*.") and/or treating it as the creation of an outside force, a seducer, or the devil. They then tried to remove that symptom as if it were simply an unwelcome visitor.

One wife became a combination of pastoral counselor and therapist. Another husband sought professional help and received "conversion therapy." When it simply converted his fantasies to activity, the wife chose a new therapist. Walking her fingers through the Yellow Pages, she inadvertently picked a counselor who was also an Evangelical minister, which she considered a sign from God. He performed several exorcisms and the husband was "saved" several times, but never permanently.

Couples who still loved each other lived in constant fear of discovery by the Church. Yet wives who no longer loved their husbands were nevertheless caught in a bind between their duty to stay married and serve their husbands and their duty to reject sin. If the husbands were seen as emotionally sick (and a few possibly were), the wives felt less guilty about the homosexuality but more guilty about leaving a husband "in sickness." Moreover, a few husbands, like Mary McDermott's, pledged their wives to secrecy, even when the separation was at their own insistence. The wives were then rejected by friends, relatives, or in-laws, for either breaking the "in sickness" vow or for leaving a "good" man for no apparent reason.

Less Fundamentalist and nonreligious women were caught in much the same moral dilemmas. The issues were simply framed as questions of ethics rather than religion, with questions of "right" and "wrong" based on personal decisions or the "spirit" rather than the "letter" of church doctrine. For example, was there a "moral/ethical" difference between homosexual and heterosexual acts in defining infidelity? A few husbands declared their extramarital affairs moral, their wives' immoral.

Political-Professional Crises

A minor yet important theme was an integrity crisis involving disparity between intellect and emotion. Religious and political conservatives had sometimes taken expressed stands against homosexuality and extramarital sex. They felt both moral and social hypocrisy. Political liberals faced a "Guess Who's Coming to Dinner" dilemma in realizing that they were not as "liberal" as they thought they were. Ashamed of any homophobic thought, they constantly worried whether occasional anger was homophobic or realistic. Sue Johnson's comment was typical:

> I feel like I'm constantly being scrutinized for homophobia, like I'm under a microscope. I get mad at him for always evaluating my reactions, but I do the same to myself. I wish I could rise above it, roll with the punches more, stop worrying about why I feel a certain way in a certain situation.

One wife in a still-happy marriage had participated with her husband in working for homosexual rights:

> It's funny how sometimes little things bother you more and are harder to work out than big things. In a sense, I felt more betrayed politically than sexually, because what he does sexually is *his* issue, but the political issue affected *my* integrity.
>
> We always had to fight the "guilt by association" battle of "if your husband cares about gay rights, he must be gay." I've never answered such accusations, no matter what cause we've worked for, but I have stated my indignation at that sort of attitude, and I was proud that my husband had gotten involved not because he was gay, but because it was "right."
>
> Well—I figure you can fight civil rights fights from the vantage point of the insider or the supportive outsider, but you should be honest about which it is. Now I feel left with egg on my face. I hope I would have stood beside him no matter what, but I'll never know. I wasn't given the choice. I feel like I volunteered to join him in a war, but he didn't tell me the kind of hill we were defending, he let me fight with the wrong weapons, and he never stopped to think that I might get hurt.
>
> Now we both struggle with feelings of hypocrisy. But if we step out of the closet now, the reality is that people will say "See, I knew it all along" and we'll have done more harm than good. I can understand his plight. We might have chosen this way no matter what. But whenever I face problems of political integrity, I also wrestle with some anger at him.

Mental health professionals such as psychiatrists, social workers, and psychologists differed in opinions as to whether their careers had helped them or hurt them. All felt that their profession had prevented worry about morality from a religious framework, had provided information about sex and homosexuality, had enabled them to be empathic and flexible, had given them communication skills, and had taught them to avoid precipitous, impulsive decisions. Aside from those aids, such a profession had not been of much use in giving them guidelines for this situation. One wife felt it had had no effect except perhaps to help her "give up" more easily. Another felt it had heightened confusion and the sense of stigma regarding mental health issues. Faced with a "shoemaker's son" problem, another was reluctant to either confide in or turn to colleagues for therapy. All felt torn between old and new professional stands on homosexuality and monogamy. As Jessie told me,

> I really think bisexuality is probably the most "normal" of everything. Maybe in the future all people will be both bisexual and nonmonogamous. But for now, I'm hopelessly heterosexual and monogamous. Accepting this intellectually is far simpler than accepting it on an emotional gut level.

Since such professionals were apt to have become political activists because of or in the line of their professional duties, they were the ones most apt to face the political integrity dilemma. In addition to fear of stigmatization from colleagues, practical considerations presented other problems. One married counseling team felt that they could not become more open for fear of imposing an added burden on patients already struggling with "transference" problems. A few wives felt hypocritical in expecting their patients or clients to "cope well" when they themselves were struggling. They felt the need for a professionals' support group where they could cry, air their conflicts, and struggle with homophobic thoughts without having to worry about appearing in worse shape than their potential or ongoing clients or reinforcing homophobia in others.

INTERPERSONAL PROBLEMS

Some interpersonal problems have already been mentioned, since they were, of course, part and parcel of other problems. Yet some problems need to be looked at separately and in more depth. They include such areas as dealing with children, parents and in-laws, coping with the husband's stress, and of course the biggest of all — the intricacies of the marital relationship itself.

Dealing with Children

Whether or not to tell children about the homosexuality, at what age to tell them, what to tell them, and how to help them cope with it were problems for both husband and wife. It was the one area in which almost all mothers specifically asked me for guidelines — and the one area in which none could be found. With great variations in the ages of children and in individual situations, there was also great variation in how each couple had handled the problem. Few, if any, wives were entirely satisfied with how either they themselves or their husbands had dealt with it. I suspect that the lack of guidelines is due to the fact that in today's society there simply is no "right" answer, but I'll give my own editorial on the topic in the last chapter. For now, however, let me act mainly as reporter.

The group of women who were least accepting of homosexuality worried about the "influence" on their children should the children be told of the homosexuality or see their fathers in a new homosexual relationship. Most of these same women, however, were also coping with husbands who were showing emotionally disturbed behavior, poor judgment, and sometimes violence. Their major concern, then, was for the safety of small children.

Eight women out of the 103 expressed past or present concern that their own children might be molested. Of those, one had been told by a psychiatrist that she *should* be afraid, since her husband liked adolescent boys. Whether the psychiatrist's assumption that this would lead to incest was valid or was based on homophobic stereotyping is not known. Another wife had been concerned at one time, but was no longer. Her husband had lost a job because of reputed molestation. The child in question was not his own, but because neither he nor the psychiatrist would talk to the wife about it, since she had children of both sexes and her husband had seemed interested in girls as well as boys, her previous concern was certainly understandable. Eventually, she had consulted a sex abuse expert who had helped her both assess reality and talk with her children in an empathic, nonfrightening way. Two had actually had to deal with a son's molestation — one by the father and one by the father's lover, with both resulting in considerable psychic trauma for the children.

Most of the women, more accepting of homosexuality, worried mainly about the stigma their children might face and about putting their children through the same kind of identity crisis that they themselves had undergone. Some wives insisted that the children be told, others that they not be told. Some with young children were waiting for their children to reach adolescence. Several felt that the husband should be the one to do the telling and were waiting impatiently for the husband to gather the courage to do so.

Those whose children had already been told varied in their reports of how the children had reacted. Small children appeared to have had little reaction, but of course were more apt to "spill the beans." Hence "confidentiality" was more of a concern for parents who were still closeted. Some adolescents handled the news badly, others calmly and saying they'd really suspected it (or known, as in Harriet's case) for some time.

Three situations became traumatic. One wife had insisted on secrecy until their child was through high school. Unfortunately, through a fluke just prior to a planned disclosure, the child learned about it from a friend. He was far more upset about the fact that the news had come from someone other than the parents than about the homosexuality itself. Both adults had at first blamed the wife, with the wife feeling guilty for not having allowed the husband to tell earlier. Eventually, however, she decided that the husband was also at fault for having broken his promise to maintain secrecy.

One older son used the opportunity to reveal his own homosexuality. Not only did the wife then have to cope with her added feelings about that (a relatively mild problem), she later watched him enter a relationship with a young woman who had fallen in love with him, without telling her. She was torn between her determination not to interfere with her son's life and her concern that he was about to bring someone else the pain that she herself had undergone.

Meanwhile, back at Laura's ranch, the third situation was far more serious. Her husband's severe emotional deterioration had finally forced her to both secure psychiatric help for him and face the homosexuality. She confronted her husband, but he denied it. The husband grew increasingly insensitive to her. She stayed with him as long as she felt he ioved her. But when she needed emergency surgery and he refused to cancel a business trip to be with her, she decided that the love no longer existed and began to prepare for divorce. The psychiatrist told her that under no circumstances should her husband be allowed custody of their children because of the possibility of sexual abuse.

There is no way to know whether or not such advice was sound, but Laura panicked at that point and called an older (though still young) and recently divorced son. Blurting out the secret she had carried for so long, she asked him for help in dealing with the situation, only to learn that he was struggling with emotional problems of his own. First he berated her for telling him at all, then he berated her for having not told him earlier.

A few months later the son was killed in a car accident. Though it was termed an accident, Laura firmly believed that he had actually committed suicide. She blamed herself for having burdened him with her problems when he was already overburdened with his own. That belief and self-blame had been heightened by her feeling that he had intimated he was having sexual problems of some kind himself and that hearing such news about his father may have increased his own worries.

The night her son died, Laura sat on her bed with a handful of sleeping pills. As with others, what stopped her from taking them was her concern about the trauma that such an action would bring to her other children.

She was the only wife who regretted having told a child. Asked what advice she would give other parents, she was conflicted, but felt that had she confronted her husband in the beginning, and had they worked out a suitable plan for their lives, they might have avoided the whole sequence of events that had brought such pain to parent and child alike.

The other parents who had told their children were glad they had done so. Nevertheless, wives tended to feel caught in the middle, torn by conflicting loyalties and feeling that no matter what they did it was wrong. Many resented the fact that their concerns about the children were simply dismissed as homophobia. They saw the children as conflicted, yet did not know how to help without sounding as if they were trying to turn the children against their father. They often felt that their husbands undermined any effort to either help the children voice conflicted feelings and talk over problems or to obtain professional help for them. Hence several husbands were praised for the sensitive way in which they had told their children but rebuked for their unwillingness to either recognize or help deal with problems that the children then faced.

That wives' concerns were realistic is suggested by an incident told me by a friend who knew of my study and thought I'd be interested. It seemed that while at the beach, he had noticed two young teenagers sitting near him. One was trying to comfort her obviously upset friend, who suddenly burst into tears. "You don't understand," he heard her say, "I'd *like* to talk it over with my father, but I *can't* because the reason I'm upset is that he's gay!"

Terri had only one complaint about her marriage. Both partners were having extramarital sex. From both an ethical decision and a practical reality, she had not hidden her activity. Her husband, however, so feared their rejection that he was unwilling to tell their children about himself. Hence when the children first realized what was happening with their mother, they accused her of being unfair to their father, and there was no way for her to adequately explain. Most wives, whether the children had been told or not, struggled with how to deal with homophobic language and jokes that the children brought home from school.

Aside from issues of homosexuality, all the parent–child problems usually found in families where divorce is either contemplated or actualized were found in these families. Problems were most acute in the "horrendous" marriages with the husband not admitting homosexuality despite blatant infidelity and verbal or physical violence. Two wives from that group had to eventually repair the damage of their own stress-related child abuse or near-child abuse.

Dealing with Parents and In-Laws

Most women lived away from their parents and were happy about that fact. They worried about the effect on aged parents who might be "devastated" by the knowledge of the homosexuality or over-protective or punitive toward the husband. Some parents who knew about the situation were supportive, but others blamed the wives (for working, being away from home, etc.) Two women reported this irrational reaction from their mothers: "I always knew he didn't like me."

Three wives lost the support of their in-laws and in one case an entire extended family. Two husbands had refused to tell their parents about the homosexuality and the wife was seen as unreasonable in wanting divorce. The other in-laws were ashamed of the homosexuality, blamed the wife, and threatened her with a lawsuit if she ever told anyone the reason for the divorce. In two cases, the rejection was so severe that the wife was asked to return approximately 10-year-old wedding presents. Conversely, one wife became uncomfortable when she received so much support from her extended in-law family that she felt she was causing her former husband's rejection by his own parents. Her breaking the family tie became as painful for her as breaking the marital tie had been. Couples who jointly decided not to tell parents were faced with the problem of how to explain divorce in a seemingly perfect marriage.

In summary, some families were supportive, some were punitive, and some were simply not told. They tried to be helpful, but were deliberately kept at arm's length. Most wives expressed conflict between wanting parental or familial support yet not being sure how much they wanted, how much was fair to ask for, and how capable a family was of coping with homosexuality.

Coping with the Husband's Stress

Some husbands were in such acute stress themselves that their needs automatically took priority, with the emotional disturbance a greater concern than the homosexuality. For example, Dr. E., a highly respected surgeon, lost his job when he suddenly began walking out of surgery. He became disoriented, calling frequently from one city, saying he was in another. He began to fly into rages, breaking furniture. One day he broke windows and tore off the garage door to get in when he had forgotten his house key and his wife was not home. He was being seen by a psychiatrist four times a week, but his wife was unable to obtain much information. She had stayed with him for almost 2 years following disclosure, but when the physical violence began, she decided to divorce.

Some husbands had threatened suicide at some point, usually when a wife had decided to divorce. A few were given in-patient psychiatric care. Whether the hospitalizations and psychiatric care were required for true mental illness or whether the husbands were also going through unrecognized acute crisis reactions is not known. Wives generally felt, however, that they were given little information about the nature of the husband's disturbance or help in knowing how to deal with it.

Three husbands showed an entire constellation of asocial behavior, erratic work histories, child molestation, brushes with the law unrelated to the homosexuality, alcoholism, poor interpersonal relationships, and heterosexual infidelity. Their homosexuality seemed almost incidental in their lives. It was the least of their wives' worries and served mainly as a "last straw" to precipitate a long-contemplated divorce. Their behaviors seemed to roughly correspond with self-described attitudes and behaviors of what researcher Brian Miller calls "trade husbands" (i.e., they used the sexual services of male prostitutes in public bathrooms, a practice known as "The Tearoom Trade").

Marital Relationship Problems

Despite the fact that almost half of the marriages had improved immediately after disclosure, not many maintained that positive effect. Approximately a third were still intact at the time I interviewed wives. A few were obviously heading toward divorce, and the rest were almost equally divided between being described as "shaky" or "struggling" and "happy" and "stable." A few had returned to and surpassed a previously "happy" status, with one or two reaching the "American Dream" description. Two divorcees did not ascribe their problems to either the homosexuality or the extramarital sexuality.

Generally, marital satisfaction and sexual satisfaction rose and fell together, with a good sexual relationship an important factor in the maintenance of a happy marriage. There were, however, some exceptions. Hallie, for instance, whose alcoholic husband had never admitted homosexuality and who was having heterosexual affairs, felt that sex was the only satisfying part of their marriage. Brenda, on the other hand, felt that the poor sexual relationship was the major factor in the "struggling" status of her marriage. A striking feature of scores measuring sexual and marital satisfaction was the wide disparity between those who rated their marriages as "happy" and those who rated them as "shaky."

THE CAUSES OF MARITAL BREAKDOWN

Why did so many marriages, even when they had been good ones and when the disclosures were "positive," fail? The direction the marriage took was based on several factors. They were essentially the same factors (the degree of mutual trust; love and concern for the other partner; the quality of communication; the amount and quality of recreational time spent together; the quality of the sexual relationship, and the degree of power and autonomy felt by each partner) that had determined the quality of marriage before disclosure.

Despite many husbands' expressed fears and beliefs, *no* wife appeared to have divorced purely because of her husband's homosexual interest or activity. Harriet, who had threatened to kill her husband and then tried to kill herself, was the only one to have divorced following a first disclosure without any attempt to save the marriage. She had faced such a strong betrayal of trust that to stay in the marriage would certainly have been unthinkable.

Except for her, almost all of the wives attempted to renegotiate the sexual contract to allow for homosexual activity. If they did not do so willingly at first, then they did it somewhat grudgingly later. The few who did not, saying it would be "sick" to stay married to a homosexually active husband, had actually described futile attempts to open up communication with their husbands and to seek ways of improving the marriage. All commented spontaneously a few minutes later, using almost the same words as Margaret's:

> You know, I've been thinking about your question as to whether I would have stayed in the marriage if my husband had acted differently. I guess if my husband had been more understanding of my feelings, if he'd shown the flexibility he was asking of me, if there had been some communication and he was showing me warmth, love, some kind of sex and all that, maybe we could have worked something out. But I was getting none of that, and I couldn't see that I would get any more in the future.

Most wives, then, stayed in the marriage as long as they felt that problems could be worked out, that they were loved, that they were either getting their fair share of emotional and sexual gratification, or that at least "staying" would be less painful than "leaving." Almost half of the divorces were at the husband's request over the wife's objections, although a few wives, in retrospect, credited their husbands with having been the more realistic of the two partners.

Male Chauvinism, Liberation Ethics, and the "I Can't Stand Blood" Syndrome

Problems faced in trying to save the marriage seemed to be related less to homosexuality per se than to three syndromes that might be called "Male Chauvinism," "Liberation Ethics," and the "I Can't Stand Blood" Syndrome. Although their causes may have differed, the attitudes and behaviors they engendered were so similar that it becomes difficult to say which syndrome was operating at any given time. All brought about extreme cognitive dissonance that added to the wives' confusion and put them in continual double binds. ("Cognitive dissonance" is the disparity between old beliefs or perceptions and new realities.)

Male Chauvinism

A few wives reported that disclosure had brought a decrease in their husbands' sexism. A few reported no change from earlier lack of sexism.

A major theme for most wives, however, was that although husbands retained or increased such outer trappings of nonsexism as help with the housework and child care and less "macho" dress, when the homosexuality came out of the closet a far more basic sexist attitude "came out" with it. That attitude, which Jo Freeman first called "male chauvinism," was that it is a man's (husband's) right and duty to discover and fulfill his desires (seen as "needs") and that it is a woman's (wife's) duty to stand behind him, help him, and be happy for him without complaint.

Liberation Ethics

The liberation ethics syndrome held the same basic tenets as "male chauvinism." It simply substituted the terms "oppressed minority" and "spouse-as symbolic-oppressor" for the original "man-husband" and "woman-wife." Any behavior to which the wife objected was defended with the complaint that she was denying the husband's homosexuality and that he was being oppressed. Those wives in struggling marriages as well as those who had already divorced reported their husbands' increasing and usually uncharacteristic insensitivity to their feelings, needs, and rights. The wives found themselves in double binds created both by their own ambivalence and their husbands' insensitivity at every step.

For example, they felt asked to decide how much they wanted to know and what sexual contract terms they wanted at a point when they had no idea how they would feel or what the consequences would be. They were then trapped into that contract by the statement "You said that was what you wanted."

Already-renegotiated sexual contract terms were often violated. Trial-and-error changes were made, with some wives starting out rigid and becoming more flexible and others taking the opposite approach. Changes were usually made, however, with a recognition of the husbands' inevitable sense of "double bind" (i.e., "damned if you do and damned if you don't"), seldom with recognition of wives' similar feelings. Most wives felt that whether they behaved well or badly, no matter what they did or how they felt, it made no difference. They were seen as "wrong" and their wishes, feelings, or rights hardly entered into their husbands' decisions.

If wives asked that there be no homosexual activity, their husbands agreed — and went out secretly. If they agreed to moderate amounts, the nights out gradually became more and more frequent. Previously considerate husbands started staying out all night, coming home drunk or stoned, going out on weekends, Christmas, New Year's — even on anniversaries and wives' birthdays.

If wives tried to hide their feelings when husbands went out, the husbands assumed they did not mind. Both husbands and therapists then later accused them of being dishonest and expecting husbands to be mind readers. If they stated their feelings, however, the husbands often went out anyhow. If they cried, they were accused of being manipulative, overly emotional, "just like a woman," and of "laying guilt trips." If they expressed anger, they were accused of being "jailers," "bitches," "irrational," "aggressive," and "unladylike." Either way, they were accused of "denying" the homosexuality and either way, the husbands fled the scene quickly. Both minor and major arguments often ended with either a direct or an implied "If you don't like it, tough! Divorce me!"

The "I Can't Stand Blood" Syndrome

Interviews with several husbands suggested that at base they were still so guilt ridden about homosexuality and so homophobic themselves that they simply assumed their wives shared those feelings. Hence they sincerely believed they were being considerate and sincerely believed that their wives were complaining about homosexuality per se.

Many husbands were truly distressed at the pain they felt they had created and were so excessively guilt ridden that they could not tolerate any sign of pain, any expression of emotion. It was as if they had said to themselves, "My God, I've hurt her. She's bleeding! I can't stand blood! I can't stand the guilt! GET ME OUT OF HERE!"

Such husbands could tolerate neither anger nor tears. Yet wives were often neither that angry nor that unhappy. Their emotion was not necessarily directed at the homosexuality itself, but rather at some specific incident or problem. The husbands would refuse to discuss problems until the wives were "in better control," or they would say "Maybe I shouldn't have told you. Maybe we shouldn't talk about it if it brings you so much pain." This left wives unable to relieve tension, sort out conflicted feelings, or find solutions to problems. It left them more angry and worried about what might be happening secretly.

Terri, who had an unusually good marriage, summarized this syndrome from her vantage point as the leader of an informal support network:

> This experience has taught us—and my husband needed to learn it even more than I did—to have a new outlook on the idea of "hurt" or "pain." Instead of seeing it only as a negative, we now see a positive aspect that occurs when it is a part of "growth." Growth can cause pain, and pain can cause growth.
>
> At first, because our good marriage became so much better, I was a bit impatient with wives who were so upset. But then I realized that if I had been treated like those wives had been treated, I'd have been upset too! The other men I've talked to just couldn't handle the hurt they put on their wives. They withdrew emotionally and sexually or left the marriage. As far as I could tell, the wives could have handled the pain. But they were given no choice entering the marriage without knowing, and they were given no choice when the husband came out. So instead of a little hurt, I've seen a lot of marriages end that need not have ended, a lot of growth that was nipped in the bud, and a lot of pain that was really unnecessary.

If this was Terri's conclusion about her small support group, it was completely consistent with my conclusion about the group as a whole.

Trust

Trust was an important ingredient for the maintenance of the marriage. A husband's strong betrayal of trust often precipitated a wife's decision to divorce. More difficult to appraise, however, were minor situations in which a husband was found to have withheld some bit of information that might have changed a wife's reaction to a particular friendship or behavior. While the husband was often mystified at the wife's "overreaction," the wife tended to feel that the spirit, if not the letter, of a contract had been broken. She felt unable to decide which of the two partners was being unreasonable or to adequately explain what she wanted for the future.

Many wives in struggling marriages trusted their husbands, but did not trust "the future." Their words were similar to Dorothy's:

> I'm always waiting for the other shoe to drop. We love each other, and I don't want to divorce on the basis of what *might* happen in the future. That would be like cutting off my nose to spite my face. But I can't help worrying that he's just not telling me something because he's afraid to hurt me. . . . I keep wondering when he's going to come to me in good faith and say he loves me but he just can't continue in a heterosexual marriage. . . . I don't want to leave him, but if we're going to get divorced, I want it to happen now, while I'm still relatively young and attractive. . . . I can't continually ask him for reassurance, yet I don't think he really understands why I'm scared or how scared I am!

Sometimes "disparity" became a problem. A wife stayed in the marriage until she perceived a disparity between her husband's commitment to her and to either his new lifestyle or a specific lover. Brenda, for example, had accepted her husband's lover into the marriage without feeling coerced, and the two had become good friends. She received some of the added companionship she had anticipated. But she was becoming increasingly upset at seeing her needs receive the lowest priority of the three.

Before "Bill" had entered the picture, she had been upset at the care and excitement her husband had shown dressing to go out on his "night out" in contrast to his lack of interest when getting ready to go out with her. Now she was seeing him buy presents for Bill but not for her. He rushed to comfort Bill when Bill was feeling rejected or left out but did not do the same for her when she had such feelings. She saw him sleeping with his arm around Bill, while their own sexual relationship was marked by lack of such expressions of affection. When the two men forgot a planned family outing and went to a party instead, she threw them both out and prepared to divorce. A reconciliation occurred and improved matters, but the marriage, predictably, was still having its ups and downs when I interviewed her.

Similarly, part of the "sexism" or "liberation ethic" was what some husbands have termed "having one's cake and eating it too" and "redoing adolescence." Many wives used exactly the same terms. Husbands, however, used such terms to describe joy and liberation. Wives, on the other hand, used them to describe what they considered irresponsible, selfish demands for the freedom of bachelorhood while enjoying the comforts of marriage.

Sexism or liberation ethics, however, was not the exclusive domain of men. Fran, for example, reported that a return to school and involvement in the women's movement, plus the fact that disclosure had not brought the increased intimacy she had anticipated, had put her in a "man-hating period" in which her husband "could not win." She herself withdrew commitment to the marriage and divorced, despite the fact that her husband had never acted upon his homosexual fantasies during their marriage. Angela, the one wife who had come to grips with her own homosexuality following disclosure, began to spend more and more time away from home. She eventually followed her own lover to another state, despite her husband's reproachful pleading, "But when I came out, I stayed committed to you. I didn't leave!"

Sexuality

A few more comments regarding problems in sexuality are in order. Both partners were often conflicted about attitudes toward female sexuality. A few husbands were called "male chauvinists" who invoked rigid double standards. Most husbands, however, whether as a way of easing their own guilt or out of a sense of justice, urged their wives to seek affairs. Yet they often became jealous and upset if the wives did so. Like Mary's husband, some considered their own extramarital sexuality "faithful" and "moral," their wives' "unfaithful" and "immoral." Phil, who had literally pushed his wife into the arms of a stranger, later asked her to stop what had finally become a pleasant affair, telling her, "Intellectually I know you have the right. In my guts, I can't take it."

Even when husbands remained true to their agreement, wives again faced a double-bind situation. On paper they had the "right." In reality, there was difficulty in using that right. Most women were not interested in "one-night stands" and often felt guilty about sex without love. Yet the couple's new sexual contract specified "sex but not love." Moreover, wives usually had less opportunity for affairs. Partly this was a function of time. As Sue put it, "I'm trying to juggle a full-time job and the responsibilities of housework, child care, and hostessing. I don't have time for a haircut, much less an affair." Partly it was a function of society's double standards: women in their late 30s, 40s and 50s were not likely to find partners as easily as their husbands were.

In the marital bed, if the wife asked for sex, she often felt or was accused of being aggressive, oversexed, punitive, and of denying the homosexuality. If she didn't, she was accused of being frigid, passive, or asexual. If she accepted a husband's erectile problems as unrelated to the homosexuality, she was later again accused by the husband as having denied the homosexuality. If she didn't, she was accused of being homophobic. Often such accusations were reinforced by therapists.

WHY DID SOME MARRIAGES SUCCEED?

Happier wives tended to have husbands who were either less active homosexually or who had impersonal encounters rather than love relationships.* Wives' own personalities, sexual needs, reli-

---

*The new problem of AIDS, however, may well change that finding.

gious and cultural attitudes about monogamy and homosexuality, etc., certainly played some part in the course the marriage took.

For example, Terri, a flamboyant and assertive woman, had viewed disclosure as an opportunity that would allow her to meet her own desire for extramarital sex. She delighted in a highly unconventional marriage and unconventional sexual relationships. Her husband, who rated himself a "Kinsey 5," was so homosexually active that he described himself as promiscuous. He had had love relationships, and one lover was brought into and had stayed in the family for almost 5 years. Terri had her own heterosexual lover, and occasionally she and her husband would become involved in a swinging group. Few other women in the study would have been comfortable with her lifestyle.

Nevertheless, comfort with unconventionality did not seem to be the whole story. No matter how traditional the wives may have been, most wives had done their best to understand and allow for their husbands' needs. Moreover, Terri had come from the same highly religious and conventional background that others had come from. Although no longer conventional, she and her husband (who once studied for the priesthood) remain highly religious. There were other wives who were as unconventional in spirit as she was, had faced a positive disclosure with the same excitement that she had, had allowed a husband's lover into the marriage as enthusiastically as she had. The results had been far different. Neither the degree of homosexuality, the wife's personality, nor her attitudes, then, appeared to be the key, nor was Terri's lifestyle necessary for other happy marriages.

A support network seemed to be helpful, with Terri and a few other happily married women stressing its importance. Certainly for Winnie an understanding support network had been a key factor in saving her marriage despite a negative disclosure. Yet not all happily married women had a support network, and as we'll see in the next chapter, it was impossible to compare wives with and without an adequate gay/straight support system, since there was no adequate one to be found.

There did, however, seem to be a few clear-cut answers. Rather than the degree of a husband's homosexuality, it seemed to be his degree of *heterosexuality* — or at least his ability to find heterosexual satisfaction, his love for his wife, and his ability to show empathy and regard for a wife's needs, rights, and feelings that were the crucial factors.

Those marriages that seemed to flower rather than wither were marked by that ability. The husband retained a primary commitment to the wife both emotionally and sexually, no matter how homosexually active he might be. The wife felt listened to, heard, understood, loved, and treated fairly. Communication was increased. Displays of emotion—even overreactions, unanticipated reactions, and conflicts about homosexuality or stigma were both tolerated, understood, and given empathic help.

The sexual relationship was maintained and was usually good. Even when problems occurred, the husband was committed to helping the wife obtain sexual satisfaction within the marriage, found some degree of satisfaction himself (as opposed to merely "servicing" his wife), and engaged in empathic problem solving rather than criticizing. Contracts were kept, and when minor problems arose, the husband was able to both assert his own needs and compromise to meet his wife's. The wife felt that she had a reasonable amount of power in the relationship and hence also had true choice.

No matter what the situation, the husband was empathic enough with the wife to know what she—as an individual—needed. Terri's husband voluntarily gave up his love relationship the moment he saw it was in danger of interfering with the marriage, without Terri even having to ask for a change. Jessie's husband retained his honesty with his wife, but curbed his eagerness to talk about a lover when he realized that it was causing her too much pain. Terri's lifestyle may have differed from other happy wives, but her stated feelings about her husband and the quality of her marriage spoke for all:

> Not a day goes by that my husband doesn't show me both verbally and nonverbally that he loves me. I know that if at some point I'm feeling especially vulnerable and tell him I'd prefer he not go out, he'll stay home willingly, without "punishing" me for it. Therefore I have real choice. I can *choose* to accept small hurts, knowing that I will be repaid over and over again with pleasure. And it's a two-way street: sometimes I do

that for him, sometimes he does it for me. We care for each other and we care about each other.

Those marriages appeared to be not merely happy—they seemed far better than average. Of course, one never knows for sure how accurately a "statement" describes life itself. I can, however, tell you something about Terri's family, both from staying with them for the 2 weeks I spent interviewing in their city and from their minister's long-term knowledge of them.

It was one of those situation-comedy households described as "warm, crazy, funny." If I had worried about imposing on strangers, I needn't have. Guests continually popped in to stay for a few hours, supper, overnight, or for several days. They were treated like family. Housekeeping was treated casually. Rather than being Terri's job, shared responsibility was simply taken for granted and was provided automatically, willingly, and cheerfully by her husband and anyone else around.

Their two sons—even the teenager—were unusually at ease with adult strangers. Other than that, they seemed almost stereotypically "all-American" boys. They roughhoused with each other, argued over the use of a new baseball mitt, and spent more time at baseball practice than they did at school homework. Parental tempers flared briefly when the youngest child forgot to keep his eye on a gigantic new puppy, who had an accident on the living room rug and ate the family flower garden.

True, the family hardly held traditional sex roles. After the children went to bed, the parents may have had atypical sex lives. But measured in terms of love, warmth, happiness, and humor, this family could have been the prototype for "Leave it to Beaver," "Happy Times," or "Ozzie & Harriet," with the laughing coming from the family members instead of an audience.

CONFUSION, ISOLATION, STIGMA, AND LOSS

Such problems as confusion, isolation, stigma, and loss have been continual themes throughout the preceding chapters. Their reciprocal and cumulative effect cannot be emphasized strongly enough. Each one of these problems was created by and added to the others.

Confusion

So much confusion resulted from the many contradictory feelings, perceptions, and options that internal dialogues resembled the "three-handed" debates that Tevye in *Fiddler on the Roof* held with God ("On the one hand . . . On the other hand . . . On the *other* hand . . ."). In this case, however, there were so many "hands" that many women felt they were struggling with hordes of octopi. As one young wife told me a few months after disclosure,

> I feel in a double bind all the time, and I put him in one too. I have a million things going round in my head, trying to figure out what's right, what's wrong, what I want, how I feel. I guess I sound pretty confused, but . . . but that's because I am!

For women used to being assertive and decisive, and whose total approach to life gave meaning to the expression, "I think, therefore I am," such confusion was as much a blow to the self-esteem as anything the husband had done. The following statement was typical:

> I kept on thinking how silly it was that I couldn't figure out what must be a simple, logical solution. I thought any day now I'd get a handle on it, make a decision, and do what had to be done. But just that day, that minute, I couldn't seem to do it.

Some women stayed in the marriage because the only thing they perceived clearly was that they were in no shape to make a rational decision. Two women left when the only thing they perceived clearly was that:

> It was no longer an issue of what was right or wrong, what was best for the children, when was the best timing, or anything else. It was an issue of "Get out now, today, or end up in a mental hospital." It was a question of survival.

Some confusion came from disparity between old beliefs or perceptions and new realities or perceptions. It is this disparity that is called "cognitive dissonance." For example, religious conservatives often felt a disparity between old stereotypic ideas about homosexuals and the realization that their husbands did not fit such stereotypes. Conversely, political liberals sometimes felt that the stereotypes they and their husbands had vigorously disclaimed seemed to be coming true in their own lives.

An even greater sense of dissonance came from sudden change — often it seemed like a Jekyll–Hyde change — in behaviors, expressed attitudes, and values, as well as the husband's stated sexual orientation. Wives were often accused by the husbands or therapists of dichotomizing homosexuality and heterosexuality and seeing the husband as a "changed" person simply because of a label. Wives' descriptions, however, suggest that the wives may have done this less than the husbands themselves did, and that many husbands did indeed "change." Reporting a change from a conservative, considerate businessman to an inconsiderate and flamboyant swinger, Aileen said,

> You have to understand that it was not what he did that was so strange, it was the contrast. He always prided himself on his sense of ethics. Now he tells me I'm old fashioned, and that it's a dog-eat-dog world. Our only fights had been about *his* violent homophobia and general bigotry. I was the one who convinced him to wear pink shirts, he was the one who sneered at hippies. He wasn't just a corporation man, he wore grey flannel underwear!

Marsha, my former client, recalled that therapy session in which her husband had been so unexpectedly cruel and humiliating that even my co-therapist and I had been stunned:

> No matter what my complaints, he'd never acted like that! On the way to the interview, he'd been especially tender, telling me how sorry he was for hurting me and how we were going to work things out. The things he was saying 10 minutes later in the interview — I was stunned! He was someone I didn't know! A strange new person!

Another aspect of dissonance added to the helplessness in trying to fit learned sexual skills to husbands' needs:

> You're taught that certain behaviors, attitudes . . . your femininity . . . is what makes you appeal to men. Suddenly that whole system falls apart. If it had been a woman, I'd have understood the attraction better. I'd have known what to do — or at least what to try. Having it be a man is easier on the self-esteem in some ways, but it's harder on the sense of helplessness.

That same theme was heard over and over again. Trying to reconcile the husband's newly stated sexual identity with his old one and with the wife's own perceptions of him and trying to understand what such terms as "homosexuality" or "bisexuality" meant to him provided more confusion, as seen in the following typical comments:

> He tells me I'm denying his homosexuality. I think I can accept the homosexual part of him pretty well, but sometimes I think he denies the heterosexual part.
>
> I can empathize only up to a point. He says he's bisexual, but I'm the only woman who's ever turned him on. I don't understand that. I don't understand why an occasional fling should color every aspect of his personality and life gay, as he says it does. If his homosexuality is what makes him the sensitive and kind person he is, I'm all for it. If telling me has increased his spontaneity in sex the way it seems to have done, I'm all for that too. But I'm not sure I understand it.

Stigma and Isolation

While stigma and isolation have already been given some discussion, the wives' perception of homophobia that rubbed off on them and of the sexist base to both their own husbands' and outer society's attitudes toward them was such a dominant theme that some added comments are appropriate. All but a few women labeled the double-barreled stigma of homophobia and sex-role stereotyping as either the worst or one of the worst problems they faced.

Many wives feared or had already experienced automatic negative and stereotypic reactions to them from others. That their fears and perceptions had some basis in fact was suggested by *a priori* assumptions and statements made to me by many people, including therapists. One young man, for instance, volunteered:

> I can tell you all about wives of gay men. They're very intelligent, assertive, capable women. Probably that's why their husbands married them. They're really more like men.

Male (more than female) therapists who asked me about the study had usually treated few, if any such wives, yet were often far more interested in stating their own ideas than in hearing new ones. One who had seen a few accurately described some of the identity crises I have described and then added,

> Of course it's important to always keep in mind the psychodynamics, the underlying needs of women who would stay in such a marriage: the power they must feel from their martyrdom.

As we have seen, if there was any need met from "martyrdom," it was certainly not a sense of "power!"

One therapist, asked what I was finding. When I answered that many women worried about what their husbands' homosexuality said about *them*, he said emphatically, "And well they might!" He had never treated such a wife. I told him that so far I had found nothing to indicate problems in the wives' underlying sexual identity. He simply gave me a condescending half-smile, shrugged his shoulders, and changed the subject. His friend, also a therapist, gave me a common therapist reaction:

> I'm sure you're finding that these women have the same syndrome of battered wives and wives of alcoholics, that they repeat the patterns of their parents, and marry men who cannot possibly meet any of their sexual or emotional needs.

Another typical therapist assumption was that the women had had a history of repeated marriages to gay men and that a high percentage came out as lesbians following disclosure. One psychiatrist told

me there was a study to confirm this and that I "should look it up."
When I told him that I had done a computer search and had found
no such study, he said, "Well, I can't remember where it is, but
I'm sure there is one. You should look it up."*

This study was not deliberately designed to determine the pre-
existing mental health or family backgrounds of the wives. But as
seen in Chapter 3, there was enough information to suggest that
although such assumptions may have fit a few wives, there was
little evidence of such group patterns, syndromes, or characteristics. On the contrary, there was considerable evidence that the fac-
tual base to such assumptions was little more than the "kernel of
truth" found in other stereotypes.

If straight therapists were most apt to focus on "battered wife
syndromes," gay therapists were apt to focus on "hysteria" and
"vindictiveness" of wives following disclosure, to ascribe husbands' dysfunctional and irrational behaviors to stigma, and wives'
behaviors to neurosis and homophobia. Dr. A., for example, had
seen several couples, and in contrast to others, was unusually sensitive in his statements about wives. Yet listen to the inconsistencies
in this excerpt from an interview with him:

Q. *What do you consider your first task with a couple?*

A. Oh, calming every one down, diffusing the exploding
emotions. When they first come in, both partners are upset.
The husband is feeling guilty and scared, the wife is hysterical
and sure her marriage is doomed. I try to relieve the guilt and
panic, stop the dichotomizing, and reassure them both that
such marriages can work.

Q. *What is your major task with husbands?*

A. Relieving the sense of stigma. The husbands are often
really homophobic, even though they don't realize it. They
dichotomize and act in ways that they think gays are supposed
to act. I try to help them realize that their behaviors are stereotypes and have nothing whatsoever to do with gayness.

---

*He may have been referring to Myra Hatterer's report on twelve wives whose
husbands were being given conversion therapy, whom she regarded as "neurotic"
and who did have a high percentage of divorced parents.

There's nothing sadder to me than to see 50-year-old men suddenly start dressing like 20-year-olds, trying to change their entire personality and project a gay swinger image, and for no reason whatsoever other than their own stereotypes and guilt, insist on riding off into the sunset and leaving long and perfectly happy marriages.

Q. *What is your major task with wives?*

A. To help them face their neurotic *need* to dichotomize, to see their husbands as "changed" and their marriages about to end.

Several women reported fears of being labeled a "fag hag." Remember Terri, who was described to me as a "fag hag" at the same time that she was perceived as sexual competition by other wives.

Isolation and stigma were handmaidens in a vicious cycle. The more stigmatized a wife felt, the more she isolated herself. The more she isolated herself, the more stigmatized she felt. As noted in the introduction, the sense of isolation was the first and most dramatic finding of the study, with women in San Francisco feeling as alone and unique as women in rural upstate New York. One of the stated reasons for participating in the study was "to help others avoid the terrible sense of isolation I felt."

Husbands often had the gay support system to help them, although admittedly, it was not always kind to married men. Most wives, however, had no one other than a therapist in whom to confide. This in itself caused problems. Fear of discovery stifled spontaneity in existing relationships. Internal dialogues simply kept women going around in psychological circles. Already confused and with no one around to provide a more objective viewpoint, wives became increasingly paranoid and disoriented, with an increasing sense of "craziness." One wife did not realize the importance of a support system until she finally found someone in the same situation with whom to compare notes:

After listening to her story I was less hesitant to share my own. I told her of a small problem I was facing. I felt it wasn't fair to bring up angry feelings I'd had 3 years ago, but hadn't been able to pinpoint or express at the time. Yet I couldn't get past that anger. She listened, then said "Well, your husband seems pretty understanding. If you told him just exactly what you've just told me, don't you think he'd understand?"

It was as if the Red Sea had just been parted for me. I'd struggled with that problem for so long. The solution was so simple (and I always knew it was, even though I couldn't find it), it was mind blowing. If that conversation had taken place with anyone else, I'd have felt like a real fool. But she'd struggled with just as stupid things. I didn't feel a sense of criticism from her, just help. Now I'm partly grateful to have met her (although unfortunately, she moved away), partly mad at myself for having wasted so much time on such an easily solved problem, and partly furious that with any other issue, the ability to share with others would have prevented such a small issue from becoming such a stumbling block.

Were such fears of confiding in others paranoid? Certainly, to some extent. Paranoia was one of the problems that isolation increased. Most women who took the chance eventually found that many of their fears were exaggerated. But caution was not unwarranted. Most women also found prejudice and lack of understanding, and many retreated quickly after their first negative experience.

While helping me with my first written report on the study, my male "editor" suddenly stopped reading and exclaimed,

My God! I just realized something! Recently several people in my office got divorced, often because of a spouse's extramarital affairs. Each time, all the others gathered around the person and gave support, and we said to each other, "No wonder! Now we understand why she's been so bitchy lately! She's been going through hell!" But when one woman gave her husband's homosexual affairs as the reason for divorce, we gave her no support, and we said to each other, "Of course! Wouldn't you know she'd have a husband like that? She's so bitchy!"

Loss

Almost all wives experienced either the threat or the actuality of partial or total loss of their husbands' commitment to them. They had to cope with the same grief of other divorcees or widows.* Added to the grief of the ordinary divorce, however, was the fact that most wives still loved their husbands and were often loved in return. Emotional separation became difficult for both partners, but especially for wives, who had no ready replacements. For a few women, there was no time to deal with feelings and prepare for single life. Like Janna, they were simply dismissed without notice, like maids. Most divorced women said "Loss is loss! Who cares whether it's heterosexual or homosexual? When you lose someone you love, it's very painful!" Many, however, felt their pain compounded by an accompanying feeling that divorce might have been unnecessary had either partner known better how to cope with the situation and had they had better help.

There was perhaps an even worse sense of loss than the loss of a loved one: the wives' loss of faith in their own perceptual skills. True, a few reported that those skills had been confirmed and sharpened by disclosure, providing them with greater faith in the "intuition" they should have respected earlier. Most, however, reported a devastating blow to their faith in their ability to evaluate reality:

> If I'd been so wrong before, how could I trust what he said or how I felt in the future?
>
> I felt like a giant fool! . . . I really got paranoid. I mistrusted everyone, not only his male friends, but female ones too. Even people who reached out and tried to be supportive of me. I found myself looking at every male, wondering about him. Sometimes I felt like the whole world was gay!
>
> What if it happens again? I like the qualities I find in gay men. How do I know I won't choose another one?

---

*Obviously, by now, some women not in the study (and I must admit that I worry about a few in the study) will have had to cope with both the stigma and the actual grief of widowhood or of their own impending death due to AIDS.

If he never loved me and I never perceived it, how do I know I won't get fooled with the next man?

Many wives wondered if their happy marriages had been a "sham." If a husband denied having ever loved a wife or having ever been heterosexual, the sense of "dissonance" increased, and the wife felt her "past" as well as her "future" had been lost. No matter what, during the interim period a wife often felt that she could no longer trust her own perception of the world and people in it, nor could she trust her own judgments. In every sense of the word, she had lost "herself."

Chapter 8

The Search for Help

To whom did the wives turn for help? How did they rate the help they received? What helped and what hurt? Although I have alluded to such issues before, this chapter will answer those questions in more depth.

As noted earlier, there was great variation in both the timing and sequence in turning to others. The quality of help seemed of prime importance. It also seemed, however, that the earlier a wife sought help, the larger the support network and the more the husband participated in and encouraged counseling or confiding in others, the speedier and more solid the wives' reintegration tended to be. Almost all who sought help eventually found it, but for most, the path to that eventuality was a long and bitter one. Perhaps the most significant finding was that although women desperately wanted and needed a support system specifically designed for this situation, the almost total lack of such a system prevented a valid estimation of its real worth.

THE HELP OF FAMILY AND FRIENDS

Generally, wives tended to isolate themselves from others and to be extremely cautious about who they told. There seems no point in repeating details about negative reactions from others, other than to note that when such reactions came from those who had been expected to be understanding, they were especially damaging. What was seen as helpful was the ability of family and friends to listen, to provide empathic, nonjudgmental support, to encourage without forcing a depressed wife's socializing, and to include a divorced wife in activities that did not make her a "fifth wheel."

Several wives learned of the study from friends who had brought them the newspaper announcement or from former husbands who had sent it to them. Aileen cited the empathic creativity of a neighbor who refrained from scolding her, but who sent her 3-year-old child over to make sure that Aileen had gotten out of bed.

"I'd have probably been angry had she come over herself," Aileen remarked,

> but how can you yell at a 3 year old who's asking you to come play with her? You can't! You get up. You have something to do immediately besides thinking about how miserable you are, and it helps. My friend knew that. She didn't preach it to me, she showed me.

Several women stated that they would have never made it through divorce without the help of their children, who both made them feel needed and who parented them. Two daughters "made Christmas" when their mother was too depressed to bother and frequently pinned notes to her pillow with messages like "It'll be better tomorrow," "We have faith in you," and "Don't be so hard on yourself. You're a great person!" Two other teenagers told their mother, "C'mon, get out of your bathrobe and take us to a movie. Stop thinking about Dad! You have US! We love you! We need you! Aren't we important too?"

In the midst of my interviewing one wife only 3 weeks after her divorce, her 8-year-old son came home unexpectedly early from Cub Scouts. After we had been introduced, his eyes went from me to the pile of used tissues on the coffee table, to his mother's red and swollen eyes, back to me again. "What's going on here?" he asked me, accusingly. Then he remembered. "Oh, I guess you're the lady who's talking to Mom about Dad." He patted his mother's hand reassuringly, telling me, "Don't worry, she's been that way a lot lately, but she's getting better every day. She's going to be all right!" He thought maybe he should finish the interview for her and was willing to leave the room only after she promised that she was feeling better and that there would be no more tears. One was reminded of stories about mother bears and their cubs. Only in this case, the cub was protecting the mother.

What was *not* seen as helpful were homophobic remarks (even when intended as supportive to the wife), false reassurances ("Everything's going to work out fine"), platitudes ("Well, you're lucky. It could have been another woman"), "sexist" advice ("He's your husband, you should serve him"), simplistic blame and solutions ("Well, maybe if you stayed home more and were a better wife"), self-righteous criticism ("I don't see how you could think of staying with him, you must be sick," "I don't see why you're so confused, it seems pretty simple to me," or "I knew it all along. How could you have not known?"). Wives also disliked over-solicitousness and an attitude of pity.

THE HELPING PROFESSIONS

The helping professions received very mixed reviews, with positives and negatives often coming from the same reviewer. Most women eventually found someone helpful, but it was usually after a long and diligent search. One wife cited Ann Landers as being the most helpful, simply by advising people in her column to keep searching for the right counselor.

The Church as Helper

Over a third of the wives had turned to the Church. Of those, several felt that disclosure had increased the role of religion in their life, although that religion may not have been in the church of their childhood. A few became "born-again Christians." A few wives felt estranged from the Church either because they no longer accepted church dogma or because they now felt unacceptable to their church.

A few liberal ministers were criticized for being so shocked and overwhelmed that they could offer sympathy but no help. Such reactions increased the wives' sense of helplessness. Two ministers and their wives in the study felt that generally liberal church policies did not extend to homosexuality and hence were afraid to confide in anyone. One couple divorced partly because the husband felt he could neither ethically keep such a secret from his parishioners nor tell them, nor could he allow his actions to hurt his wife, who was also a strong church leader. He moved to another city and changed professions. The other couple are still together. Living in an isolated area, they are still searching for a support system.

More often, however, people who confided in liberal ministers praised them for providing support and spiritual faith without religious dogma, for relieving guilt about the wives' own breaking of the marriage vows, for providing help in problem solving, and for a generally nonhomophobic, nonjudgmental, and nonsexist outlook. The Metropolitan Community Church is a primarily but not entirely gay/lesbian church with branches in many large cities. Although ecumenical, its Fundamentalist roots made it a strong support system for a few Fundamentalist couples.

A few wives found conservative and even Fundamentalist ministers helpful, nonjudgmental, and able to help them regain their self-esteem. One wife was helped to recognize her husband's severe emotional deterioration and to obtain needed psychiatric help so that she could stop focusing on the homosexuality and start making decisions about her own life.

Another saw her inadvertent choice of an Evangelical counselor as a sign from God. She was conflicted about his futile attempts at exorcism to cure her husband of homosexuality but praised his ability to help her face the fact that her husband did not wish to be cured. He helped her to recognize her own strengths and to leave an unsatisfying profession. Accepting her husband's decision to divorce, she entered nursing school as her way as her way of dedicating herself to God.

Most Catholics were too fearful to tell their priests of their secret. Dorothy went to hers for marriage counseling but never found the courage to tell him what the problem really was. Homosexuality never occurred to him. Counseling was focused on communication problems. At the end of the sessions, the priest was pleased at her progress. She thanked him for his help and kept her secret until she saw me almost 10 years later.

Two wives, however, urged others to lose that fear. One said that her own parish priest had not only been understanding, he had given sensitive counsel in maintaining a sexually open marriage contract that allowed for homosexual expression. The other had found similar help from a gay priest through DIGNITY, a Catholic gay organization. I might also note here that since the study, both lesbian wives and gay husbands in my own clinical practice have also found at least one Catholic (nongay) priest to be similarly supportive.

Despite the positives cited, the most prevalent theme was that of extreme conflict in wives who were the most strongly committed to Fundamentalist churches but who vehemently denounced church dogma. They blamed the Church for having created a situation in which men felt coerced into both heterosexuality and marriage, for inadvertently aiding and abetting emotional and physical wife abuse as the husband's way of coping with guilt, for contributing to wives' naiveté about sex and inability to assert their own rights, and for—as several wives put it—"professing love while teaching hate."

Divorced Fundamentalist wives seemed to abandon the Church for a brief but dysfunctional period of frantic sexual activity (self-defined as "promiscuity") and then return to be "born again." When they returned, however, they were totally changed in their religious outlook. They had learned to "use" the homosexuality to obtain the Church's approval for divorce, for gaining sympathy and even financial help. But they were upset that wife abuse had evoked no concern or understanding. June's attitude toward the Church was typical:

> Tell women to turn to the Church. But not the organized Church. I mean the Bible and Jesus. The organized Church can give companionship, a belief in Jesus, and can point them toward the Bible. But tell women to choose a sect that lets them keep their deeper interpretations of religion to themselves. The antisex, antiwomen, homophobic attitude of the male church establishment is really nutty. What does the organized Church know about Christianity? Nothing!

Whether divorced or still in happy marriages, most strongly committed Fundamentalists declared themselves "closet feminists" and were working hard (albeit surreptitiously) to change their church's attitudes toward both homosexuals and women.

The Mental Health Professions

The Church had been criticized for hypocrisy about "love." The mental health professions were criticized for professing expertise and understanding where none existed. No theoretic orientation or profession seemed to be better or worse than any other. Complaints ran as follows:

1. Therapists either pretended they knew all about such a situation when they didn't, or simply admitted lack of knowledge and left wives to flounder around by themselves.

2. They lacked empathy, were unskilled in reading between the lines, and either misread, ignored, or glossed over the wives' concerns and feelings.

Zelda, for example, was afraid to even talk about sex, much less voice her suspicion of homosexuality. Her marriage counselor neither recognized her indirect cues nor opened up the area of sexuality herself. Cindy and John's therapist glossed over her anger about John's deceit and her anxiety about the marital sexual relationship, misinterpreted her depressed "giving up" as "feeling calmer," and allowed John to focus discussions on housekeeping problems. Cindy never felt heard or understood.

Elizabeth's first experience in seeking help was with a family doctor who told her that her husband couldn't possibly be gay, he was too masculine. She was shocked at the misinterpretation of her concerns when a later counselor (one of a series), seen regarding her husband's reputed child molestation, asked her, "Do you think you could live with the homosexuality if your husband was more discreet?"

3. The professionals hid behind confidentiality as an excuse for either inability or unwillingness to provide information and guidance in coping with a husband's homosexuality or even mental illness. They turned the wife into "the problem" and inadvertently increased the wife's guilt and fear.

Connie called her own therapist in panic one night, when her husband came home from a therapy session acting either so catatonic or drugged that she was amazed he had been able to drive home without an accident. The therapist, ordinarily helpful and certainly concerned, promised to talk with the husband's doctor. The husband was seen again immediately and his symptoms were relieved, but Connie was never allowed to talk to the doctor herself, nor was she able to find out from her own therapist what had caused such symptoms or what to expect in the future.

Dr. E's wife was never able to obtain from her husband's doctor any information about the potential for violence toward their children. She thought that his nonverbal communication supported her concerns, yet he told her that legally he did not think she could prevent the children from visiting him. Her concerns, which could have been seen as homophobic, were really based on inadequate help in coping with mental illness.

Elizabeth, whose stream of counselors included her husband's therapist, spoke for many when she told me,

> I did get help in clarifying my own ideas and making my own decisions. But most of the time I felt I was treated like the patient or like a child. I needed information, guidelines, and professional knowledge so that I didn't have to rely on hearsay and stereotypes. . . . I understand and respect the need for confidentiality, but I needed help not as "the" problem, but as an intelligent adult trying to cope with "a" problem.

4. The professionals were unwilling to take risks and put wives in untenable positions.

Ruth was asked by a therapist to help him confront her husband with his overdramatization of symptoms. Reluctantly she complied. When her husband became furious with her for "ganging up" with the therapist against him and for even coming to "his" interview, the therapist made no effort to either support her or to let her husband know that she had come at his request.

Zelda's husband had seen a therapist regarding psychosomatic symptoms. When the therapist asked her to come for an interview and to provide some background history, Zelda was finally able to voice her suspicion of homosexuality. The therapist stated that her history "painted a whole new picture" for him and asked if she would come to an interview and confront her husband with her concerns. She agreed on the condition that he would give her some idea as to whether her concerns appeared reasonable, since if she was wrong, she feared violence. When he refused to supply any indication of his thinking, she refused to be the "confronter."

5. The professionals were punitive toward the wives. At the more positive end, one usually helpful therapist told a wife that had she been more understanding of her husband's erectile problems, the husband might have become more heterosexual. Gloria was incensed at a church-selected therapy team that had tried to cure her of child abuse without either asking her reasons or allowing her to talk about the wife abuse. "Well," she added, reconsidering, "one social worker did at least ask. But she never waited for the answer. She simply agreed with the others that the cause was 'penis envy.'"

At the more negative end, two women reported extreme reactions when psychiatric help was sought around beginning suspicions of homosexuality:

> I told the psychiatrist I thought maybe my husband had had some homosexual experiences, but I needed help in how to tactfully broach the subject. I still can't believe his response. He said nastily, "What's the matter? Can't you say *cocksucker*?"
> He never bothered to ask anything about the situation. He just laughed a long nasty laugh, and then said, "Boy, if that isn't just like a woman! Let a man not get it up once and they're ready to castrate him. No, your husband's not a homosexual, he's just not a damn robot."

Other complaints were that therapists recognized the existence but not the depth of wives' confusion, depression, and loss of self-esteem. They focused on the unconscious and early childhood while ignoring "here and now" practical concerns or played trivial "behavior modification games" while ignoring basic issues. They terminated treatment prematurely and inadvertently created anxiety and guilt about the need for future help.

They were sometimes automatically discouraging of efforts to save a marriage. When Ruth was seen regarding her husband's hospitalization, for example, she was told that such marriages usually fail within a few months. Conversely, a few counselors treated the counseling exactly like any other marriage counseling case, without recognizing the wives' sense of stigma.

A common complaint was that professionals failed to go beyond the narrow limits of their job description. When Dorothy was given a pretrial interview following her husband's arrest, for example, the counselor's concern for her was focused solely on whether or not she truly understood the nature of the arrest, the psychiatrist's report, and the legal proceedings. The fact that she was 8 months pregnant and in acute shock was not even noticed, much less given attention.

What was seen as helpful, of course, was behavior that contrasted with behavior described in the complaints. Not required but often the most vividly remembered were symbolic but concrete gestures of support like the pinning of an invisible "winner's badge," providing physical (not sexual) comforting, or humorous empathic drama. Nan told me,

> My husband had been complaining that I was frigid. When I walked into our social worker's office for the first time (my husband had already seen him), I was scared to death. He looked at me a long time. Then he burst into a big grin and said, "Hell, you're not frigid! Don't ever worry about that!" I don't know how he knew that, but at that point I didn't care! That support was wonderful!
>
> I don't remember half of what he said, and my husband wasn't being honest at that point, so there was a limit to how helpful he could be. But that badge and that statement — just funny, nice ways to tell me I was "OK." I clung to them and treasured them for years.

Summarized advice to therapists almost always started with, "Please check out your attitudes toward women and gays," reiterated pleas to avoid the mistakes cited above, and often added, "Please give encouragement and hope to couples trying to make a go of their marriage. Be realistic, of course, but don't defeat them before they've even started." The advice often included, "Realize that the wives need different things at different times, and may need either long-term help or many periods of short-term help." As Elizabeth said,

> At one point I needed to be told very concretely what to do and where to go, specific information, and considerable assistance in following advice. At another point I only needed help in clarifying my own thoughts and wishes. At still another point, I needed only brief information and counsel on how to handle a specific problem.

No matter what their complaints, almost all wives who had sought professional help were glad they had done so, wished they had done it sooner, and had found someone helpful. All but one urged other couples and other wives to seek professional help quickly, "without waiting for confusion to set in," and to "shop around" if necessary.

Support Groups

Approximately a third of the wives had used some kind of support group: Marriage Encounter, EST, Reevaluation Therapy, a Unitarian peer confrontation and support group, or a woman's consciousness-raising group. With few exceptions, each wife was highly enthusiastic about her own particular group and urged others to seek the same or a reasonable facsimile.

What was missing in all of these groups, however, was the one ingredient women most wanted — the ability to talk with others in or who had gone through the same situation. An adequate homosexual/heterosexual support system simply was not found, even in those cities selected because of their promise of one.

Five women had attended one of two gay/straight couples groups. One had been a time-limited formal group. The other was a highly informal network headed by Terri. It had dwindled to a few friends, two of whom were wives of Terri's husband's former lovers. Appraisals of both groups were exactly the same: the group had provided an excellent "starter" for relieving the sense of isolation and guilt, giving a modicum of support in first attempts at sharing. The fact that nobody had any information or answers also decreased guilt about confusion and forced self-reliance — a benefit that was noted without much enthusiasm.

Complaints were that partly because of lack of publicity, the groups were too small and contained people in about the same state of confusion. Newcomers found three types of members: (1) a few complainers, (2) a few in "bizarre, at least to me" situations and who would not admit their obvious unhappiness, and (3) at best, one "exuberant" wife like Terri, whose avant-garde lifestyle was intimidating to more conservative women. With no professional at the helm to deal with severely distressed women, to guide discussion and channel complaints into constructive problem solving, or to assure "risk-takers" of adequate support, some women were unable to voice complaints, and others were unable to get beyond them.

San Francisco supposedly had a support system. It either did not exist at the time of the study or had not been located by me, three members of a divorced wives' group, or the social workers who had started the group. That group had started only 1 month before my interview with the wives and was designed as a therapy group for divorced "spouses." The one straight husband who showed up had, to the others' regret, been intimidated by being the only male and had left. The wives, however, had already found it helpful. They praised the peer support, the therapists' knowledge, empathy, and willingness to share their own personal experiences and feelings as appropriate. It was noted that far from finding a gay-supportive city helpful to them, many wives in the group, suffering the same sense of isolation and stigma others had felt, had made arduous attempts to find a support group while still married and had found the gay/bisexual community unresponsive to their requests for help.*

In summary, a theme repeated by 101 of the 103 wives stressed the need for a comprehensive gay/straight (or, as it is sometimes called, "mixed orientation") support system that is ongoing and well publicized, and that provides a wide variety of interventions: psychotherapy, marriage counseling, peer support groups for cou-

---

*Since the study, however, and in some instances because of it, support groups have been formed in many more communities.

ples, individuals, and children, and feedback from both gays and straights, males and females. It was also suggested that even peer support groups have professional leaders with well-defined responsibilities, that "neutral" names and locations be used because of the stigma attached to a "gay" identity, and that a "hotline" be established for women who are not yet ready to risk the loss of anonymity or to identify with a stigmatized group.

Chapter 9

Wives Speak Out

This chapter is divided into two overlapping sections. First we'll explore the long-term effects of disclosure on wives' attitudes toward homosexuality and gay men. Some of their statements, however, could just as easily fit into the second section, their "capsule comments" on the total situation and the "messages" they wanted me to deliver to others.

THE EFFECT ON WIVES' ATTITUDES TOWARD HOMOSEXUALITY

One of the commentaries on wives found in the literature or heard from the gay community had been about their vindictiveness and homophobia. The findings discussed earlier certainly seem to negate the supposition that as a group, wives instantly rejected husbands or vindictively tried to take children away from their fathers simply because of homophobia.

Those few to even consider a custody fight did so for one of three reasons: (1) They had been advised (rightly or wrongly) to do so because of the potential for sexual abuse. (2) There had been actual sex abuse. (3) There was ample reason to fear negligence or violence not because of homosexuality, but because of emotional disturbance. Out of almost 100 couples with children, there were only six such cases. Three wives reconsidered when they finally located adequate, knowledgeable counselors. One reconsidered when the husband became more emotionally stable.

But how did the wives really "feel" about homosexuality? Did the situation change their attitudes? And if so, was the change in a positive or negative direction? The measurement of attitudes and changes in attitude can be a tricky and unreliable business, particularly in the area of prejudice. To arrive at a valid estimate requires far more sophisticated techniques than could be used in a study of this type. Nevertheless, I was able to obtain clear impressions and was impressed with wives' sincerity and thoughtfulness as they struggled to be honest not only with me but with themselves.

Assessment included comparing answers to forced-response questionnaire questions, spontaneous interview comments, my direct questions to them during the interview, such questions as "How do you compare your life with that of women who married heterosexual husbands?", "Would you have reacted differently had your husband been interested in other women?", "Are you glad you married your husband?", and to the "capsule" statements they wished to make to the world in general or someone in particular.

In the questionnaire, about 45% said the experience had had a "positive" effect on their attitudes toward homosexuality, approximately 30% cited a "mixed" effect (positive in some ways, negative in others), and only 2% cited a "negative" effect. Approximately 18% said "no effect." Of those, 6% had started with a "very negative" attitude, 6% with a "very positive" attitude, and the rest had been either "neutral" or "moderately positive."

Assessment of attitudes at the time of the interview was based on the following criteria:

1. The extent to which a wife stereotyped, generalizing from her husband to all gay or bisexual men (or the other way around).

2. The degree and kind of stereotyping: for example, "All homosexuals are artistic and sensitive," "All homosexuals are sick (or immoral)," "All homosexuals seduce children."

3. The extent to which a wife cited a negative change in her attitude toward her husband or left a marriage purely because of the homosexuality, regardless of the situation. This was tested further by the degree of rigidity shown when a hypothetical question was posed. For example, did a wife who cited her husband's irresponsibility and lack of affection as the reason for divorce still rule out continued marriage even if the husband had hypothetically behaved differently?

4. The extent to which a wife held a double standard of consider-

ing homosexual expression or infidelity more immoral or more of a betrayal than heterosexual expression or infidelity.

5. The surrounding context of a particular word or comment. For example, words like "fag" could not simply be considered derogatory and counted; they derived their meaning from the context in which they had been used.

Some statements were easily defined as positive or negative, homophobic or nonhomophobic. Others were more difficult and depended on subjective interpretations of "implied" attitudes. For those I used consultants from the University of Hawaii and from the gay community to help me make a judgment.

Six strongly negative or stereotypic statements were made. For example,

> ... Well, discreet homosexuals, I don't know how I feel. But to see grown men prancing around with little wings, bizarre outfits, puts me off. I don't know if I think it's really normal, and maybe this experience has made me—well, I may go through life not being so accepting of homosexuals. I wouldn't want to live in San Francisco. I realize I might be acting very narrow and self righteous, but it's the way I feel.

One wife who saw homosexuality as "sick" ascribed her choice of husband and an occasional homosexual dream to the "sick" part of her own personality. Arlie, who had been treated so unfairly by her husband's gay friends and lover, stated honestly that although she had always prided herself on her lack of prejudice, she no longer liked homosexuals—male or female—as a group. Another wife found it difficult to understand what she considered the "adolescent" flitting from one romance to another in the gay community. A few damned with faint praise: for example, "I don't mind homosexuals. I get along with them at work. I don't bother them and they don't bother me."

A few negatives were implied by attempts to prevent children from using derogatory terms simply because "you don't know what the term means" or by providing a definition of homosexuality without any attempt to change the negative attitude implied by the

term used. Some conflicted comments were made within the course
of one interview. For instance,

> I'd like to see the world open up so that gays do not need to
> hide their feelings in the first place. I want to tell Anita Bryant
> she was wrong, all wrong! Gays are decent people! . . . I don't
> know if you can blame society. My husband tried that line on
> me, and I told him, "Bullshit!" Nobody forced him to marry
> me, we fell in love. I didn't dichotomize, *he* did. I loved him.
> There was no reason he needed to leave me. . . . This has not
> changed my views toward gays. They can live life the way
> they want, they have that right. I've always felt that. Just so I
> don't see people kissing in public, doing it in the park. . . . Be
> gay, I'll work with you, play with you, be friends with you—
> just don't have the nerve to marry a woman!

Despite these instances, the most striking feature of the wives'
overall attitudes was not the relative presence of homophobia, but
the relative *absence* of it. Complaints were usually registered
against "liberation ethic" or sexist behaviors and attributed to political pressures or individual dishonesty. Bitterness toward a dishonest or "con artist" husband was not usually generalized to the
gay community:

> My husband is a bastard, that's all! I didn't realize it then, but
> I do now. Before, he was a straight bastard. Now he's a gay
> bastard. The gays I know who also know him don't think any
> more of him than I do.

Usually, conflict between intellect and emotion was recognized.
Wives noted their own contradictions, struggled with them, and
eventually summed up their attitudes as "basically positive, but
obviously conflicted." Winnie, one of the most positive and least
homophobic wives in the group, stated,

> I have as much homophobia as anybody. How can you grow
> up in this country and not have it? I had such stereotypes
> . . . but it's important to recognize that and deal with it. I don't
> know why my husband became homosexual—maybe his early

childhood—who knows? Who cares? What's important is knowing that it had nothing to do with the wife, getting beyond black-white, good-bad views, and really examining your ideas, your contracts; changing and growing, with understanding of each others' feelings, making sure that the marriage is held together because you both want to be there and that you really *like* your spouse. I think we've *both* become better people since he told me.

Neither positive nor negative attitudes were usually globalized. Several women noted changes over time from their earlier tendency to overgeneralize, based on their getting to know more people from the homosexual community. Ruth told me,

I used to go with him to gay bars, talking to a few men, feeling really turned off by their gossip, thinking "Oh God, is this what my life is going to be like?" I felt I had to like all gays, and I felt guilty about possibly stereotyping. Thank goodness I met C. and a different crowd! The more gays I know, the more I see them as people rather than labels, and the freer I am to say I like So and So, I don't like So and So.

Marsha recalled an anguished and bitter comment she had made to me while she and Tony were still fighting:

I remember I told you once that the experience had made me anti-gay, that Anita Bryant was right, that homosexuality wrecks families. Well, I don't feel that way any more. I still have some conflict about allowing anything in the name of gay rights, for gayness to be the new "in" thing, that sort of stuff, but I've done a lot more reading and talking to different people. I think I have more understanding now. I'm mad at certain people or certain attitudes, not at all gays or homosexuality in general. Tell Anita Bryant I've changed my mind! She was wrong!

The more people met and the better the experience had been with the gay community, the more positive (and realistic) the statements tended to be. Some women reported that their strongest support had come from gays or even, as in Nan's case, from a husband's lover:

> If it hadn't been for D., I might have become a Moral Majority type person. But how can I hate gays? I know there are bad ones, just like with straights, but I have never met one. When my husband was being so nasty, it was D. who helped me. He was the one who told me about my husband, who helped relieve my guilt, who went places with me when I was alone, who shared his own feelings, who helped me talk to others, who perked up my self-esteem. Now that I know how a really good sexual and emotional relationship feels, how can I deny that to my own husband?

Many women expressed increased sensitization to the prejudice against homosexuals:

> I'm trying hard to get over the feeling that my husband "used" me. I'm conflicted, but I'm really beginning to understand how scared he must have been. We have a friend who came out recently, and the shit I've seen him go through is unbelievable! I'm getting madder and madder at the bigotry I see!

A good relationship with the husband contributed to even stronger positives. Of course, as might be expected, the strongest positives came from wives still in happy marriages. Nevertheless, many of the same comments came from wives in struggling marriages and even divorcees:

> If my husband is gay, then that says something for homosexuality. He's a wonderful person. I realize my son stands a slightly better chance of being homosexual by living with my husband, because he'll meet more people and see that he has options. That's okay with me. All I want is for him to be happy, to have the same fine qualities my husband has, and maybe without the bigotry we grew up with, he'll avoid some of our mistakes.

Happily married wives were especially apt to see their husbands, with some but not total generalization to all gay husbands, as less sexist, more sensitive because of their own experiences with oppression, often more "sensual" in their sexuality, more "alive" and "free," and more loving and tender with their sons than heterosexual men. "Nonsexist" here meant less apt to engage in sex-role stereotyped marital "duties," more considerate of women generally, and less constricted by stereotypes about male and female behavior and thinking.

The few women who maintained rigidly homophobic attitudes had nonetheless tried valiantly (from their perspective) to understand and adjust to their husbands' needs, but had been given no reason to change their attitudes by either their husbands, the gay community, or their therapists.

The single most overriding theme of the group, expressed by every woman in the sample at some point, was that, at base, *"This is not an issue of homosexuality."* Then what is it? The explanations of what that meant ran as follows:

> It's an issue of *loss*. When you lose someone you love, straight or gay makes no difference. It's just very painful.
>
> It's an issue of trust and honesty.
>
> It's an issue of monogamy versus open marriage and extramarital sexuality.
>
> It's an issue of interpersonal relationships.
>
> It's an issue of stigma, isolation, and bigotry.

Did those who divorced later regret not having done so immediately after disclosure? Some did. Most, however, stated that despite the pain they had endured, they at least knew they had honestly tried to make the marriage work. They would not have to spend the future wondering "what if . . . ?" Had they not waited until they were absolutely sure that problems could not be solved, the pain of divorce would have been unbearable.

Why did women who had described such pain and such lack of consideration from their husbands still express love and respect for those husbands? Why weren't they more homophobic? The following answer was typical:

My husband is a good person. He did not mean to hurt me. He was in as much pain as I was. He simply did not know how to handle the situation any more than I did. We both made mistakes. We had no guidelines, no real help. That's why I'm here. I'm not here to recite a list of grievances against my husband or gays, I'm here to help others ease the terrible pain I felt and avoid the mistakes we made, and to see that other couples get better help than we got.

Would they have reacted differently had their husbands gone out with other women? A few said, "Not at all!" Two were uncertain, but thought they might have felt less degraded as women. Several said it would have been easier to understand, that they might have felt less betrayed and might have tried harder. Most, however, felt that their confusion, identity crises, and sense of betrayal and isolation came from stigma and lack of guidelines rather than feeling that homosexuality was more immoral or sick than heterosexuality. In fact, if there was any double standard involved, it appeared to be (1) a temporary dysfunctional willingness to put up with inconsiderate behavior that they would not have tolerated for a minute had the infidelity been heterosexual or (2) a permanent, usually more functional willingness to view homosexual extramarital sexuality as less "unfaithful" than heterosexual extramarital sexuality.

Asked to compare their marriages or problems with those of women married to heterosexual husbands, many felt that the sense of stigma, isolation, confusion and helplessness they had undergone was far worse. Women in still-happy marriages (also some in struggling marriages and even some divorcees), however, gave a favorable comparison. Comments ran as follows:

I can honestly say that my husband is far more sensitive than most I've seen, that I've never once had sex when I didn't want to, that my children have the best parent–child relationship, with a model for fatherhood that few children have.

I think we had far more understanding, companionship, and equality than other couples I see. I hear the same complaints from other wives, even worse ones. I don't hear or see any of the talking and fun together that we had. I sometimes feel other couples live in the same house together, but they don't even like each other.

I guess I really like gay men better than straight ones today. I have a straight lover I'm very fond of. He's warm and sensitive. But sexually, he was so constricted. He's gotten better because he's learned from my husband, through me. But we could never have the good marriage my husband and I have. The minute he gets away from a "pleasant affair" relationship, the old "straight" sex roles come right back.

I consider myself very lucky. I have a better, firmer relationship with my husband than any other couple I know. When I see women in tight, constricted marriages, with blinders on them — couples with walls around each of them — when I think of the way my husband and I used to be — it makes me feel tight and horrible just thinking about it.

Women who had been married previously cited "no comparison" between their gay husbands and their former straight husbands.* As Iris, the fugitive from the Black ghetto, told me,

My former marriage was just a disaster. My current husband is a fantastic person. I help him a lot, but he helps me a lot, too. He's the warmest, kindest, most sensitive man I've ever met. Our sexual relationship is fantastic. I don't know what will happen, but if it all fell apart tomorrow, I wouldn't regret having married him for a moment.

Even bitter and homophobic women sometimes commented spontaneously that when they thought about it, they had not had a bad life, compared with other women they knew. A common theme from divorced wives who had once had "American Dream" marriages, however, was expressed sadness at what could be called the loss of Camelot:

---

*Of course, women who married again after divorcing gay husbands were also apt to be more positive about their new husbands.

I guess I feel the loss so much because I had so much. But at least I had it. What I had for a long, long time, some women never get to experience in their entire lives.

The most common theme of all came from women who found it hard to make general comparisons. Asked to take inventory of their neighbors, friends, and colleagues, they all had essentially the same reaction, starting with a laughing, "Well, that sure puts it into perspective quick enough!" followed by:

My neighbor on the right is divorced and went through a terrible, messy custody suit. My neighbor on the left is so tied to such a traditional wife-subservient marriage that though she seems happy, I wouldn't trade places with her for a minute.

A neighbor across the street has an alcoholic husband. A neighbor down the block is a battered wife. My child came home from school the other day and announced that her teacher had taken a poll, and that she and her best friend are the only two children in the class whose parents are still married. My child complains she feels left out!

I'm practically the only still-married person in my office. A neighbor down the street has a husband who goes to bed with every woman he can find, and she retaliates by doing the same with men and using her husband as a mere meal ticket.

My husband and I are having trouble finding friends. Everyone we know has divorced. Our friends, none of whom know about the situation, call us the last perfect couple in America. I don't envy other people, they envy me.

In summary, there was little evidence from this study to support the assumptions cited by others that wives are unable or unwilling to change old prejudices or that they become even more rigidly homophobic and vindictive. The degree of homophobia expressed in the study sample again seemed little more than the kernels of truth to be found in stereotypes. There was considerable evidence to suggest that most wives, even those from strongly Fundamentalist backgrounds, had exerted every effort to grow and change their attitudes and had actually done so to a surprisingly high degree. Both the degree of growth and its timing appeared to depend strongly on what incentives their husbands gave them to make changes, whether their attempts were rewarded with reciprocal growth and understanding, and how much help they received from the homosexual and professional communities.

CAPSULE COMMENTS

At the end of the interview, each wife was asked if there was any comment she would like to add or emphasize. Most women had expressed their own desire to write a book. They were asked, "If I could be your ghost writer but I only had room for one or two sentences from each woman, what would you like me to say for you?"

The answers fell into three categories: (1) There was a reiteration of earlier advice. (2) There was a personal statement about the wife. Some women restated the pain they had undergone; others restated the increased happiness that disclosure had brought to their marriage. Most gave a message of hope (whether or not they were still married), symbolized by their own increased happiness and self-confidence. For example:

> Tell people I'm a survivor. I look forward to the future with confidence in myself. I haven't gotten it all together yet, but I know one thing. I've learned I have strength I never knew I had, skills I've just begun to discover. I know I was put on Earth to do something good, and when I know just what that thing is, the world will know it too.

Or more modestly stated by others:

> Tell people not to feel sorry for me — I'm okay. I'm a survivor!

(3) The largest category by far was a combination of pleas for understanding of women, messages to husbands, the Church, and to the Moral Majority, and political statements about homophobia, sexism, and societal values. Two ardent Catholics, for example, said:

Tell the Moral Majority to look at people as people! Tell men to look at women as people! Look at me for what I am! Women have feelings! They're human! If I could do it all over again, it's not homosexuality I'd change, it's attitudes toward women and sex.

I'm not so mad at homosexuals, but sometimes I wonder what it takes to get through to *Men*!

From ministers' wives came statements like:

I don't understand a church that looks the other way when it comes to acts of violence and condemns as sinful acts of love.

We are still in the closet because the Church is so narrow. I want all this to come out! I feel we are so wrong in thinking the world must be 'straight.' People in Columbus's day felt the world must be flat. We have persisted with false assumptions, and to address the truth of reality, we need a whole new flexible set of groundrules.

Tell my church I love it, but it's got to change!

Sue Johnson reversed the interview schedule by insisting that she be allowed to make the following statement before she would consent to holding the interview:

I can't start this interview without expressing my resentment that it has to be given. Why are so many people so worked up about lesbian or homosexual affairs? They aren't about heterosexual affairs! Men starved themselves to death for a cause last week, two-thirds of the world population do not have enough to eat, and it makes me mad! There are more important things to worry about than whether a person has homosexual feelings!

Other typical political comments ran as follows:

I do think our society gets upset about the wrong things. We should be concerned about violence, not who's touching whom.

One 70-year-old women had faced this situation in the 40s, when she was stigmatized by a "triple whammy" of attitudes toward not only homosexuality, but toward psychiatric help and divorce. She thought about my question and then said,

> I don't know whether this is appropriate, but I have to make a political statement. I am . . . what can I say? Appalled? Yes, simply appalled! . . . at the trend our society seems to be taking! The Moral Majority simply terrifies me. It is taking us right back to my day, to the 30s and 40s, with the same attitudes toward men, women, marriage, divorce, and sex roles that created so many problems in the first place. I thought we had progressed. Now we seem to be going backward.

If these had been "social message" comments, some of the messages to husbands provided capsule comments on the interpersonal relationship:

> Tell my husband I'm not mad at him about the homosexuality, I'm mad at him about his deceit. His lack of faith in me.
> Tell my husband how scared, confused, and mad I am. I'm not mad at him, just the situation. Tell him how trapped I feel because I can't share my feelings with him for fear of adding to his pain and guilt. Tell him I don't want him to feel guilty, I just want him to understand and help me with my feelings like I'm trying to do for him.
> Tell my husband I'm trying to understand. But I don't know what he thinks or how he feels. Tell him not to shut me out. Tell him to talk to me!

And finally, a message delivered by many women, both married and divorced. It was simple:

> Tell my husband I love him.

Chapter 10

Advice to Other Husbands and Wives

The guidelines and advice in the next three chapters are based on consensus among wives, on my general conclusions from the study, on responses I have received to my presentations on the research, on my own experience as a therapist. If you are experiencing the circumstances we have been discussing, it may help you to feel less isolated, unique, and "abnormal" if you remember that many — perhaps most — of the issues, comments, and guidelines apply not only to people in or connected to this situation, but also to other individuals, couples, and situations.

ADVICE TO WIVES

(Husbands, please eavesdrop!)

1. Having company in one's misery doesn't necessarily make one happy, but it does help to relieve the sense of isolation. So *try to remember that you are not alone.* You are in an extremely large crowd. Moreover, whether or not you fit the description of most of the women I studied, they were what most societies consider "the cream of the crop." You need hardly be ashamed of the company you keep.

2. Try to remember that you are not alone in the kinds of feelings you have had, presently have, or may have in the future. Whether those feelings are positive, negative, or simply confused and ever changing, no matter how "crazy" they may seem to you, they have been shared by others. The same is true of your actions.

3. If you have just learned of the homosexuality, try not to panic, and avoid hasty, impulsive decisions. Your marriage is not necessarily doomed, and it may well improve. You have many options.

You need time to let the dust settle a little in order to explore and assess them.

4. Try not to blame yourself and don't accept others' blaming you for either your husband's homosexual thoughts or behaviors. Neither has anything to do with your looks, your sexual competence, your personality, your sexual orientation, your general mental health, your femininity, your adequacy as a wife, or anything else about you or your behavior. You did not cause either his homosexual feelings or actions, nor will you in the future. Of course, your opinions or decisions may affect his own decisions about what to *do* about his feelings, but in the final analysis, his decisions are his responsibility. You can only be responsible for yours.

5. Avoid letting this issue take over your life. Think and talk about it until you reach the point of diminishing returns (solitary thinking can sometimes reach that point in about 10 minutes) and then force yourself back to "business as usual" for the time being.

6. Conversely, benefit from Laura's experience. Shutting the door and pretending the homosexuality doesn't exist is not helpful to you in the long run. It does exist. It won't go away, not even if your husband decides to forego extramarital sex or tries to keep it away from your consciousness. Life may or may not be much different, but it will never be "exactly" the same for you. You need to confront the issues squarely if you expect to either prevent future problems or solve them with minimum, rather than maximum pain.

7. If you are new to the situation and are feeling relatively calm and positive, that's great! Be glad. Perhaps with the new information and guidelines that this book and future ones will provide, nothing will happen to change those feelings. You should be prepared, however, for periods of confusion, anger, depression, discouragement, turmoil, stress, and mood changes. If or when you are in the midst of one of those periods, try to remember that they are natural and that eventually confusion, anger, and grief will abate. Pin up on your wall (or in your mind) a reminder that judging from others' experiences, *you will eventually find happiness for yourself no matter whether you stay married or divorce.*

If the preceding advice sounds easier to give than to take, the next will be even more so. Often it will be merely common sense advice applicable to any marriage. You have probably given it to yourself over and over again. So Advisory No. 8, a transitional one, is simply:

8. Be patient with yourself if you find that you can't or don't know how to follow such advice, that you seem to have lost your "common sense." No matter how simple it *should* be or how simple people tell you it is, the situation you are facing can be complex and confusing. In essence, you and your husband are blazing new trails. So don't be distressed with yourself if you sometimes lose your way. You'll eventually find it, no matter how lost you feel.

9. Try to look beyond the homosexuality in assessing your options and in how you solve both big and little problems in your marriage. For example, you need to try to be understanding of your husband's needs and worries and flexible in working out ways to meet them. However, you need to evaluate what problems are intrinsic to homosexuality, what problems are intrinsic to all open sexual contracts, whether homosexual or heterosexual, what problems are related to personality, and what problems are related to coping with stigma. As one wife put it, "Render unto Caesar only what is Caesar's."

In short, your husband really has not changed simply because of a label or even because of a change in attitude or behavior. He is the same person he's always been; he has simply let you know a part of him you haven't known before. What you liked before you can still like. What you didn't like before, you probably will still not like. If unknown qualities emerge, they may be likable or unlikable, but they are not "homosexual." You might be able to be more understanding now that you know, and you may be able to allow changes in your contract on the basis of that understanding. But you should not blame all problems on the homosexuality, nor should either of you excuse all problems on the basis of homosexuality. "Flexibility" and "empathy" are two-way streets. You also need to stand up for your own rights, ask the questions you need to ask, and insist on the same flexibility, consideration, and understanding from your husband that he asks and expects from you.

10. Don't blame yourself for your choice of husband. You probably had good reason: he filled your needs at the time. Now you need to examine those reasons. Do they still exist? Are the qualities you liked before still there? If not, why not? Are they simply buried in

confusion? Can they be brought back? Have old needs changed? Are your present needs being met? If not, why not? Can the two of you find ways to meet them? If not, maybe it's time to move on to new relationships (marital or other) that will better meet your needs. If you decide to stay married, do so only because you want to. Recognize that that's why you're there, and take responsibility for creating some of your own happiness, without expecting your husband to satisfy "all" your needs. *All* wives (and husbands) need to make that assessment. You're not the only ones.

11. In making those assessments, use your new knowledge (disclosure) to facilitate your own personal growth and development. Evaluate your own needs and wishes, your own strengths and weaknesses, your options, and the ways in which you might increase your options. Then choose among the options you want, taking the steps necessary to enhance the old and adding new ones.

For example, if the marriage is generally good but neither of you is feeling sexually satisfied, you may need to explore new sexual options. Aside from the risk of AIDS, which we'll discuss at length in Chapter 11, can you accept the possibility of an open-sexual contract that allows for extramarital sex? If so, what ground rules can you set that will provide both safety and mutual satisfaction without either partner feeling coerced or oppressed? No matter what rules you set, be sure you build in allowances for unanticipated feelings and situations, with periodic reevaluations.

Can you explore new ways of enhancing your marital sex? Perhaps one or both of you have equated "sex" with "intercourse." Performance anxiety often becomes a roadblock. When the bedroom becomes an arena in which erections, intercourse, and orgasms are do-or-die "tests" to prove love, sexual desire, competence, or self-worth, all lovemaking and expressions of affection can stop purely from fear of eventual "failure" and rejection.

Intercourse is only one of many avenues to sexual fulfillment, necessary only for making babies. In fact, self-stimulation, which takes only one person, is probably the most effective route to sexual orgasm. Except for achieving a goal of pregnancy, it is mainly the emotional pleasure of the relationship and some (but not all) of the sensual caressing that requires two people and provides much of the sense of self-fulfillment people get from sex.

Use this as an opportunity, then, for redefining "sexuality" as "sensuality," exploring or more fully enjoying such sensual activities as manual stimulation and caressing to orgasm, erotic massage, nonerotic backrubs, oral sex, and so on. Far from being "foreplay," such activity is often all people need for sexual fulfillment. You and your husband might even want to agree to "forbid" intercourse at some point, until you feel more relaxed. You should not allow yourself to feel coerced into activities you don't like or don't even wish to try. If you've never allowed yourselves such options, however, you might be pleasantly surprised to find that although lack of erections is disappointing, it does not need to mean an end to marital satisfaction. You can both please and be pleased by your husband in a variety of ways, and occasional exchanges of "sexual gifts" (*not* performance of "duties") in which you each do or allow something strictly for the pleasure of pleasing the other person can enhance the "human" relationship.

In deciding whether or not to have extramarital sex yourself, try to give yourself permission without feeling coerced or railroaded into doing so. Remember, however, that it is not apt to be helpful to you if it goes against your moral code, if you use it as a "test" of your desirability or sexual competence, or if you use it simply as a way to hurt your husband or "help him come to his senses." Of course trying to assess one's motivation was exactly the problem that became so difficult for many wives in the study. If you make a mistake in judgment, try not to be too hard on yourself. You have been neither "immoral" nor "uptight." You have simply used a "trial and error" way of dealing with difficult decisions. It almost goes without saying that all decisions about all sexual behaviors in and out of the marital bedroom must be weighed in the light of risks for AIDS.

TIP: Remember that gay/straight couples are not the only ones who need to learn such lessons. After all, the rush of "how to" sex manuals, the vast amounts of money and time spent on sex therapy, and counseling around issues of "open" marriages started with and remains mainly focused on the sexual problems of exclusively straight couples!

ANOTHER TIP: If you've tried some of these options and are not finding them helpful, you may be muttering under your breath those @$#$%!!!* (*@ words that the Watergate transcripts coined as "expletives deleted." So remember that empathic communication is the crux of both sexual contracting and of overcoming problems in both the marital and the extramarital bedroom. One reason those suggestions can fail is that people often — usually — need more specific direction in order to use them effectively. You might try the "programs" in a professionally authored "how to" sex manual. In the appendix I list three that have proven helpful to many people. Even with excellent books, however, people often need more individualized help. If you haven't gotten very far after a few weeks, don't be ashamed to seek professional sexual counseling. This brings us to the next guideline.

12. Don't try to struggle with this situation alone. It simply becomes too confusing. Even if you are in that happy second honeymoon aftermath of a positive disclosure, get professional counseling quickly before confusion sets in. Few wives disagreed with this advice. One or two saw no need for help — they were doing fine. The first therapist Ruth and her husband had seen told her such marriages seldom worked and he predicted divorce in a few months. (What they did — and I consider it a wise decision — was to eventually change therapists.) Ruth suggested that a wife should think through what she wants to do and find someone (peer or professional) who will help her do it.

This tactic, however, has severe problems that Ruth herself noted. Part of the confusion comes from not knowing what one wants to do and if "wants" are realistic. Still happily married Winnie, for instance, had immediately "wanted" divorce and heaved a sigh of relief that her accepting marital counseling allowed her to find better solutions. Conversely, Cathy would have saved herself months of agony in an untenable marriage had she entered a support group earlier.

My own view agrees with the "seek help before confusion sets in" view of most wives. In the first place, there was no wife, no matter how positive she was after a positive disclosure, who did not undergo some internal turmoil and confusion. The mild "stun" reaction helped immediate functioning, but without *competent* help, in the long run, it trapped her and her husband into unrealistic solutions, messed up future communication, and usually resulted in often needless and far greater future distress.

Second, I have emphasized the word "competent" because even ordinarily competent therapists may not provide competent help in this situation. In an "acute crisis," you may be unable to find a therapist quickly, much less evaluate or cope with therapists' mistakes, and you simply won't have the time to run around looking for the "right" one. Ruth and her husband, for instance, were trapped into sticking with the first therapist for some time before the acute crisis of her husband's suicide attempt calmed down enough for them to find someone better. Recently she wrote me that with the help of their new therapist, the "happy-but-struggling" status of her marriage when I interviewed her has now changed to "very happy." But had she and her husband had adequate help earlier, their excessive pain might have been prevented.

Third, as in general health care, an ounce of prevention is worth a pound of cure. Also, when people are seen only after they have broken down, rather than as they usually are, professional errors of judgment are far more frequent. We think nothing of using well-baby clinics, having periodic checkups and PAP smears, or going to dentists for a first checkup, the filling of a tiny cavity, and periodic professional teeth cleaning. Only in individual, marital, and familial emotional health do we consider utilizing professional knowledge such a sign of "weakness" or "inadequacy" that we are ashamed to take that step until a serious crisis forces us to do so. To me, that makes no sense.

Finally, you'll just feel more relaxed if you already know and like the person and can get down to brass tacks without having to start from scratch in explaining the situation and its history and in establishing a relationship. I'll talk more about the therapeutic relationship when I answer "Common Questions." Right now, however, it's more appropriate to proceed to guidelines for overcoming the sense of stigma and isolation.

13. Try not to isolate yourself. Professional counseling should help allay your confusion and sense of stigma and "uniqueness," but therapy is not enough. If you withdraw from family and friends, they may or may not sense the pain underneath, but they will be apt to feel rejected, helpless, hurt, and angry. You will have *decreased*

your options for finding satisfying emotional relationships, rather than *increasing* them. You simply need companionship. If you are afraid of bursting into tears, "being a drag," etc., you might plan some strategy. Winnie, for example, told a colleague,

> I'm facing a really stressful situation right now. I need your help to start the day. I'm really not comfortable about talking about it, but if you could just hold me and let me cry a bit, I think I'll be okay in a few minutes.

Her friend "could" and she "was."

You might just explain in advance to friends that if you seem snappish or unfriendly, it's not that you're mad at them, but that you're struggling with a personal problem and you're afraid of crying or being "no fun." You might tell them, if you've burst into tears, just what you'd like them to do for you: hold you, just sit and let you cry, ignore the tears and pretend they don't exist, get you a tissue, etc.

Part of peoples' reaction to someone who cries is simply that they feel they should *do* something but don't know what to do and may even worry that they've said or done something wrong. If you let the tears flow and either change topics or just go on with your present conversation, you'll probably find that you stop crying sooner than if you divert all your attention to stopping the tears and the thoughts that caused them. True, your friends may be curious. But they will usually offer help and then respect your wishes if you tell them that "not talking about it" is the best way to help you or that you're just not ready to talk about it for now.

You may really *want* to talk about it but are afraid to do so for fear of really breaking down, giving the impression of more pain than you feel, being criticized or pitied, or creating more hurt for your husband. It may help you to be more open if you simply tell people that, giving them the framework for understanding what you say.

Want to or not, you *need* to be able to talk about it with others. After all, most people engage in a bit of Kaffeeklatsch sharing that includes informal, everyday problem solving, griping, commiserating, laughing over comical events, and sharing good things. It's part of a general support system that helps people survive marriage, child rearing, and life in general, keeping little problems little by releasing tension and providing new perspectives. If you are so closeted that you don't permit yourself such help, you may prevent some hurts, but you will also add to the already excessive intensity in your marriage and prevent the relief that comes from both support and finding many of your feelings and problems shared by others, no matter what the sexual ballpark in which they play.

14. In short, you need to learn the art of coping with stigma. Everyone learns it to some extent, but for most people, it is a minor subject. They simply audit a class session to help them deal with being the new kid on the block, being teased about their braces, having an accent, being the only Republican in a crowd of Democrats, and so on.

For many people it is a major subject. They take a full and usually lifelong set of classes in copng with racism, anti-Semitism, anti-Catholicism, etc. You may be in that category. If so, for a change you can consider yourself lucky. Recognize that you are simply attending a special seminar on the same subject, and your experience and the automatic skills you have learned will stand you in good stead. If you have not had the dubious pleasure of that kind of "luck," you can benefit from the experience of those who have. (Still, just being a woman has given you some lessons in coping with sexism. You may simply be attending some extra sessions that weren't in your class outline.)

Closets are one form of ghetto. They are stifling. They hurt you. Yet in some ways they are safe. There's no way around it, getting out is risky. You may — and probably will — get hurt at some point. Taking into consideration both your own needs and the needs of your family, only you and your husband, either independently or together, can decide whether the risks of staying in are better than the risks of getting out, and only you can decide how "out" you dare be. But make no mistake about it, isolation is hazardous to mental health, and getting out may be far less hazardous than you think.

15. In dealing with straight society, you do need to be cautious. In a war against bigotry and ignorance, however, you can develop some strategy. In *Loving Someone Gay*, Don Clark cites a clever

strategy developed to help gay men overcome the pain of rejections. One simply treats them as the trophies of war. Marathon runners ease the pain of "losing" by wearing T-shirts that proclaim them winners simply by virtue of running the race. Writers paper walls with rejection slips and consider them part and parcel of being a professional. They might prefer "trophies" to come in the form of checks, but at least they allow themselves the privilege of enjoying a tax writeoff.

You might try writing down the insults you receive. Who knows? Some day they may pay off in the form of an article. This does not mean you should be an "insult collector" who actively seeks rejection and finds insults in every nuance, disagreement, or question. Bigoted or not, people are often simply unknowledgeable and are seriously trying to gain information and understanding from the only resource they know—you! Educating other people gets tiresome and has its limits, but it is part of the "dues" one pays to make the world a safer place to live.

Nor should you set yourself up by proclaiming your situation to people most likely to hurt you. A desensitizing attitude simply puts stings and barbs—particularly from unexpected sources—in better perspective. If you retreat after your first bad experience, you will never learn what others have learned: that although some surprises may be bad, more will be good. By and large, people will respond empathically.

There are two pitfalls following a "disclosure" of your own: Remember that this is simply a way of maintaining or reestablishing the ordinary informal support system that everyone uses. It is not therapy. If you turn understanding friends into therapists and every social encounter into a therapy session, you'll lose friends not because of homophobia, but because you yourself have stopped *being* a friend.

Chances are that you don't want your friends to be therapists any more than they want to be. The real crunch may come right *after* you have confided in somebody, particularly if you have broken down. You may feel foolish. You may worry that your friend thinks less of either you or your husband, that you have been misinterpreted, or are now being pitied. You may even be a bit miffed at some particular response. You may wish you hadn't told and wonder what to say next time you see your friend.

Your friend, on the other hand, may also be worrying about what comes next and what to say the next time you meet. You may try to avoid each other. Don't! Avoid waiting for your friend to make the first friendly overture or to mention the subject again. It is really up to you to break the ice and ease that transition period, even if you have to make a phone call to do so. If you don't, you may both end up feeling needlessly rejected and hurt.

You might plan some potential ice breakers here. You could simply be honest about feeling foolish or whatever feelings you have. Or say casually, "Hey, thanks for listening the other day. I appreciated it and it helped a lot. Hope you'll also feel free to use my shoulder if you ever need one." Have another topic ready to mention or chat about and then do so immediately. If you snapped at something your friend said, you can apologize, say you may have been hypersensitive (if you were), and you know she or he was only trying to help.

You can correct potential misinterpretations by some sentence like "Hey, I hope I didn't give you the impression that my life is terrible. Most of the time it's fine. I just need to let off steam every so often. Thanks for letting me blow off to you." If you keep your next conversation off the subject and then mention it again *briefly* at some appropriate point in a future conversation, you'll be apt to find that from then on, you and your friend will both feel freer and your relationship will be back to normal and perhaps closer.

Confiding in straight friends may or may not be the best "first" step, particularly if you are up to your neck in turmoil and confusion. A women's support group, a mixed-sex support group, or an actual therapy group may be both safer and more helpful, since it will allow you to struggle with real problem solving without ruining your social relationships. Moreover, there may be safety in numbers. If one person is hurtful, another will be helpful. You'll have the checks and balances of a wider variety of viewpoints, with some help in standing up for your rights.

When and how to deal with gay society will depend largely on your individual situation and your predisclosure starting point. You may know very little about homosexuality and know few homosexual men. Your knowledge may be based mainly on stereotypes or on knowing the highly visible minority of people who fit those stereotypes. If so, now is the time to obtain a more accurate picture. Do some reading by creditable authors (the appendix provides references). Talk to your husband. Meet his friends or talk to someone you already know. Don't be afraid to use the gay support network: a gay minister, counselor, or a gay rights organization may be your best starting place. Attending a rap group or speech, entering the doors of a gay counseling agency, or a similar action will not label you. Share the concerns you have, ask the questions you would like to ask.

You will probably find that except for sexual preference and the problems of stigma, gay society is no different from straight society. You will meet some people and attitudes you like, some you don't. You will hear both common experiences and feelings and many opposing perspectives on both homosexuality and heterosexuality. You will meet men who "like" women and men who don't. You will meet people who are empathic with you and people who are not. Most important, you will gain more understanding of the problems, confusions, and feelings that prevented your husband from being more honest earlier or that affect his current behavior.

You should be prepared for the fact that you may meet counterprejudice toward straight society. You may—particularly if you are coming from a gay supportive stance and are talking with people you already know—feel that you have been "betrayed" by friends. You may worry that you are a fool in the eyes of militant gays who do not believe in "bisexuality" or the compatibility of homosexuality and marriage.

You may find yourself wondering if "every" man you meet has had relationships with your husband. You may or may not wish to meet a person with whom he is involved (and you should make your wishes clear), and you might find that your husband's friends are even more embarrassed with you than you are with them. You may also find, as Sue did, that you feel like an "outsider" whose every move and remark is treated with suspicion and that you are constantly being unfairly tested.

For the most part, your fears will be unwarranted and are simply a natural phase of learning to cope with stigma. You need to move cautiously, but you do need to move. The more people you meet, the more you, like Ruth, will learn to treat people as individuals rather than labels, to differentiate between those you can turn to as confidantes and those you can't, and to find people who will be supportive and helpful friends. Remember that several women found their greatest allies in the gay community—and even in a husband's lover.

As for being treated like an "outsider"—well, some of that is inevitable. Any oppressed group trying to ward off danger from without develops its own weapons: a sense of stubborn cohesiveness and its own subculture. Part of that cohesiveness is what I call "the in-groupness of the out-group." You may recognize it in what some call the "clannishness" of Jews or the "soul brotherhood" of blacks. The group provides a safe haven, develops its own in-jokes and communication patterns, and establishes ways of recognizing, criticizing, and joking about its own weaknesses without fear of being misunderstood. For instance, blacks or Jews sometimes tell ethnic jokes that they would not allow others to tell, because the distinction between an "ethnic" joke and a "racist" joke is so subtle that often only the "insider" can recognize it. Moreover, they sometimes allow racist remarks from one another that they would not tolerate from outsiders.

Sometimes their jokes are deliberately designed to shut out others, and sometimes they show the same suspicion of and prejudice toward others that others have shown to them. The same is true of gay society. As a wife sincerely trying to understand and to be an "ally," you need to understand this and try not to take it personally. At the same time, you have every right to speak up when you sense that you are being treated as an enemy or when you encounter homophobia or heterophobia. Not only is it your right, it is your obligation to yourself, and it may also be helpful to the other person. Remember that if your concerns are couched in terms of "This is how I feel" rather than "This is what you are doing," your chances of being heard and understood will be far greater.

In short, being a minority is not a question of numbers but of status and role. It changes according to the situation, and this is one situation in which your heterosexuality has made you a "minority" instead of a "majority" person. Frustrating though it may be, you can use your own feelings to help you understand what has happened to others who are constantly in a minority position.

As for dealing with gay/straight society, remember that being in a minority position is not the greatest position, even at best. You too now need a "safe haven" where you can have the spontaneity, support, and security that comes from being with others who have shared or presently share some of your feelings and experiences, who do not need everything spelled out in order to understand, who can validate your feelings and help you clarify them without your feeling patronized, who can disagree without your feeling criticized, and who can simply be social friends without your having to watch every word you say. In short, you need a support group specifically designed for your situation.

There may be a support group in your area. It may be a gay/straight (or "mixed orientation") couples group, a "spouses of gays" group, or a "divorced wives of gays" group. It may be a "gay fathers" group with subgroups designed for wives or former wives. It may be a therapy group or simply a social group. You may need more than one of these groups. There may simply be one or two wives willing to share with you. No matter what, make every effort to find and join that support system. If none exists, make every effort to start one. I list some specific resources in the appendix. I'll also talk more about support groups when answering common questions asked me by husbands as well as wives.

This last section is not really "advice." It is simply some information about husbands that may be of help. Into any group of people, some "heels" inevitably appear. A few husbands in this study certainly seemed to fit that category, deliberately deceiving their wives from the start, with apparent lack of concern for anyone but themselves, and as deceitful in other relationships (including gay relationships) as they were with their wives.

The vast majority of husbands either in the study or in my own clinical experience, however, no matter how hurtful they may have become, were not acting out of "heel-ism" and did not intend to use or deceive their wives. They married in good faith, out of love, either unaware of homosexual feelings or truly believing those needs were either already eliminated or would be, and truly intending to be faithful. Unless there is strong evidence to the contrary, you can rest assured that your marriage was not a sham.

For the most part, you can also believe a husband when he says he does not consider his extramarital homosexual liaisons "unfaithful," that they fulfill needs that cannot be met in heterosexual marriage, and that those needs are more than a question of simply physical satisfaction but are an important "part of him." This may be difficult, if not impossible, for you to understand, but you might try asking yourself how easily you could shut out and hide your heterosexuality, your outlook toward life, your view of God, etc., or how well you could separate out any of those items from your total personality. Chances are you couldn't, at least not without serious consequences for your own integrity and your own ability to relate to others as a "whole" and "integrated" person.

The same may be true of your husband. His homosexual relationships may indeed hold "different" emotional and sexual nuances that are truly important to him yet that may in no way detract from the importance and value of either his sexual or emotional relationship with you. What is important, then, is not so much what he seeks from and brings to other relationships but what he seeks from and brings to his relationship with you.

In fact, many of the problems you have encountered or may encounter in your relationship may stem from the very fact that in order to "compartmentalize" and shut out an important part of his personality, he has had to shut out other feelings as well. In short, compromising integrity in one area tends to compromise integrity in all areas. He has paid a large price indeed for conformity, and unfortunately, you as the innocent bystander have had to pay part of that price.

You should also know that seeming deceit may truly be based on concern for your feelings: Fear not only that you will leave him but that knowledge of homosexuality will hurt you more than it will help you, and a true belief that he can meet his homosexual needs without hurting your relationship. This may be entirely unrealistic, but unless you have evidence to the contrary, you can believe he is sincere.

Finally, you should know that suddenly "strange" and uncharacteristic inconsiderateness and insensitivity may be temporary conditions associated either with your husband's own stereotyped notions of what it means to be gay or bisexual or with some hard facts of "liberation." Any oppressed group or group member trying to become liberated faces two needs: the first is to defend against prejudice and the other is to defend against guilt. The deceit that hurt you is born of guilt and self-hatred. In trying to overcome it, your husband may become paranoid and may indeed put on blinders, shutting out recognition of your pain, misinterpreting the cause of your pain and anger, and truly believing that he is being honest and helpful rather than insensitive and hurtful.

To some extent, his putting blinders on is as necessary as it was for you to close your eyes to your parents' pain the first time you refused their advice, went on a date instead of taking part in a family tradition, or took some other step toward independence. Those same blinders will be necessary for you if you need to confide in someone over your husband's objections or if you decide to divorce even though you know it will be hard on your children. For now, your husband's blinders are simply a fact of life and may be part of the insensitivity shown in requests for immediate divorce, denial of past love, criticism, etc. You need not take them literally, nor need you devalue yourself because of them.

That does not mean you should accept unfairness simply because it was not deliberate. Whether or not you can get beyond such problems depends partly on your willingness to share your feelings with your husband and partly on whether or not he can remove his blinders. Whether he can or not, however, your understanding of what is happening may ease your own self-doubts and some of the bitterness you may feel.

ADVICE TO HUSBANDS

(Wives, please eavesdrop!)

In reading advice to wives, you will have received guidelines for your own actions. To avoid repetition, then, I'll simply emphasize some highlights and make a few additions.

1. There is no pat rule for whether to tell or when to tell a wife about homosexual needs and either past or present activity. You

would do well to use professional (or peer) help in thinking through that decision, *if* you remember that advice to maintain secrecy was what created many "negative" disclosures and disastrous consequences.

Honesty is usually (though not always) the best policy. Usually, the sooner you talk with your wife, the less "betrayed" she will feel, the more positively she will respond, and the better chance you will have for either improving your marriage or separating with the least amount of pain for everyone. You will probably be pleasantly surprised to find that, as with the wives in this study, your wife will neither fall apart nor throw you out, but will be relatively understanding and helpful.

In making your decision, realize that not asking about homosexuality does not mean a wife is either unaware of it or deliberately closing her eyes to it or that, aware or not, she is either helped or at least not being hurt by secrecy. The evidence from this study suggests that wives were indeed suffering during and because of secrecy. No matter how difficult "knowing" may have been, they could cope better with reality than with not knowing what reality was.

In fact, the most severe pain I encountered in this study was from wives who were seen but who could not actually become part of the study because they could not confirm their hunches that homosexuality was — or had been — a cause of marital problems or divorce. They could neither assess the past nor prepare for the future and were in far worse emotional shape than any of the actual study wives. In short, even divorcing without telling a wife, either blaming her or letting her think it was because of a heterosexual affair, is apt to be far more injurious and unfair to a wife than honesty.

2. "Honesty" should not become equated with "cruelty" and must be tempered with sensitivity. While almost all wives advised honesty, a few noted that special circumstances might call for exceptions to that rule based both on knowledge of oneself, one's wife, and the details of a situation. Winnie, for example, noted that had her husband told her at the beginning, when she was about to give birth, it would have been far more devastating. Had he not waited until they had a support system available, faced with such deceit she might simply have divorced. (It should be apparent, how-

ever, that had he not then waited for 9 years, she would not have felt so deceived).

Try to assess your motivation for telling at a certain point. Certainly guilt over deceit is an appropriate motivation. It should not, however, be the only motivation, nor should it obliterate sensitivity to the effect on a wife. Mary McDermott's husband, for example, should have told her far earlier. One can only assume that his guilt got the better of him at the last moment, but relieving himself of that burden at that point did not show much sensitivity to her feelings, nor did his subsequent behaviors. As Mary herself suggested, given the fact that he had waited that long, he might have done better to wait a few months longer, preventing excessive shock and paranoia on her part and thereby giving the marriage a better chance to succeed.

3. The components of "positive" versus "negative" disclosures are not simply to be read as entertainment: they provide clear guidelines for husbands' behaviors. Try to make your disclosures as positive as possible in your timing and sensitivity to your wife's feelings.

4. Although you cannot know what the future will bring, do your best to avoid making promises that you do not intend or may not be able to keep, and be scrupulously honest in obeying both the spirit and the letter of any contracts you make. This is particularly important now that AIDS has entered the scene.

If you feel that your wife has not been understanding, take another look at your disclosure (or disclosures) and the events surrounding them. Ask your wife how she recalls them. You may discover unrecognized "negative" aspects that you may be able to correct or at least modify. Try to lift the blinders that prevent you from separating issues of homosexuality from other issues. You may be amazed to realize how "blind" you have been.

Winnie, for example, had cited her husband's empathy with her anger as a major factor in their ability to save their marriage. When at her request I interviewed the two of them together, however, it became clear that he had not been empathic at all. He had merely followed his peer counseling group's rule of letting people express their emotions without interference. He had believed then—and still sincerely believed—that homophobia had been the reason for her anger. Only during that interview, when she suddenly exploded in amazement at what she was hearing, did he realize that her anger not been about his homosexuality, but about the fact that he had spent 9 years breaking an explicit promise of honesty. Had he not truly listened to her at that point, I would have ended up doing frantic marriage counseling instead of research interviewing.

5. Honesty, then, is simply not enough either in an initial disclosure or in the future. If you have been unfaithful to marriage vows that specified "forsaking all others" without exemption for "homosexual others," you have betrayed a trust. Even if you have simply unintentionally caused pain, allowed your wife to blame herself for problems that were not hers, or broken a later promise in a small way, you have been unfair.

Should you feel guilty? Of course! Should you go around in sackcloth and ashes and label yourself totally despicable? Of course not! All people sometimes deliberately or unintentionally hurt the people they love. But as you probably taught your children soon after they learned about Washington and the cherry tree, "I cannot tell a lie" and "sorry" are just beginning steps in correcting one's errors. You need to be prepared for and willing to suffer through your wife's anger, grief, and hurt. Try to meet her feelings not with defensiveness or excessive guilt, but with empathy and understanding. Painful though it may be, you need to reach out to her, help her talk about her negative feelings, and provide help in problem solving.

6. Although you have the right to ask your wife to listen to you and try to understand, you do not have the right to insist that she agree and accept your logic. After all, how kindly would you take to even a business partner's announcing and then insisting that you accept his decision to break an exclusive contract with you simply because he decided he could make some extra money by also dealing with another firm? You might be able to reach a compromise, but it would not be without some feelings on your part, and you would probably be less trusting from then on.

7. Help her cope with stigma. It is as real a problem for her as it has been and will be for you. Remember that she has a "double whammy" problem to face of homophobia and sexism. Recognize that her stereotypic views are probably no different from the ones you once had (and may still have), and try to remember that her

sense of stigma is less a question of how she feels about you than it is of how *she* will be viewed. You have spent a long time struggling with feelings and building coping devices. Instead of trying to talk her out of her new and overwhelming feelings, share with her the feelings and problems you have had and what has been helpful to you. Work with her to develop new strategies to help you both, and encourage without forcing her to utilize the gay support system.

8. No matter how positive the disclosure and her reaction may have been, no matter how calm she may seem, remember that emotions may be churning underneath and that even small, unrelated incidents may make them bubble over. Try not to be unnerved by tears or anger. Partly she is angry at the situation, not you. Partly she is confused and scared. Partly she is just releasing tension. And of course she may be justifiably hurt or angry at some insensitivity on your part. You need to deal realistically and empathically with all of the above. You may not know why she is reacting a certain way at a certain point, nor may she. If you help her to talk through her tears or anger, trying to understand, you will be more able to clear the air and find solutions than if you retreat out of anger or guilt.

9. Read the chapter on AIDS. Reread the guidelines for wives on sex. Remember that affection need not lead to sex, that "sex" need not include intercourse, and that touching and caressing may be far more important to her than intercourse — or even orgasm. She needs not just a physical act but a feeling that you love her and appreciate and enjoy her body.

10. Fair is fair. If you are having extramarital sex, she also has that right. You might encourage it. But try not to force her into it in order to relieve your own guilt, and try not to make her feel guilty for not having it. She may not need or want it. As a woman, she is apt to have fewer opportunities than you do. Moreover, society's socialization has created barriers to her ability to enjoy casual sex. If she is able to use that option, it will have to be in her own way, in her own time. And if you then discover that you're not as pleased about it as you thought you'd be? Well, unanticipated feelings are as much your right as they are hers. Use them to enhance your understanding of how she feels about your extramarital sex, be honest about them if it will help, renegotiate back to monogamy again

if she is willing, but do not ask her to be monogamous when you are not.

11. Try not to feel railroaded by others into choosing between marriage and homosexual expression. You will meet many people who tell you that your bisexuality is simply your dishonesty with yourself. That is a possibility. It is also possible, however, that you are simply hearing another version of bigotry, and you need not rule your life by it. You have options. If you and your wife can work out a mutually satisfying contract, there is no reason why you should not do so. You simply need to realize that your wife will want to be the primary person in your life and that when a conflict of heterosexual versus homosexual interest arises, her needs will have to come first.

12. If you cannot honestly commit yourself to and be happy in a heterosexual relationship, don't string your wife along out of fear of hurting her or resort to nastiness in the hope that she will decide to leave. Even if she eventually does, you will have inflicted excessive pain on her and increased bitterness and potential recrimination toward you.

True, a request for divorce will hurt. Feeling unloved, second best, or merely tolerated by a husband who feels trapped, however, hurts more. Even worse, it prevents a wife from finding the more satisfying relationship she deserves. She will cope with reality once she knows what reality is. Just remember that she will need — and deserves — your help in rebuilding her self-confidence, preparing for single life, planning for the future, developing a new support system, etc. How long that will take depends on your situation. Trying to achieve a happy balance between "firing" a wife as if she were a maid and prolonging the agony is difficult. One of you may eventually have to have the strength to set the date or end your contract. Chances are, however, that if you let her set the pace, she herself will make the break when she feels strong enough to do so. Your own empathy will help speed that process.

13. Just as wives go through crisis, you are going through it too. Be patient with yourself as you go through periods of guilt, depression, irrational anger, physical symptoms, and plain, simple confusion. Don't panic that you're going crazy — get help and use your own feelings to help you understand your wife's.

14. What do you need to understand about your wife? The loss of trust your wife feels is far worse than simple loss of trust in you. She may have learned the hard way that she needs to pay more attention to her hunches, and it may show up in occasional paranoia. She has definitely learned the hard way that life is not always as it seems or as she perceives it, or even as you may perceive it. Her faith in her own perception has been shattered.

Both of you will have to live with the fact that she can never again afford — if it were possible for her to do so — to believe totally in your love for and sexual satisfaction with her. No matter at how low a level it may be, her defense against possible future hurt is as necessary for her future health as your defense against homophobia is for you. Moreover, if you married prior to the gay liberation movement, she is enough of a realist to know that had you been born in a different era, you might not have married. No matter how much she trusts your love, no matter how happy you both are, and whether she tells you or not, that knowledge will always hurt just a little.

There is nothing you can do to completely erase that hurt or fear. Nor can you waste time feeling guilty about it. There is much you can do, however, to ease it. You can be empathic and reassuring when her need for reassurance seems excessive. You can and should provide her with verbal, physical, and sexual (or sensual) expressions of your love frequently, without her having to ask for them. That does not mean plying her with gifts, obeying her every wish, or giving false reassurance. It simply means showing her the same sensitivity to her wounds that you want her to show toward yours.

Chapter 11

The Impact of AIDS

This chapter requires a warning: There are still many unknowns about AIDS, and information given here may be obsolete by the time it reaches print. It is important for you to check what I say against current information.

When I started my study in the early 80s, AIDS meant nothing more to me than a 2-inch newspaper article about a strange new "gay" disease. I remember thinking that label was probably some new Far Right way of denouncing homosexuality. The women I was interviewing at the time had—at worst—worried about such sexually transmitted diseases as syphilis and herpes. By now one of the few good things to say about AIDS is that it makes those other worries suddenly seem almost mild.

THE EFFECT OF THE AIDS CRISIS
ON REACTIONS TO DISCLOSURE

What effect has today's AIDS crisis had on my earlier findings about disclosure? The mass media have dramatized such incidents as the wife who sued her husband for giving her, not AIDS, but an "AIDS phobia." Even in less extreme cases, how could a positive disclosure occur with a potential death threat hanging over a couple? Wouldn't a wife's immediate reaction to disclosure be "Oh God! We're all going to die!"? And wouldn't that fear put the disclosure of homosexuality into an extremely negative category that inevitably ruins the future relationship?

One would certainly think so. Yet, although AIDS is still too new for already-published research to really answer that question, researchers Dorothea Hays and Aurele Samuels report that unless coping with an actual diagnosis, women interviewed after AIDS had become well publicized still did not seem to put it highest on their list of concerns. Samuels finds that women in the support groups she now runs range from being unwilling to either be tested or protect themselves, to being "devastated" when they test positive to the AIDS antibody. She feels that many factors enter into a wife's degree of concern about AIDS.

My own thinking (based on poststudy letters and conversations with women, my present private clinical practice, and the counseling I do in an AIDS antibody testing clinic), supports that view. Certainly the threat of AIDS has had an impact both on people themselves and on the individual and couple counseling they need. Still, wives' reactions, whether generally to a husband's disclosure of homosexuality or specifically to his real or possible exposure to AIDS, seem to be consistent with reactions to pre-AIDS disclosures of homosexuality. How a husband deals with AIDS seems to be consistent with and part of the way in which he deals with his homosexuality in general.

For example, if a husband's disclosure is positive in all other respects, AIDS does not seem to be the wife's first and foremost concern. To the extent that it is or becomes an issue for her, it is again her husband's attitudes and behaviors that define the category of the disclosure and dictate her immediate and future reactions.

Say, for instance, that he has had completely safe sex with men, has been tested, and has voluntarily reassured her about AIDS. Or perhaps he has had one recent unplanned, low-risk experience, has already had one negative test result, still feels guilty, and does not want to do anything to put his wife at risk.

In both cases he tells her quickly, is empathic with her feelings, encourages her being tested for her own peace of mind, and also accompanies her and plans with her realistic and safe ways to satisfy their sexual needs. In both cases, the disclosure can still be considered relatively positive. Accordingly, her reactions are also relatively positive.

If she already knows about the homosexuality but a recent risky sexual behavior has precipitated a new disclosure, we are obviously starting down the road of "increasingly negative disclosures" mentioned earlier. Nevertheless, angry or not, unless such behavior seems to be turning into a pattern, wives seem able to remain positive about the honesty and to assume that the husband's own distress is "punishment" enough. In fact, as with Samuels, I sometimes find wives inclined to err on the side of being too trusting and understanding following such an event. If that trust is violated with new "accidents," however, a wife is likely to grow more negative, unduly suspicious, or even paranoid about the husband's possible extramarital activity.

At the extreme negative end of the continuum, let's imagine a worst-case scenario: a "very negative" disclosure of long-term, ongoing, high-risk homosexual behavior is forced by a diagnosis of AIDS. The husband has known of his infection for a year, yet has continued to have unprotected intercourse with his wife, has allowed her to become pregnant, denies homosexuality, refuses to go with her for testing, and when she too tests positive, he blames her for his condition. To predict that she may be less than understanding would be a masterpiece of understatement.

So far, although I have been faced with real or potential negative disclosures in both the clinic and private practice, I have never seen such extremes. Even in a public STD (Sexually Transmitted Disease) clinic I am more apt to see frightened, guilt-ridden men wanting the AIDS antibody test the day after one unplanned, "low risk" homosexual experience. Afraid to either tell or to have sex with their wives, they are often suicidal.

I'm sure exceptions will eventually occur, but so far women have been supportive and understanding when such men have gathered the courage to tell them and have brought them in for testing and to talk with me. This has held true even in the one instance when such a man tested positive for the AIDS antibody.

So far, in over a year at the clinic, I have seen only two infected men who had been and remained insensitive, deceitful, and seemingly unconcerned about the wife's feelings or rights. Both wives were more far more compassionate, I must admit, than I myself would have been under the circumstances.

HOW GREAT IS THE RISK FOR WOMEN?

Anecdotal experience is of limited help. How concerned should wives of bisexual men be? Unfortunately, research also fails to provide adequate answers, and those that it does provide bring both good news and bad. Let's start with:

The Good News

1. Although a husband's homosexuality puts both partners into a "high risk" category, remember that it is actual behavior, not a category, that creates the risk. So far, statistically the risk for wives still seems low. The Centers for Disease Control (CDC) statistics at mid-January 1988 listed adolescent and adult women as accounting for 7% of all AIDS cases. Of that 7%, approximately 29% had been infected through heterosexual sex. Of that 29%, about 18% (26 women at most) had reported sex with a bisexual man. This was in comparison with 32,799 homosexual/bisexual men, and constituted less than 1% of the total adult/adolescent AIDS cases. CDC figures can change weekly, but relative proportions still appear to be holding constant.

2. Many of the women who contracted AIDS through heterosexual sex became infected only after repeated — and one remained negative after 200 — acts of unprotected intercourse with their infected partner. Moreover, many of those women could not be considered innocent victims of dishonest men. They knew of their partner's infection, had been counseled, and yet had disregarded the advice and warnings of their physicians and other counselors.

3. *As far as is known*, *proper* use of condoms seems very effective as a barrier for preventing sexually transmitted infection.

4. Although the virus can be transmitted through vaginal intercourse, anal intercourse seems to be the most hazardous practice.

5. No other family members have become infected from everyday contact with their fathers. AIDS in children has been related to hemophilia or other blood disorders, transfusion, possibly breast-feeding, and, most often, being conceived by an infected mother. Although a child could become infected through sexual abuse, so

far there are no documented cases to suggest that this has actually happened.

WHAT DO THESE STATISTICS MEAN?

Do these low figures mean that most bisexual men have taken care to protect their female partners? That most bisexual husbands do not have intercourse with their wives? Or that most couples divorced before AIDS became a problem?

At present there is no way to know. One fact, however, seems clear: unless there are specific causes for concern in a certain situation, women need not hit the panic button simply because a sexual partner is gay or bisexual. Even if he is infected or has AIDS, that fact alone does not automatically mean that his wife, girlfriend, or child is or will be infected.

The Bad News

That was the good news. Unfortunately, that's not all there is to the story. The primary bad news is that CDC statistics cannot give us the rest of the story. If wives need not panic, they do need to be concerned and careful for these reasons:

1. There are two major problems with CDC figures. First, the all-important category of "heterosexual transmission" does not adequately distinguish between five possible risk factors. Also, within a category – particularly in the large high-risk "drug user" population – are men who are also bisexual or who have risky homosexual experiences while under the influence of drugs. In the end, we don't know the actual transmission route for women infected through "heterosexual sex with an infected partner."

2. The biggest problem with CDC figures is that they report only diagnosed AIDS cases. True, researchers in some communities study women who are at risk, who are sero-positive (i.e., infected but asymptomatic), and/or who are sexual partners of men with AIDS. These are studies on small, readily available homogeneous groups such as hemophiliacs or participants in a drug program. Married men, however, are often unwilling to either participate in

studies or to reveal their homosexual experiences. When tested, they are often not asked and may not mention their marital status. Many women do not know that their husbands or lovers are bisexual and hence are not tested.

Why haven't such women shown up with AIDS? Simply because AIDS has not been around long enough to get past a long time-lag between infection and illness. Once infected, it may have taken a man years to become ill enough to be diagnosed with AIDS. It may take years for his partner to become infected and more years before she too is diagnosed and becomes part of the AIDS statistics.

3. Another problem with the lack of nationally coordinated research on "sero-positives" is that we do not yet have consistent and reliable data on exactly how a virus is transmitted heterosexually. We know, for instance, that anal intercourse is the highest-risk sexual behavior. Yet we also know that women have contracted the virus through vaginal sex alone. We know that oral sex is low risk; we don't know how low "low" is. We know that kissing is theoretically risky; we don't know if it is in fact risky.

Laboratory tests prove that well-made condoms are effective barriers through which the virus cannot pass. We know that if properly and consistently used, they are very effective in actual intercourse. But we don't know nor do we always collect or report on the data needed to tell us exactly how effective, necessary, or reliable they are in actual use. In one study of 80 couples, for example, one wife remained negative after 200 acts of intercourse with her sero-positive husband, whereas another wife became infected after only one act. But the report did not state how many couples had used condoms, how consistently they had been used, or if there had been any condom failure.

4. The reliability of condoms depends mainly on how consistently and how properly they're used. Many condom failures result simply because people do not know enough about condoms and are ashamed to ask for instructions.

5. The virus can attack the brain, but we are not yet adept at spotting the first signs of dementia. Hence we may not be aware that someone actually lacks the capacity for good judgment.

6. Poor judgment, risky behavior, and even loss of memory may result from drug or alcohol abuse. Some people do not remember

what they have done. Some people are at risk from both sexual behavior and needle sharing. Although the latter is the most dangerous, when there are two or three risk factors going in one person, the chance for infection increases, and there is little way to know exactly how a virus was actually transmitted.

7. Remember the dysfunctional behaviors cited earlier as part of reactions to crisis? Crisis and its high emotional stress can also lead to risky sexual behavior on both partners' parts, both in and out of the marital bed. People having extramarital sex must take precautions with an extramarital partner no matter how safe he or she may seem. Intravenous drug use is probably not a common coping device for wives of bisexual men, but it is a particularly dangerous one. The same logic applies to both single and married women: if a man refuses and is so angered by a request to use condoms that a women is afraid to insist for fear of losing him, that attitude itself may signal danger ahead.

8. The biggest danger for husbands and wives alike is not from people who know they are infected (most of whom are concerned, careful, and honest), but from people who do not know, who think that they and the people they have sex with are too "nice" to be infected, who consider themselves immune because they've tested negative despite the risks they've taken, who consider safety the other person's responsibility, or who think that either having been in an assumed monogamous marriage or having tested "negative" once classifies a person as "safe."

9. Finally, although there may be few "heels" who knowingly risk their wives' health, such husbands do exist. I see few of them in the HIV (AIDS) antibody clinic, but I do see men who out of fear, like their counterparts in earlier chapters, are taking themselves and their wives down potentially disastrous roads. Some see only three possibilities: to desert their wives, to divorce for some fabricated reason, or to kill themselves to avoid revealing either homosexuality, sero-positivity, or actual illness. Some men see avoiding the marital bedroom as their way of protecting their wives, and avoiding any communication in other rooms of the house as their way of protecting themselves.

Some use condoms spasmodically or only with marital sex. If a condom breaks, some avoid their wives until the test results come in. Others continue unprotected marital sex to avoid arousing suspicion, on the grounds that they do not want to frighten a wife needlessly. Some try to convince themselves and me that they have simply had a one-shot "drunken" homosexual experience that will never happen again, hence no need for honesty. My own feeling is that eventually wives will learn the truth. Whether or not infection has occurred, such men will again have set up the exact angry, unforgiving, and vindictive scenarios they were so worried about in the first place.

SO WHERE ARE WE?

What we do know is this: wives and former wives of gay/bisexual men need not panic, for the number of women known to be seropositive or to have AIDS because of a bisexual partner is still low. It is indeed amazingly low considering the estimated size of the married or once-married gay/bisexual population and the number of husbands apt to have been having furtive, risky sex during the years when the AIDS virus was active but unknown.

What we don't know is how many infected wives, former wives, or other female partners of gay/bisexual men are waiting in the wings about to become sick. We only assume that there are many. We do not have a completely reliable estimate of the degree of risk from either a "category" or a specific sexual behavior. We don't know whether today's figures are reliable indicators for the future or if researchers have not asked the right questions, have been given misleading answers, and received false impressions.

In general, AIDS may not have changed either the "disclosure" picture or the male–female sex game all that much. On the bright side, it may be making women more aware of bisexuality and more able both to ask about it and to assert their rights. It may be forcing people, no matter what their sexual preference or marital status, to talk more openly and honestly about sex, to realize that "sex" is more than "screwing," and to work harder at finding and sustaining committed, monogamous relationships.

On the dark side, many men still see women simply as "objects" (perhaps "subjects" is more apt here) and will be honest or use safety measures only if forced to or if it suits them. They will say anything to get their way, use a written test result or a verbal "Trust me, I've been tested" as a line, and will blame a woman for their woes rather than taking responsibility for their own actions. Many women still tolerate such abuse, will themselves refuse condoms, or will delegate all responsibility (and blame) to men and assume none for themselves.

The bottom line is that wives need a balance between panic and dysfunctional denial. They can relax quite a bit, but they cannot afford to simply trust their husbands or any other men without taking any responsibility for their own safety.

Reclosing the Closet Door

A major concern, however, must be the potential results of new stigma and closeting. While we "see" many more men being honest and responsible, we may be "seeing" only those willing to be "seen." We know that even with anonymous testing, many men are too wary (often for good reason) to come for testing. When they do come, they may not mention that they are married; hence neither they nor their families receive adequate counseling.

Moreover, I see many men who come for testing in order to be "clean for marriage" before they embark on a frantic search for someone to marry. In the meantime, they have sworn themselves to celibacy (often ruling out even masturbation) and have joined a Homosexuals Anonymous group or become born-again Christians in order to cure themselves of homosexuality. Already-married men are also turning to religion and vowing extramarital abstinence.

These tactics, unfortunately, are no more likely to provide long-term solutions now than they ever were. Fear, although a powerful temporary deterrent, has never really sustained its effect over long periods of time. It simply drives both desire and honesty underground. When the desire resurfaces, fear of ostracism may still prevent honesty, but activity is apt to resume furtively and probably with little more safety than furtive sex ever had. In fact, it seems to me that the men who try hardest to erase all homosexual thoughts are the ones most apt to return to the clinic in a panic because in one drunken moment, they engaged in the highest-risk behavior possible.

Unless we can stave off panic, bigotry, and punitive societal attitudes, men with homosexual desires are likely to simply return to or stay in the closet. The last generation's mistakes will return to haunt our children and grandchildren. Until medicine provides a cure for AIDS, the future results of stigma may be even more devastating than they had been for the men and women described in earlier chapters.

So What Do We Do Now?

Enough about statistics and society. What many of you want and need to know is how to cope with the fear of AIDS in your own life. There's no question that right now, no matter how small your risk may be, AIDS is a very real concern. Unless you have a diagnosed case to face (in which case you probably already have individualized help), you are part of a group rapidly becoming known as "the worried well." In helping you to find that balance between undue worry and dysfunctional denial, again there's both good news and bad. This time, I'll start with:

The Bad News

1. Even if a husband has decided on homosexual abstinence for now, it may be too late. Don't worry about every little cold symptom, but do keep alert, talk with a *knowledgeable* professional, and receive individual guidance if either one of you is concerned. If either of you has avoided the other sexually for fear of giving or getting AIDS or other STDs, you should discuss that fear honestly. Not only may a spouse be feeling sexually rejected without knowing why but there are better strategies to plan. Honest talk may even allay both your fears.

2. Even infrequent or monogamous activity does not necessarily make one safe. As with other sexually transmitted diseases, or the nondisease of pregnancy, one can become infected in only one sexual contact with the medically wrong person or even with a highly trusted spouse or lover who has had only one sexual contact with an infected person.

3. Ordinarily reliable doctors are not always as well informed and helpful in this area as they should be. With new reports coming in

almost daily, getting a consistently clear story sometimes seems impossible. Also, early medical terminology used to explain AIDS has often served to confuse instead of help.

4. Finally, safety measures may limit — or at least modify — sexual options you would ordinarily have had with each other.

The Good News

The good news, on the other hand, is threefold:

1. Fear of AIDS need not put an end to your marital/sexual and parent–child relationships. Much fear of communicability is needless. New research has already provided and will continue to provide better preventive, diagnostic, and treatment measures.

2. Despite the insecurity that the "all it takes is once" reality creates, the fact is that the AIDS virus is actually difficult to transmit. Like other sexually transmitted diseases, the risk increases with the number of risky behaviors. You may even be willing to gamble on a few *low*-risk activities, although you should not relax totally just because years have passed, you are still negative, and you and your husband are symptom free.

3. Despite the uncertainties about AIDS, given the short time it has been around and the confounding nature of the virus, we know a surprising amount. When it first started, testing and counseling helped prevent transmission but offered little else. Now it can do much to either allay fears or provide couples with relatively good guidelines for a safe but enjoyable sex life. At that time, there was almost no help that doctors could offer. Now there are possibilities for tracking the progress of the virus, medicines, and other health measures that seem helpful, with enough potential cures to give people hope.

For the rest of the chapter, let's answer some common questions about coping with a "worried well" status and give a few tips on coping with a sero-positive status. I'll write as if I am addressing a still-married couple and will leave it to you to translate advice and pronouns to fit your own needs.

COPING WITH A WORRIED WELL STATUS

Q. *Should my spouse and I get tested?*

A. If you or your spouse think you may have had risky sex or some other risk factor since around 1978, you should both be tested if only to establish a "baseline" to tell you where you stand at the moment. If you have had a recent possible exposure, you might want to be tested even though it is too soon, simply to establish that baseline. If you are negative, retest 4 to 14 weeks after the risky episode, making sure that you stay completely safe from any new potential exposures in the meantime.

As a wife, you might want to be tested if you think your husband is gay but are divorced and no longer in contact with him; if you fear he is less than candid about his homosexual activities; or if there has been a possible exposure no matter who or what the source and you are planning, are in the midst of, or have just finished a pregnancy.

The Pros and Cons of Testing

To test or not to test, however, is not a decision to be made lightly. There are many factors to consider. Blanket testing is not a useful idea. Become as informed as possible, talk over your individual situation with a counselor at the testing site, and take as much time as you need to think it over.

Q. *Why shouldn't everyone be tested? I'd certainly want to know if I had AIDS. Wouldn't you?*

A. Yes, I would. But the antibody test will not tell you that. It will only show whether you have formed antibodies to the virus. Sometimes it does not even tell you that much. You may have to be retested either because antibodies have not had time to form or because special factors render the test potentially false. Waiting for results is often stressful. Waiting weeks or months for a retest greatly increases that stress.

More important, having a "positive" test result is often devastating to people. True, the need to know is more compelling for couples with one high-risk partner than for other couples. Still, unless there is risk for an unborn or nursing baby, do not ask the question until you have thought about and discussed with a trained HIV counselor how you will cope with the answer. Some research even suggests that despite good intentions, people who test negative are less apt to stop high-risk behavior than people who assume they are positive and act accordingly.

Q. *Then why get tested? Maybe it's better not to know.*

A. There are two advantages. The first, of course, is to prevent the spread of the virus. Research also suggests that despite good intentions, high-risk people who have confirmed that they are sero-positive are less apt to take risks than those who have not been tested. The second is that the sooner infected people are linked up with the medical system, the greater their ability to stay healthy, to keep their families healthy, to plan wisely for the future, and to have immediate access to any new vaccines, medicines, or treatments that come along.

Q. *What exactly does testing positive mean?*

A. It means you have formed antibodies to the HIV (AIDS) virus. For all practical purposes, that means you are both infected and infectious: you can transmit the virus to others through blood, semen, vaginal secretions, amniotic fluid, or breast milk. You may become highly vulnerable to opportunistic infections and should do everything possible to stay healthy.

Q. *Don't antibodies mean you were exposed and became immune?*

A. With some viruses, yes. With this one, no.

Q. *I hear it can take 10 years for the virus to incubate. So a negative result is meaningless. Right? A positive result means that you're going to die when the virus incubates, whether that happens in 2 days or 10 years. Right?*

A. Wrong on both counts. Like many people, you may need a better understanding of how the virus works. The following explanation is not the most complete or accurate one you could get. If you're a doctor, forgive me. I usually find, however, that it gets the general idea across better than more complicated, albeit more technically correct ones.

Essentially, our bodies contain an army of cells that help defend us against disease-producing organisms. That army is part of our immune system. One set of cells sounds the alarm when the body is under siege, another does the fighting. Suppose a measles virus comes to attack. The first time around, the virus takes us by surprise. A helper cell fights and eventually kills the virus but cannot prevent it from incubating (i.e., multiplying to a sufficient number for the alarm to be sounded and the body to start fighting it). The specific symptoms of measles show us that a battle is in progress. When the virus is killed, we get well. The alarm ringer has also produced a chemical substance called "antibody," which stays around to act as guard. Next time a measles virus appears, the antibody recognizes and kills it immediately, and we can consider ourselves immune to measles.

The AIDS virus, however, does not work that way. True, an antibody is formed, usually in 4 to 14 weeks. It stays around to show that it at least tried. We may develop a few symptoms of infection if a battle was at least attempted, but the virus cannot be killed. In fact, it hides out in the fighter cell itself, usually too quickly to even be spotted and fought at all. Then it waits to see what will happen next.

Although we do not yet know all the factors that trigger the virus into action, what happens next seems — at least in part — to be related to infection from other sources. Eventually, we are exposed to some other kind of disease-producing organism. Our body's army is alerted, but so is the AIDS virus. It multiplies, kills the cell it has invaded, and then it and its new squadron of clones start traveling, staking out and hiding in new cells. Whenever we either become sick or even have to fight off infection from any source, the AIDS viruses repeat that process, growing in number and destroying our defensive army cell by cell.

As our defensive army becomes more and more depleted, we begin to pick up disease-producing organisms that we'd normally fight off. Flu and symptoms of infection stay longer, return more frequently, and are far more severe than normal. Eventually, we begin picking up illnesses usually associated with poor immune systems, like shingles or certain forms of cancer and pneumonia.

Whatever the symptoms, they are the symptoms of their particular diseases. It is mainly the combination of a known risk factor, an observed antibody, and a lowered "T-helper" cell count that tells us that the AIDS virus is indirectly responsible for our contracting those diseases. We call that condition ARC (AIDS Related Complex). ARC patients are treated for whatever illnesses occur. Some physicians keep careful watch on the cell count and give preventive medicine if it falls below a certain level. Others prefer to do nothing unless a person actually becomes sick. At any rate, if all goes well, we recover from whatever disease we have contracted. ARC, then, can be like a headache. Its illnesses and symptoms may mean nothing or everything, be mild or severe, be temporary, long lasting, or fatal.

What happens next is even more uncertain. Some patients seem to have recovered, to have shown an improved helper cell count, and to have avoided further symptoms. Although nobody yet knows how long that can continue, it provides hope that some people may be able to avoid actual AIDS. More often, however, the virus seems to return to its task of depleting the immune system. When that system is so low that the body picks up and can no longer fight fatal diseases, we say that the person has AIDS. But it is a misnomer, for there is no disease called AIDS. The person has cancer or pneumonia or some other disease. AIDS is simply a name given to the state of the body at that point, since it is the AIDS virus that has rendered the person so vulnerable to the actually fatal disease. It would probably be more accurate to say that one is *in* AIDS rather than that one *has* AIDS.

Q. *How reliable are the tests?*

A. Although some authorities would disagree (and certainly even better tests are in the making), by now, given a reputable lab and skilled counselors, results are very reliable. But of course you can see that much depends on the honesty of the person and that if someone is exposed to the virus and takes the test 1 week later, no antibody will show up. Although one never knows if new data will change the picture, the present rule of thumb is that most people form antibodies by the end of 2 months. A small group takes 14 weeks. Although a few people form antibodies in 2 weeks, testing at that point mainly establishes a baseline and cannot be considered reliable.

Hence though you can take the tension level down a notch by testing at the strategic points, if the potential exposure has been high risk, you cannot consider yourself home free until you pass the 14-week mark. The chance for either false positives or false negatives is slim, but various factors can produce an "indeterminate" test result. Your test counselor is the best person to help you decide if and when to be either tested or retested, and your degree of honesty can make a difference in how accurately the test results are interpreted.

Testing will not tell you about an exposure that occurred 5 minutes after being tested. Women often assure me that their military partners were tested. But the military tests every 6 months at the most. Lots can happen between tests.

You can also see why it's so difficult to know what will happen after one tests positive. Much depends on how long the virus has been active before testing. Much depends on how many viruses are at work: one may work slowly, 1,000 can work very quickly. Much depends on how healthy a person is and how healthy he or she stays. If sickness acts as an invitation to viral activity, it obviously pays to do everything possible to stay healthy. Hence a normally sickness-prone person may be in full-blown AIDS within 2 years of infection, whereas a normally healthy person may stay symptom free for 10 years or more.

For now, in general we can say that 30% to 50% of sero-positives develop symptoms within 5 years and 50% within 10. Only time will tell whether the remaining 50% stay healthy until they die of old age or not. Only time will tell whether research finds ways to either cure or stave off illness. One thing is certain: eventually everyone will die of something, for life itself is an incurable illness.

To sum up, then, the virus does not "incubate" into a specific disease with specific symptoms like measles. Until a test to see the actual virus is available for general use, the only way we know it's there is that in around 4 to 14 weeks, an antibody can be observed. Even then, we simply assume that the virus is alive and well until we have the circumstantial evidence of a low helper cell count and symptoms caused by other organisms that have incubated into other diseases.

Q. *Where should I go for testing?*

A. You can use your own doctor, a public health facility, or some other officially designated testing site. Most cities have a hotline to tell you the resources in your area. Public clinics are free. Whether or not they're convenient will depend on your locale. Private physicians may be more convenient, but are costly — and — this may surprise you — may *not* provide you with the best information, advice, or counseling. Moreover, your test result may then automatically become part of your medical record.

Q. *How confidential is testing?*

A. That depends on your locale. Some states provide confidentiality: identifying information is required, but is kept confidential. Some provide anonymity: no identifying information is asked. Test results are identified and given out only through a coding system. Some states provide neither — and may in fact require that positive test results — with names — be reported.

Q. *Coming back is difficult. Can I call in for results?*

A. Most clinics and doctors will not give results by phone. Why? Think how you might feel if your result is positive. Do you really want to be told by an impersonal voice over the phone? And do you want to take the chance of someone else calling in to learn your results?

Q. *Are "home testing" kits reliable?*

A. "Home testing" usually means that you take your own blood sample, send it out for testing, and receive your results by mail. Some will probably be reliable. But in my opinion, you should still not use them unless in-person counseling from a trained HIV test counselor is both provided and required prior to taking the test and when the results are given. Nor should you be tested by your own doctor or anyone else unless he or she has either been specifically trained to counsel you or is having your counseling provided elsewhere.

Q. *Why? What's the problem?*

A. No matter how intelligent, well adjusted, or well informed you are, you need someone to help you evaluate whether to take the test, evaluate even negative results, know whether or when to be retested, and know how to stay safe in the future. No matter how well prepared you think you are, you absolutely need information and counseling should you test positive.

In the clinic where I work, people watch several TV programs and read brochures about the test in the waiting room. They have pretest counseling to make sure they understand what they have read and both need and want the test. They go home armed with a bunch of new pamphlets and have posttest counseling to make sure they understand the results. Even then, an overwhelming amount of complex information combined with stress leads to forgetting or misinterpreting much of what they've been told. Getting results on a mere piece of paper or by telephone message is apt to create either panic and undue depression or unwarranted relief that increases risky behavior.

Q. *What kind of sexual relationship can we have? What is safe in or out of the marriage?*

A. Much will depend on the nature of your relationship, and how open and honest you are with each other. Good communication is essential. The decision to take an HIV test should be seen as common sense, not a lack of trust. The same goes for deciding on a sexual contract and whether or not to use condoms. Obviously, trust is important, but trust can and often needs to include a recognition of human failings.

A husband in or past his 40s who has had relatively infrequent "safe" extramarital sex or who has one homosexually monogamous relationship with a noninfected partner is probably not at high risk. Of course, the same is true of a wife. Starting with testing for each partner (twice, if necessary, and staying safe between tests), you need simply avoid casual encounters and practice "safe" sex outside the marriage. The same is true in the marital bedroom. "Safe" will need to be determined individually.

Remember that intercourse itself is not necessary for good sex; there are options for both marital and extramarital manual caressing to orgasm and oral stimulation. The one fly in this ointment, unfortunately, is that if there is any risk whatsoever and you wish to avoid subjecting your spouse, yourself, or your lover to danger or even frequent inquisitions, you will need condoms for vaginal, anal, and oral (penis-mouth) intercourse. Of course, again we're really weighing the amount of risk you're willing to take for yourself and the person you love. Only you can discuss the issue and decide on the contract you need to make. You may need counseling to help you decide on a realistic and fair plan.

Let's take the risk factor for each sexual activity, going from highest risk to lowest risk:

1. Anal intercourse is far and away the most risky of all sexual behaviors. Being the "receiver" is the most dangerous, since anal tissues are so delicate that even without penetration, tiny tears provide entry points for tiny viruses. Moreover, there are now indications that the virus can infect cells in the bowel itself, without waiting to enter the bloodstream. In all intercourse, it is better to give than to receive. But "better" does not take "giving" anally out of the highest-risk category.

In heterosexual relationships, the woman is obviously at most risk. Yet some women become infected without anal sex; others seem to have so far avoided infection despite unprotected anal sex with an infected partner. Nevertheless, it would seem wise to avoid anal sex, since even condoms can break. But at least use a condom—(and consider the new "extra strength" brands). In addition, use a lubricant with Nonoxynol 9 in it.

2. Vaginal intercourse is the next most dangerous. Women are the most at risk here, but it is also possible for the man to become infected. Moreover, new research suggests that the cervix itself can become infected simply from contact, without the virus needing to enter the bloodstream through tiny vaginal cuts or tears.

3. With oral (mouth–genital) intercourse, we come to the "iffy" areas of risk. We simply don't know the risk here. Until recently there were no documented cases of transmission through oral intercourse alone. Now there may be three cases of mouth–penis transmission. Documentation is difficult, however, since people engaging in oral sex are apt to be having other sexual activities too. Obviously, though, an open sore or even a minute, unnoticed cut in the mouth from brushing, flossing, or dental work can provide an

entry point for a virus. The CDC hence suggests the use of condoms for penis–mouth contact. If no condom is used, a man should at least withdraw before ejaculation. Further, since the pre-ejaculation fluid also contains virus, withdrawal should take place well in advance of ejaculation. Since even condoms are not foolproof, you may decide to forego oral intercourse — especially in extramarital sex.

One might avoid vaginal tongue kissing just prior to or following a menstrual period, since unnoticed particles of blood might again transmit the virus through unnoticed cuts in the mouth. There's never been a documented case of such an event, but this is one time you don't want to be first on the block. Some people suggest always using dental dams or sponges for complete safety in vaginal kissing. That might be safe, but so is watching a documentary on cactus. The two activities sound equally erotic.

4. How about deep tongue kissing? Again there is absolutely no documented case of transmission through kissing alone. Although the virus is found in both teardrops and saliva, the concentration is so low in each that an estimated quart or two of tears or saliva poured directly into a vein would be necessary in order to transmit the virus. Nevertheless, again we simply don't know if there's any risk or not, and we don't want you to be the one to prove that there is. So though you needn't eliminate deep tongue kissing, if either of you has a cut or sore in the mouth, wait until it's healed. If your kissing tends to be very wet, you might try modifying your kissing techniques.

Of course, we're being extra safe with all these rules, simply because (1) either partner might unknowingly have become infected since the last test, and (2) it was probably not a lack of trust that put you in this situation. No matter how slight it may have been, it was probably a breach of trust. Still, you needn't go around scared all the time, nor do you necessarily need all these safety measures. What you'll need really depends on you and your individual situation.

At the very least, however, you do need to have *and strictly obey* a contract that if either of you strays, you'll either use condoms or engage only in such safe activities as manual stimulation. If a slipup or a condom breakage occurs, you'll bite the bullet, confess immediately, and do anything necessary to both protect yourselves and repair the emotional damage.

An ounce of insurance, by the way, is in order now. I mean that very literally. If you don't have enough life or health insurance, *this* is the time to get it. Be sure it covers mental health workers (including social workers) and prescription drugs.

Does this sound like a double message? It need not be. You can be very clear about the difference between "giving permission" and "recognizing human failings" just as you stress the importance of birth control and safe sex to teenagers without giving them permission for premarital sex. You need to be very specific, however, on what extramarital sexual activities you do give permission for and what you don't. If you are not worried about a potential breach of trust, you needn't spell out the consequences of a future one; if you feel you have been given cause for concern, you may wish to be quite specific about what the consequences of a future slipup will be.

Does this put everyone in a double bind? Yes, to some extent. Trust is necessary if you are going to keep your marriage together and happy. But it's one thing to take risks with emotional hurt and another to take risks with life and death. When I started this book I was telling husbands that what their wives don't know can and does hurt them. By now, I'm telling both partners that what they don't know can kill them.

Of course, a wife may be angry about even having to worry about such things. A husband may feel added guilt. There's not much to do about that except understand, empathize with each other, and secure added counseling if necessary.

Try to remember that AIDS is only one of many dangerous diseases in world history. Long before homosexuals became easy prey to such STDs as syphilis, heterosexuals both unintentionally and deliberately had wiped out or all but wiped out whole societies with such diseases. They were not blamed for being heterosexual, nor was any related promiscuity blamed on their heterosexuality. Society simply knuckled down to the task of preventing and curing sexually transmitted illness. That's the task we face today, no matter what the illness is. The same caution that prevents AIDS also prevents other STDs.

COPING WITH ACTUAL INFECTION

If you and/or your spouse have the virus or are coping with the illness it has created, you should already have more help than this book can provide. Unfortunately, what "should be" is not always what "is." So here are a few elementary guidelines:

Crisis Theory Revisited

Reread the chapter on crisis, for a sero-positive test result can mean another emotional rollercoaster ride. Again, remember that "sero-positive" is not synonomous with either AIDS or "death." It does mean, however, that you need to face the same potential for sickness and death that middle-aged people face and that we should all have faced in our 20s. You are simply being forced to do so immediately. You need to do some contingency planning:

1. Find a knowledgeable and empathic physician and any legal help you may need. Your test counselor may be helpful with this.

2. Get relief from stress through professional therapy, relaxation techniques, and the like. Again, support groups can help relieve isolation, sense of stigma, and general stress. They can provide information and aid problem solving in such areas as who to tell, when to tell, and how to tell. If only one of you is positive, you will each need your own group.

3. This is another point for taking stock of your life: Where have you been? Where are you now? Where do you want to be in 1 month, 6 months, 1, 3, 5, and 10 years? Set immediate, short-term and long-term goals and plan accordingly. For example: Are you planning to see Europe when you retire? Do it now. I often see tourists who waited to see Hawaii until retirement and who were then too disabled to fully enjoy it. Let sero-positive status help you prevent that from happening to you. Don't give away all your possessions and burn all your bridges simply because you're frightened; however, you might well live to die of old age. But if you've been delaying a return to school or a change in career directions, if you've always wanted to take music lessons—maybe this is the time to go for it.

Conversely, if your career goal requires 10 stressful years of expensive education, you might see if a related field will bring similar satisfactions more quickly and easily. Are you filled with fear of death and anger at the unfairness in your life? Put your fear and anger to work in a political cause or in helping others. Make your life meaningful NOW.

Don't hold off on a new stereo in order to save for a rainy AIDS-filled day. That day may never come, and it's drizzling now. The money you save won't help much with the expense of AIDS, but the pleasure the stereo will bring will be invaluable.

4. Try to keep sex, sensuality, love, and intimacy in your life. HIV-infected people often feel or are treated as if they are untouchable. You needn't be afraid to hug, massage, kiss, share dishes, share food, roughhouse with the children. In short, try to live a normal life. Your test counselor or doctor will advise you about the few household precautions needed.

You needn't be afraid to have sex, assuming you have by now redefined "sex." No more playing Russian Roulette, of course— you must take precautions. Although some authorities disagree, that holds true even if you are both positive. You may decide to forego deep tongue kissing or oral sex. But the only sexual activity you need seriously consider giving up, condoms or no, is anal sex. Even here, experts disagree on the degree of risk. Hence, with better condoms and new information constantly coming in, ask your local experts about the sexual precautions needed.

Of course, positive or negative, you may not consider condoms wildly exciting. Remember that any loss of sensation is relative and will be less noticeable in time. Try different brands and use creativity to eroticize condoms. Use creativity for completely safe sex that does not require condoms: the combination of fingers, feathers, and fantasies can be highly erotic. Remember that your goal is neither pregnancy nor wild, pornographic orgasms but intimacy, affection, sensual pleasure, and tension release.

5. Remember that this chapter is just a starting point. Get individual help, try to lead a normal life, and have hope for the future. Let humor help you out. And speaking of humor . . .

6. Whether you're struggling with AIDS-related issues or not, the following story might be useful. Recently, a sero-positive support group member came to a meeting wearing a sweatshirt with a motto. Its first sentence said "Life is uncertain." The second sen-

tence told me immediately who had inspired it. A psychiatrist I'd known 20 years ago was a refugee famous for his sense of humor in the face of adversity. His two-liner philosophy has helped me out many times over the years.

Twenty years ago, AIDS was not the problem. What was? The fact that in an airplane on the way to a conference, just as lunch was being served, an announcement over the loudspeaker told us to fasten our seat belts, we were having engine trouble. A tense silence filled the cabin. Into that silence floated my colleague's voice, as he turned to his seatmate and said gravely, "My friend, life is uncertain. Eat dessert first!"

Chapter 12

More Guidelines:
For Couples, Children,
Helping Professionals
and Concerned Others

ADVICE TO COUPLES

It bears repeating that in contract negotiations, in day-to-day living, or for that matter, even during and after divorce, empathy is a two-way street. You both need to be honest and open, yet sensitive to each other's feelings. That balance is not easy to achieve. The following are questions I am often asked and their answers. Most are aimed at creating or maintaining a happy marriage. A few are aimed at dealing with the aftermath of divorce. Again, remember that many — perhaps most — of the suggestions and guidelines also apply to other individuals, marriages, and situations.

Q. *My girlfriend and I are considering marriage. I've had homosexual experiences in the past. I don't plan to have them in the future. People don't tell about their past heterosexual affairs. Should I tell? If so, why?*
A. Again there's no pat answer to that question, and you'd do well to ask a professional to help you think it through. Generally, however, wives and I agree that you should tell. There are several reasons for the seeming double standard. First, women today generally assume men have had premarital sex. They are not likely to assume homosexual sex. Hence "silence" here is more "dishonest" than it would ordinarily be. Second, you don't know what the future may hold, any more than the study husbands knew. Until the

issue of stigma is eliminated, a future disclosure of homosexuality
will plunge your wife into problems she could not have anticipated.
If you have been highly active, that situation may even include the
potential for AIDS.

You take a big risk in telling, of course. Your girlfriend may
reject you needlessly. Study wives appreciated that risk, but all believed that women have the right to make an "informed" choice.
You can decrease the risk of present rejection or future anger by
avoiding the mistakes of earlier husbands. The following example
seems a model worth emulating:

In contrast to Mary's husband, Marilyn's fiance told her of past
and supposedly terminated homosexuality before she had committed herself and changed life plans. He told her he had no way of
knowing what the future might bring. He could only assure her that
his love was real, that he foresaw no problem, and that he could
promise honesty. He recognized her potential qualms, including anger that he had been too afraid to tell her earlier, and suggested that
she might want to talk with either his therapist or another counselor.
Her reaction?

> I thought it over for a few minutes. Then I decided that all
> marriage involves risk. Given the honesty and sensitivity he
> had shown, the risk for my marriage was probably less than it
> is for most marriages.

Marilyn's husband did indeed face a resurgence of homosexual
feelings later in life and acted on them. After a brief "predisclosure
buildup" he told her in a typical "positive disclosure." They both
went through a mild version of the problems other couples faced. In
her thirtieth year of marriage and eight years after disclosure, her
summation was this:

> When he told me, I did not feel deceived. I did ask myself if
> I'd been neurotic to walk into the marriage with my eyes wide
> open, and wondered what the future would hold. It didn't take
> much time to come to the same conclusion I'd reached earlier.
> True, I've had some turmoil. As in any marriage, we've had
> some minor conflicts. But I have never regretted either deci-
> sion.

Q. *My fiance and I have discussed the homosexuality, and we are planning an open contract right from the start. Can we expect a good marriage?*

A. Your discussion has increased your chances for a good marriage. Open contracts, however, are not the panacea people often think they are. Although they can sometimes enhance a good marriage, they are likely to be disastrous for shaky ones. They may be the most difficult to maintain, although in this situation, they may be more necessary. It requires an especially honest and strong relationship, especially sensitive communication, flexibility, and self-esteem to withstand the pressure of unanticipated feelings and issues.

Moreover, you cannot know ahead of time what the homosexuality may mean for your life. You should treat your present status as a "positive initial disclosure," realize that you are pioneers, and prepare in advance for the potential problems you now know may lie ahead. Premarital counseling may help you with that task.

I firmly believe that gay/straight marriages can work and be very satisfying. You need to truly commit yourselves to each other. At the same time, you should be realistic about the possibility that your needs may change over time. If your marriage does not last forever, you will be no different from thousands of other "straight" couples whose marriages (or "living together" relationships) do not last forever, but you may have to remind yourselves and others of that fact.

Q. *We seem to be constantly arguing and can't seem to solve problems, even though we love each other. Why?*

A. Such problems often occur because Person A, instead of listening to Person B, is frantically trying to defend against an accusation and figure out what to say next. The natural response, then, is to say "Yes, but . . . , " completely overlooking what has been said and going on to make a counteraccusation. Person B responds similarly to the new accusation. Soon they are lost in a maze of new complaints, so far away from the original issue that they may not even remember what it is. No solution has been reached, and both partners feel hurt, angry, and hopeless. The following communication exercise interrupts that process and forces you to listen rather than "Yes, but" each other. It is a little like breaking your child's habit of saying "Um" or "like" every 2 minutes. It is tedious, frustrating, and irritating, but partly because of those qualities, it is effective.

Pick the easiest issue and toss a coin to see who goes first. Then A briefly expresses his or her feelings or wishes regarding the situation. B listens, without trying to answer them even mentally. B checks out whether he or she has heard and understood by parroting back A. If B has totally or partially missed what has been said, it is repeated and checked back until A feels completely heard. If the discussion has not included *why* A feels the way he or she does, the same procedure is repeated until A feels completely understood. Then—and only then—B responds with his or her feelings about either the situation itself or what has just been said, and it is A's turn to listen and repeat until B feels completely heard and understood. If there are many aspects to that one particular problem, the procedure may go back and forth several times.

You'll be surprised to see how often you try to interrupt each other, change topics, misread, and accuse. You'll be surprised to see how hard it is to get through one or two simple problems or even sentences without turning corners. You might also be surprised to see that a long-standing issue suddenly gets resolved in 2 minutes, once you both feel heard and understood.

TIP: Try to remember to talk in terms of your own feelings, rather than in how the other "makes" you feel. Also focus on what you would like in the future, not what you dislike.

In contract negotiations, it may help to ask yourselves if homosexuality is really the issue. As a heterosexual husband, would you go out on your wife's birthday, stay out all night, leave her home on Saturday nights, put others' needs before hers, tell her your extramarital sex is none of her business? Would you insist on telling her intimate details of your sexual activity and the joys and woes of your relationships with other women? If you would, the problem is not your homosexuality, it's your lack of consideration. If you wouldn't, why do it now? As a wife, would you tolerate such behavior from a heterosexual husband? Would you even tolerate it if he were simply going out with buddies, golf partners, or work associates? If you would, the problem is not his homosexuality, it's your lack of self-esteem and inability to stand up for your rights. If you wouldn't, why do it now?

Conversely, would you as a wife be upset if a heterosexual husband went out occasionally (or even once a week) with friends or had friendships with other women? If you would, you already needed to give yourselves more autonomy. If you wouldn't, why be upset now? Would you mind a heterosexual open contract? If not, why mind it now? The issue is not homosexuality, but stigma.

In short, the issues are of consideration for yourselves and each other. Lack of consideration is neither homosexual nor heterosexual. It is simply lack of consideration.

Try to remember that you are pioneers. The issues are not as simple as I made them sound in the last paragraphs. There are no "right" and "wrong" answers. You will have to be creative. In doing so, you will need to share with each other your worries, confusions, mixed feelings, and unexpected feelings. You will have to have empathy for the "double binds" that will be inevitable for both of you, avoid blaming yourselves or each other when one solution proves untenable, and go on to try to find a better one. You need to use humor in doing so. When some problem seem unsolvable, you may temporarily settle for recognizing that you are both in pain and providing each other with mutual comforting. Try to remember that most of your problems and the advice I have given here are not the special provinces of gay/straight marriages. They are part and parcel of the problems and needs I see in most marriages.

All this advice sounds good, but can be hard to follow. Again, you need peer support and professional help. Get it!

Q. *How do we deal with the children?*

A. That will depend on such factors as the age of your children and how uncloseted you can allow yourselves to be in the community. I do, however, have some thoughts on the subject, based partly on other research, partly on wives' and even some children's suggestions, and mainly on my own clinical experience and experience with many forms of stigma.

If you can afford to step out of your two-party closet, take a tip from the experience of such minority groups as blacks and Jews. Nobody can promise children that they will go through life without pain. They come into life inheriting the strengths, weaknesses, joys, and woes of their parents. Often that means they are born into a stigmatized segment of society.

The earlier parents begin helping them to cope with that fact, the easier it will be for them to do so. The later it comes, the greater the shock and the fewer shock absorbers they will have. If you have toddlers, you can make your education as gradual and as natural a part of life as your religion or politics (which themselves sometimes put children in a stigmatized position). Blacks and Jews begin fortifying their children when those children are first exposed to others, through their own conversations, through keeping alert to cruel remarks by others and helping their children understand and deal with each situation as it occurs, through the words they do *not* allow, and through self-esteem-raising tactics. So do people who are poor, who have a handicapped child, or who fight for some unpopular cause. True, you will feel your children's pain and indignation right along with them. You will feel terrible every time they say or show that they wish they had other parents. Just remember that all children wish that occasionally, and that parents need to provide children with something even more important than happiness. That something is integrity.

Adolescents are more able to keep secrets but present more serious problems because they are the most vulnerable to stigma. If your children have already reached their preteens, you may wish to delay disclosure a few years for that reason alone. But if you decide to stay closeted from them, then do so completely. Remember that the best-kept secret is the one you keep yourself. Benefit from the "fluke" that occurred with one study couple which we mentioned earlier, and the shock and sense of betrayal their child felt in hearing the news from someone else. You can count on confidentiality from only one or two sources: a support group in which confidentiality is a stated rule or a professional counselor who is professionally bound to keep confidentiality. A personal friend or lover may or may not feel so bound.

Of course, that puts you in a double bind, since the one thing you need is relief from isolation. There is no right answer. You'll simply have to use your own judgment about your friends, and if you take cautious steps out of the closet, be prepared for the worst and hope for the best.

Just to confuse you further, what little research exists suggests that children of all ages, including teenagers, handle such news from their fathers pretty well. They are not rejecting, they are often very accepting, they are often pleased at the faith you have shown in them, and if anything, are upset that parents had not told them earlier. Often they have already sensed it. Like wives, they may be relieved to find that marital and/or parent–child tension was not due to lack of love, a parent's "fault," or their own fault.

So what do you do now? You simply throw your hands up in the air, roll your eyes to the heavens, shout "Lord, is NOTHING simple?" and do what your instincts tell you to do.

Whenever you tell, remember that, as with wives, telling is not enough. No matter at what age they learn or how positively they may respond, your children will have to cope with stigma, conflicted feelings toward you, and worries about themselves. Mothers can assist, but fathers must bear the major burden in helping them. As father, you need to give permission, both verbally and in reality — and really encourage them — to share negative feelings, come to you with problems, or talk to their mother or friends. You may need to help devise techniques for dealing with "fag" jokes. You may need to encourage the use of professional help as the only way to enable them to discuss negative feelings, and you need to be quite clear that they need not feel disloyal, no matter who they use as a confidante.

Q. *Will my child be subject to sex abuse?*

A. As we've already seen, anything is possible, but such a problem is not probable. In fact (and I'm afraid this is not a fact to cheer about), your children would be in far more danger from a heterosexual husband. One never knows what changes the future will bring, but to date, research has shown time and time again that approxi-

mately 95% of incest and other child molestation cases are heterosexual, not homosexual.

Q. *Will a child become homosexual because of a father's modeling?*

A. As one mother noted, when children lose stereotypic ideas
about homosexuality and see that they have options, they may feel
more comfortable about following their own orientation. That is a
plus, for it helps prevent the pain created when people face their
feelings only after they have tried to "cure" themselves through
marriage. Although current research is limited, it suggests that children of gay parents are no more apt to become gay themselves than
children of straight parents. Also remember that most homosexuals
come from heterosexual parents. Their true feelings came popping
out despite every conceivable form of heterosexual modeling, including deliberate and strong efforts to force them (or to force themselves) into a heterosexual mode.

Q. *I am divorced. I consider homosexual relationships immoral.
My children say their father tells them such relationships are all
right. What do I do now?*

A. You have every right to state your own convictions. Your
husband has every right to state his. You need to devise a common
statement that keeps children from being caught between conflicting views and torn by conflicted loyalties. No matter how strongly
either of you feels, "religious" views of morality are questions of
opinion. You need to validate the right to disagree, stress your areas
of agreement (such as the need for love, integrity, consideration,
etc.), and encourage your children to think for themselves and make
their own decisions in the future.

Also remember that children are seldom helped by thinking of
their parents as "immoral." Moreover, if you push the immoral
view too rigidly, your children may be fearful of your rejection
should they ever face homosexual feelings. You need to make it
clear that no matter how you feel about homosexuality in general,
you will love them and want to be of help no matter what sexual
orientation they eventually have. (Of course, I assume you *would*
feel that way. If you wouldn't, all you can do is be honest.)

Q. *How do we judge a competent therapist? What do we look for? And how do we find one?*

A. The ideal therapist should have professional credentials, including at least some professional training and experience in the areas of marital counseling, human sexuality, and sexual counseling. He or she should be both nonsexist and gay/lesbian/bisexual supportive, should believe that homosexuality can be compatible with heterosexual marriage, and should have some knowledge about and experience in counseling couples in this situation.

For now, you may have to settle for less than "ideal" simply because there is so little written about this situation and so few gay/ straight couples willing to seek the help they need. You should at least ask about professional credentials. Usually, they include a doctorate in clinical psychology, a doctorate or master's degree in social work, or a medical degree with accreditation in psychiatry.

Lack of degrees does not rule out competence, nor do degrees guarantee it. They simply put the odds in your favor. Many competent counselors come from psychiatric nursing, the Association of Marriage and Family Counseling, educational psychology, the ministry, sexology, etc. Often graduate students who have not yet earned their degrees are highly skilled, even though they are required to work under supervision. In many states, professional licensing or certification is an alternative or an additional credential.

There are several ways to locate legitimate counselors. Your own friends may recommend their own therapists. The Yellow Page listings (try various categories) usually specify credentials. Your local branch of the Mental Health Association, the national associations of social work, psychology, psychiatry, marriage and family counselors, etc., can supply names. Often the chairperson of such professional departments in a university can suggest resources. A Family Service Agency may be the best place to start, since not only does it provide counseling, but part of its service is to help people find other needed resources. Most communities now have a "hotline" referral service. Finally (or perhaps first), the gay/bisexual support system usually has some center—perhaps a social agency, a gay/straight organization like Gay Fathers International, or the Metropolitan Community Church — that either has counselors or provides a list of supportive therapists.

Apart from credentials, competence is mainly a question of individual values, sensitivity, personal style, and compatibility. No therapists are going to consider themselves sexist or homophobic. You yourselves will have to ask the questions you consider worth asking and decide how you feel about the answers you receive. Experience with this situation would be best, but even more important is a therapist who can be authoritarian when necessary but whose basic approach is that of cooperating with you in a joint problem-solving effort, who both teaches you and learns from you, and who is honest enough to admit areas of less than adequate knowledge without leaving you to simply flounder.

TIPS: Though you should bear in mind that discomfort, disagreements, and anger are bound to occur at times, treat the first interview as a consultation. If you do not feel basically heard, understood, and relatively at ease with and about a therapist by the end of the first interview or two, do not hesitate to shop around before making a final decision. True, that may mean a bit more money and repetition, but it will save you much more money, time, and agony in the long run. Don't hesitate to ask about credentials or what a person's degrees mean in terms of education and experience. No true professional will take offense.

Q. *I can't afford much and I don't like to go into debt. But don't you get what you pay for?*

A. The size of fee or the grandeur of the office should not be what determines your judgment of competence. Many professions are not covered by all insurance companies or by Medicaid, even though their practitioners are highly trained and skilled. Such practitioners often carry on limited private practice, work in their own homes, share offices, and charge lower fees or use a sliding scale. Many skilled practitioners work in agencies so that they don't have to worry about fees and have needed support services readily available. Many private practitioners donate services to struggling service agencies.

Conversely, if you have to make a choice between cost and expertise, by all means bite the financial bullet and pick the most knowledgeable person. Often professionals do their best to work with you by lowering fees, letting you make partial payments and paying the balance in installments, or providing a combination of arrangements. This is your marriage and/or your mental health. Not only are both worth it, but trying to get by without needed help can cost you far more later.

Q. *Can a gay therapist understand a straight client or vice versa? Can a male understand a female or vice versa? Can a person who has never been in this situation understand?*

A. Yes and no. No one can ever completely replicate another's experience, nor is that "completeness" needed for a therapist to empathize enough to understand how and why you feel the way you do. Being or having been in the same situation may or may not enhance one's empathy with someone else. Your own sense of whether or not you are understood is a better test than the gender or the sexual orientation of the therapist. Often a male-female team or a gay-straight team provides a "check and balance" system that enhances empathy for both partners.

At the same time, therapy is not enough. It *does* help to have input from and companionship with people "who have been there." That kind of help should supplement, not replace, individual help and may come in the form of a therapy group, a support group, or some combination of the two. It may be a couples' group, a wives' group, a former wives' group, etc., and it may involve couples in which the wife is the "gay" partner.

Q. *How do we find such a group?*

A. Your therapist may know of one. The same resources (see p. 216) used for finding a therapist may know of a peer support group. Read the newspaper's calendars and personal columns, and watch for news releases or advertisements. If you don't find one right away, keep your eyes and ears open. Support groups are growing rapidly. If none exist, make every effort to start one. An agency or a private practitioner may be willing to assist you. A national support group may provide assistance or at least put you in touch with a correspondence system. (Specific resources are listed in the Appendix.) An individual private therapist may be the most knowledgeable and the most willing to help you. Many support groups have been started simply by one courageous person or couple renting a post office box (to protect confidentiality) and placing an ad in the newspaper.

A few words of caution are in order. If you get an instant response, great. But don't be discouraged if that doesn't happen. There are people out there, but they are afraid. They join only at some "magic" point when they feel both the need and the ability to "risk" themselves. Publicity, then, needs to be ongoing. Place a new ad every few weeks or months. If you have found a group of people and do not have a professional leader, get one! Either ask an agency to provide one or hire a knowledgeable private therapist or therapy team. Work out a suitable fee and a contract that specifies his, her, or their responsibilities.

Whether you are working with an individual therapist or a support group, remember that all of you, professionals and nonprofessionals alike, are carving out new paths and that you are on the same team, not playing a chess game. Professionals should be helpful and intuitive, but they are not mind readers. They cannot help you with a problem if you do not tell them what the problem is. If you feel that you are not being understood or that you need more help than they are giving, you need to tell them. If there seem to be no ready answers, you need to work together creatively to solve puzzles. That's true in all therapy. In this situation, however, you may need to take extra responsibility in order to obtain the kind of help you truly need.

For example, a common problem at this point is finding enough people for a viable support group, maintaining proper publicity, and managing costs. In this era of cost cutting, an agency may not be able to take on such special projects. It may or may not have the most knowledgeable person. A knowledgeable private practitioner, on the other hand, is limited not only by time and money but by lack of access to the free news releases, public service announcements, and calendar listings that the mass media allow nonprofit organizations. You may have to pool financial resources to purchase an ad or figure out some creative way to obtain publicity. Your professional helper should help and will probably be dedicated, but he or she should not be expected to carry the whole burden or even more than a minor burden.

Q. *Why should I (we) join a support group? Who wants to be dumped into a group of people with nothing in common but a husband's sexual orientation? Won't it be mainly a bunch of angry women feeding into each others' complaints and misery?*

A. Such questions suggest that you are taking another seminar in coping with stigma. Your anger at others' assumptions that you will automatically want to be with everyone in your stigmatized group is realistic. You want and expect absolute freedom in choice of friends. You do not want to be placed in a social prison, forced to associate only with prison society. You certainly do not want to do that to yourself. That, however, is a lesson to be learned at the end of the course. You have not yet had the prerequisites for putting that lesson to good use.

The lessons for today are:

1. Whether you like it or not, no matter how you try to deny it or how quickly you try to leave it, you have been thrust into a stigmatized segment of society. No matter what you say or do, there will always be people who think less of you for being or having been there. You have no choice about stigmatization by others. You can only ignore them or try to educate them.

2. You may refuse to admit group membership, but that does not give you the choice you seek, for much of your prison is a self-imposed, psychological one. Your questions and the attitudes they imply are the true badge of membership in the Society of the Self-Stigmatized. Your badge bears the inscription "Bestowed by the bigoted in appreciation for your self-hatred and identification with the aggressor."

3. You will lose your sense of stigma and have true "choice" only when you come to see your group as an enjoyable extended family or country club you are pleased to call your own, in which you feel welcome, in which you can be selective about those members you want or don't want as friends, and which you both enter and leave freely and joyfully.

Are you saying to yourself "Oh, come on now! Are you kidding?" I'm not. It's a difficult lesson to learn, because in truth, it is one that should not be needed. But until we have a perfect society, many groups of people must learn it. Let's take a look at what has happened to you. It involves several complicated thought processes.

First, you are a member in good standing of a homophobic and sexist society. No matter what your sex or sexual orientation, you have absorbed many of society's stereotypes about homosexuals, women, and anyone who associates with stigmatized people. You expressed those stereotypes when you first struggled with such questions as "What does it say about me that I am in such a situation and what will others say about me?", came up with negative answers, and began to lose self-esteem.

Next you realized that you and your spouse do not fit some of those stereotypes. How could that be? Perhaps without realizing it, you decided that you were an exception. That made you feel better. But then, of course, you didn't want to be classified as one of "them," nor did you want to think of yourself in the same way that you think of "those weirdos." As one wife put it, "Well, I guess I knew there were others in the world in this situation, but I certainly didn't think there were any in *my* world." You are now putting yourself through a crazy combination of bigotry and self hatred. Perhaps Woody Allen put it best in his joking that "Any club that would have me for a member can't be all good." Staying at that point is like being stuck in quicksand. It drags you down. You never quite get rid of your sense of shame, isolation, and sense of "difference." You never get the support, help and companionship from potential new friends. You are caught between two worlds.

In short, ironic as it may be, you need the identification with the stigmatized group in order to rid yourself of your sense of stigma. Only when you learn that lesson will you learn that far from being chained to a group of disreputable prisoners, you will have much in common with others in addition to the issue of sexual orientation, and that much of what you have in common you can share with pride.

Perhaps one of the saddest moments for me during the study involved two wives I'll call Wife A and Wife B. Both were in happy marriages, but both were feeling isolated and desperately wanting to talk to someone else in the same situation. Wife A was one of those who bristled at the idea of a support group. "I don't see how that would do any good," she said. "I don't see what we'd have in common except for our husbands' homosexuality. I just wish I knew *someone*. Maybe I wouldn't feel so alone."

What she did not realize was that not only did most of the wives I saw run in her own social circles, she already did know "someone." Wife B had just learned from her husband that I would be seeing Wife A, and that Wife A was the wife of one of her husband's gay friends. Moreover, it seemed that the two women were already friends at work and had often talked about the two couples getting together. But she was afraid to talk to wife A. She did not know how Wife A felt about the situation or how she might feel if the two mens' friendship became more than platonic. Lonely as she was, she was so afraid of losing her existing friendship with Wife A that she withdrew an offer she'd made to act as contact person for a support group. For all I know, the two women may still be sitting in lonely isolation.

As for the fear that a support group will just be a bunch of complaining women—well that's not even a new stigma. That's plain old simple sexism based on stereotypes of women. There is one caution about support groups, however, based on reality, not on stereotypes. Any group of already confused people struggling with new problems and without knowledgeable leadership is apt to waste time in random, unproductive motion. That's why the need for a professional to provide information, channel discussion, and keep the group safe and productive for all members is stressed.

ADVICE TO CHILDREN

If you are the child of a gay parent, you too probably have mixed emotions. You too need to know that you are not alone and that the feelings you may have are natural. You may be feeling torn in your loyalties, particularly if there is tension between your parents or divorce, but even if you see one parent being treated unfairly. You may be proud of one or both parents at one moment, ashamed of them and angry at them at another moment.

You may feel embarrassed and worried about how others would feel if they knew. You might wonder about your own sexuality or worry that you will be labeled by others as gay or lesbian, particularly if you have an occasional sexual problem, stand up for your parents or for gay causes, refuse to laugh at homophobic jokes, etc. You might feel caught between anger with your parents for putting you in this position, guilt about having such thoughts, and the need to talk it over with your parents or someone else, yet not wanting to hurt them. Moreover, you might think that talking to a professional or joining a support group would be embarrassing and humiliating.

Of course, how you feel will depend largely on your age, what is happening with your particular family, and how their way of coping with the situation affects you. You should know that as far as is known, homosexuality is not inherited and that occasional homosexual thoughts and occasional sexual problems are common to everyone. Because there are so many different issues according to age, I won't try to cover all bases. The main point is that though you should try to understand how your parents may feel (including a gay father's worry about *your* potential rejection of him), you also have your own rights and needs.

You needn't be afraid to discuss your mixed feelings with your parents. True, you don't want to hurt them. But as adults, they can be expected to take responsibility for understanding your feelings and helping you to solve problems you may face because of their situation.

You also need the ability to talk things over with someone other than your parents. Your first step may be easier with a professional — not because you are "sick" or incapable of dealing with the situation, but because you can count on being understood and helped to sort out your feelings without fear of either hurting parents or of becoming the subject of gossip.

When it comes to confiding in friends, it's true that you may meet some prejudice. It's more true that you are apt to find your fears worse than reality. Several study adolescent and adult children, for instance, finally told a friend, boyfriend or girlfriend, and, greatly relieved at the positive, understanding, and casual attitudes of their confidantes, wished they had taken that risk earlier and urged others to do so. Some, in fact, reported learning that their own fears had created needless problems for them.

Two young women, for example, worried that their fiancés

would think they were lesbians. Not only were their fears unfounded, one received the response, "Whew! What a relief! Yes, well I guess I was beginning to wonder why you always get so uptight whenever the subject of homosexuality comes up. Now I understand, I can stop worrying. Thanks for telling me. I wish you'd done it earlier."

One young man who had worried about occasional erectile problems received the same sigh of relief from his girlfriend. She had been upset about his seesawing between "macho" insistence on intercourse and avoidance of all sexual behavior toward her. Once she understood his need to "prove himself" and he understood what she wanted from him and stopped trying to prove himself, they both became more relaxed about sex and his erectile difficulties disappeared.

ADVICE TO CONCERNED FRIENDS AND RELATIVES

I am often asked by parents, friends, colleagues, or other relatives how they can be helpful to wives or couples. If you are one such person, you will have already obtained some guidelines from this book by seeing what wives viewed as helpful or not helpful to them, and you will automatically be more helpful simply by understanding the problems they have faced. The following is a summary of both my own and wives' guidelines to others. The overriding rule of thumb is that you should treat wives in this situation (and their husbands) just like you would treat any other friend or relative and probably like you would want to be treated yourself. Keeping that in mind, realize that:

1. You need not view them with pity. They are basically strong, capable people. Their lives may be temporarily in turmoil, but they are no worse off and may be considerably better off than most other people, and probably they will eventually come out well ahead of the game.

2. If pity is not needed, understanding is! Partly that means understanding that the situation is a complex one and that you may be hearing or seeing only one seemingly simple aspect of it based on what has happened recently or on a wife's feelings at the moment.

You may be hearing so much pain and anger that you wonder why a wife would stay in such a marriage. Remember that people seldom need to "unload" positive feelings, so of course you're hearing about negative ones. Those negatives may be far smaller once they are aired and tension is relieved. Tears may simply represent the release of tension accumulated under the burden of being closeted, not unhappiness with the marriage. Conversely, right after telling you of the situation a wife may be so afraid of negative reactions that she overstresses positives, leaving you to wonder why she is upset. And she may simply be struggling with so many feelings and issues that she finds it impossible to explain why she is having trouble coping with one seemingly simple problem.

You will show your understanding by simply being an active listener. "Active listening" lies somewhere between acting purely as a listening post and as an advisor. You are showing empathy for feelings with your nods, your "uh huhs," your facial expressions, your hugs, and your acceptance of tears, rather than by trying frantically to soothe, correct, or advise.

3. You can often go a bit further, perhaps giving information from this book that seems helpful, offering a corrective perspective, suggestions, or even advice, *if* you avoid what wives found unhelpful: homophobic or sexist remarks, platitudes, unrealistic support, and direct or implied criticism, and if you remember that you are dealing with someone who may be hypersensitive at the moment. A few communication techniques may help you. In fact, you have probably often used them intuitively. They include use of (1) the "Many People Principle," (2) open-ended questions, (3) paraphrasing, and (4) empathic sharing of similar feelings and experiences.

The "Many People Principle" simply lets people know that they are not alone. It allows you to ask questions or offer new ideas to consider without giving advice or sounding critical. Open-ended questions combine asking questions without asking questions and avoiding questions that can be answered in one word. They keep people from feeling either put on the spot or that they are being given a third degree, and lead to more honest and open thinking and communicating. Paraphrasing somewhat reflects what a person has said, and lets you either clarify for yourself or demonstrate that you already understand. And, of course, sharing is sharing, *provided* that it is true sharing, not "comparing." It eases that sense of being "different." Because the person can then empathize back, it returns the conversation to the two-way process of "giving" and "getting" that strengthens a friendship and symbolically restores a sense of strength and power to the person you are helping.

For example, instead of saying, "Boy, you're confused. Get help!" try, "Boy, I can imagine how confusing it must be. I understand that's one of the worst parts for people. I read that many people find counseling essential. I wonder if you've tried that and what you think about it."

Instead of "If you think you felt like a failure, at least you weren't comparing yourself to another woman like I was" or "Wow! And I thought *I* felt like a failure. At least it wasn't a man!" try, "You know, I (or my friend) had some of those same feelings of failure when my (or her) husband had an affair with another woman. It's a lousy feeling, isn't it!"

Instead of saying "If I were you, I'd tell him . . . ," try "How do you think he'd respond if you told him . . . ?"

Note how each example turned potentially critical or useless remarks and advice into supportive ways of obtaining and providing information, new perspectives, and potentially useful ideas.

4. Even though you want to avoid giving unwanted advice, it is also possible to be overly cautious. There is one piece of advice that true friends sometimes need to give even though they risk receiving an angry response. Remember that you may be dealing with someone in acute crisis, that it is a high-risk situation, and that you are not a therapist. Advising professional counseling is always appropriate. If you feel that someone may be dangerously depressed or confused, make that suggestion firmly, help the person get the counseling needed, or tell your friend's spouse or other appropriate person of your concern. If the person is already in therapy, you may need to let the therapist know of your concern. Just be aboveboard about it. Of course, it's difficult to know when "help" stops and "interference" begins. Sometimes you just have to go on intuition. One wife, recognizing that difficulty, told me

I learned later that my sister-in-law had refrained from saying anything for fear of interfering. I appreciate that quality in her — that's why I can turn to her. But I'd also turned to her because I needed help. I was so confused and overwhelmed, I didn't know which way to go. I desperately needed someone to take me by the hand and lead me to some professional help.

5. You can also help by encouraging (but not forcing) a depressed or immobilized person to socialize and include a divorced (or alone-for-the-night) wife in social activities that will not make her feel like a "fifth wheel."

6. Finally, if you have been a confidante, realize that your friend may now feel foolish and vulnerable and may try to avoid you. Although I have advised wives to initiate the second conversation, you yourself are probably in a better position to do so. You too can plan an ice-breaker. For example,

Hey, I felt good about our talk yesterday. I hope I was helpful, but to tell the truth, it helped me, too. I considered your trusting me a compliment, and it's nice to know there's someone to talk to on days when I feel down.

If you also have a sense of humor and another topic on hand, the transition back to normal will probably be smooth. You'll help both yourself and your friend if you do indeed make use of her shoulder some time, even if only for some trivial gripe.

ADVICE TO PROFESSIONALS

Every wife's message to professionals started with the same advice: "Please check yourself continually for sexism and homophobia." It is a message worth heeding. Most of the advice to be given is not new advice — it simply tells us that at least in this situation, we have fallen down on the job and that we must try harder to be the skillful, sensitive, ethical, and knowledgeable helpers we think we are. Professionals need only look at the criticisms given them to see that, and the corrections needed should be obvious.

There are, however, some general guidelines for counseling that accrue from the findings in this study of a "special" population.

They have already been mentioned in various ways, but they are worth emphasizing:

1. Therapists dealing with this situation need an underlying conviction that homosexuality (or some degree of it) can be compatible with heterosexual marriage. They need to bring to gay/straight marriages the same supportive attitude that they bring to any other marriage. They need to recognize and help the partners recognize that most of the issues of concern are the same as they are in any other marriage.

2. At the same time, professionals must recognize and help the partners cope with one major difference – the combined effect of stigma and isolation, confusion, cognitive dissonance, and *perhaps* a greater need for a sexually open marriage contract. They cannot wait for people to present them with clearly understood feelings – they must open doors to discussion. They must be sensitive to the stigmatization of *both* partners and provide direction in coping with it. They must also recognize that some of that stigmatization is directed against bisexuality and help both partners allow themselves the option of heterosexual marriage.

3. A crisis-theory orientation needs to be used for both partners, with care that it is not used simplistically or rigidly. For example, one needs to be aware of the past history of "disclosures" before assuming that a wife is reacting only to the one that serves as a "presenting problem." One needs to be prepared for – and to help the couple be prepared for – the kind of cyclical confusion seen in this study, without expecting "stages" of crisis to occur in the neat order of textbook examples. Until better information is available, therapists too are facing a crisis. They must set up a contract that allows for experimenting and new techniques even within the client–therapist relationship. Helping people through one crisis does not mean that a therapist's job is done. One must build in ability for people to return for help periodically, growing in sensitivity to the depth of confusion, despair, and depression that occurs, even under a seemingly calm surface.

4. Contracts around confidentiality must allow for providing a wife with the information and direction she needs in order to cope with the reality of a husband's sexual orientation, emotional state, or interest in marriage. She cannot cope successfully with reality if

that reality is withheld from her either deliberately or unintentionally.

5. Professionals must take their own risks and allow themselves to be the target of anger, rather than unfairly put a wife in an untenable position.

6. Therapy is not enough. Therapists need to offer help in obtaining peer support, and they may need to set up creative contracts. They need to be willing to assist in networking and and to share cases with other colleagues in the field. In short, they need to be innovative.

7. Both therapists and allied professionals need to open doors that allow closeted people to specify their problem. A physician seeing unexplained stress-related symptoms might help a patient to talk about what's going on in his or her life. A minister might include discussion about sex in pastoral counseling.

Of course, "opening doors" can be risky. You would not want to make unwarranted assumptions or be offensive. There are many ways to open doors. You might put a copy of this or some similar book or article on your coffee table, hang up a notice of a support group, or include mention of gay/straight couple counseling in your brochure. In talking about marital or sexual problems that create stress, you might provide a "shopping list" of common problems, including coping with the homosexuality of a spouse. You might pin it on me, stating that you have promised to mention to all patients that such situations are common and that help is available, and asking that the patient (client, etc.) help spread the word. Of course, you may just be overwhelmed by someone bursting to talk. If you are not a therapist, you can explain that you yourself are unable to offer adequate counseling but you can provide the name of a counselor or suggest this book. No matter what techniques you use, the message needs to be given that "sex, homosexuality, bisexuality, and homosexuality within heterosexual marriage are spoken here."

SUGGESTIONS FOR "JUST INTERESTED" OTHERS

If you are reading this book simply because it looked interesting, you, like many professional helpers, may be wondering how to utilize your new insight when you neither know anyone in a gay/

straight marriage nor expect to in the future. Remember that you probably *do* know someone. You simply don't know who that someone might be.

The same "door opening" techniques I suggested to others will enable you to be helpful — perhaps in an indirect way and perhaps directly to a specific person. One never knows how one's words might help. Simply using this book as a "door opener," mentioning it in a conversation with your friends, colleagues, relatives, or children, spreads information and helps to create public awareness. Your willingness to discuss the subject and the sensitivity to feelings that you display with your children helps to prevent problems in future generations.

Moreover, you may be more specifically helpful than you realize. The seeds you sow today may help your own children in the future. One never knows what is happening with someone else.

An old friend I was visiting during my research asked what I was studying and like most people, was interested in what I had learned. After awhile she said, "How ironic that you should have picked this, of all subjects. Remember how upset I was 2 years ago? I had just learned that my ex-husband was gay. Even though we'd been divorced for 2 years, I had many of the feelings you've described. And until this very minute, I'd thought I was the only one in the world. I'd often thought about telling you, but at that point, I was still too embarrassed."

Recently, I called in a news release about a workshop I was offering on coping with homosexuality in marriage. A few minutes later, my phone rang. The caller said, "I'm the person you just talked to. I could hardly believe my ears. I'm in that situation. I want to come to your workshop." I frequently hear from friends, "I can't believe it! Every time I mention your study, someone in the group gets all excited because a relative or best friend was in a gay/straight marriage."

So you see, "door opening" can have a ripple effect that is far reaching indeed.

Chapter 13

Comments and Conclusions

"The time has come," the Walrus said, "to speak of many things."

— Lewis Carroll

This chapter will present my own comments and conclusions. It will cover a variety of questions and issues, including the possible applicability of insights from this situation to other people in similar kinds of situations.

COMMENTS

Implications for Counseling

The study findings raise several questions and issues relevant to mental health professionals and the people who use their help not only in this situation but in similar ones. Many are issues that have long been debated within each profession.

How can counselors protect confidentiality for one marital partner, for example, providing the needed freedom to sort out feelings in private, without infringing on the other partner's right to information that will affect his or her life? To what extent should counselors state their own value judgments or share experiences from their own lives?

Such debates are usually in-house, carried on in professional journals and conferences, with professionals talking only to professionals. Wives' critiques of their therapy, whether or not they were always justified, might suggest that professionals also need to engage in public dialogue with the people they serve, raising general questions, issues, and concerns, and grappling together with common practical and ethical dilemmas.

Other issues have to do with oppression and liberation. For example, long before I undertook this study, I had begun to sense but never could pinpoint what I call "subtle sexism" in marital counseling. Pondering one issue in this study has helped me see what I had earlier sensed.

That issue was whether problems between study husbands and wives or between wives and therapists were due more to sexism or liberation ethics. In the therapeutic relationship, I am now inclined to think that male chauvinism, whether it comes from a male or a female therapist, is the biggest culprit. Since the study, I have been continually impressed that even with all my newfound insight, and despite our allegiance to the principles (albeit not the label) of feminist therapy, my co-therapists and I must continually guard against a tendency to either blame the wife or at least to burden her with the major responsibility for "understanding," "nurturing," and "changing."

I have also become increasingly aware that it really makes no difference whether the gay partner is the husband or the wife or even whether the couple is a gay/straight couple or strictly heterosexual. Unless a husband is behaving at the moment like an out and out Archie Bunker, wives tend to be confronted with their irrationality far more quickly and directly than are husbands with theirs.

And if a husband is indeed an Archie Bunker? Then after a few vain attempts to reach him, the decision is often that "it will not help the wife to back the husband into a corner." The husband is protected. Any feelings of anger or frustration on the therapist's part are quickly redirected the minute the husband shows a glimmer of pain or sensitivity, and the wife is then chided (gently, of course, in good therapeutic fashion) for not responding promptly and warmly enough.

I exaggerate, but I am convinced that such double standards, while subtle and unintentional, still exist in the most "feminist" of therapists. Such a double standard is as insulting to men as it is unfair to women, for it suggests that men are fragile, weak creatures who cannot tolerate truth.

When it comes to the relationship between husbands and wives, however, the male–female issue becomes muddied. Certainly it exists. Disclosures of a husband's extramarital affairs and thinly veiled male chauvinism that turns his sudden "request" for an open marriage contract into a "demand" are hardly limited to homosexual husbands. They are common components of a therapist's caseload with heterosexual couples. The attitude that a man's needs come before a woman's has been a time-honored tradition. It is not so surprising, when one stops to think about it, that a gay or bisexual husband, having affirmed his right to feel "masculine" in spite of his homosexuality, reclaims all the privileges of "manhood," including male chauvinism.

If male chauvinism is the only issue, then are lesbian or bisexual wives more sensitive to their straight husbands' needs and feelings? Are they treated more vindictively by their straight husbands than the study men were by their straight wives? It would seem logical. I have, in fact, heard many rumors to that effect, including the one that straight husbands are apt to become physically violent and abusive. When I planned my own study, I made such assumptions.

Yet the men I have seen in clinical practice, far from being vindictive, have been (like the wives in this study) supportive and have often needed help in standing up for their own rights. During the study, several straight husbands of lesbian wives volunteered to participate, and several lesbian wives requested that I do a similar study for their husbands. Although I had excluded such couples precisely because I felt that the factor of different sex-role expectations would become overly complex, I certainly listened, asked questions, and made mental notes. Those husbands sounded supportive of their wives. A therapy team who had offered assistance in one city turned out to have seen only couples in which the wife was the one to come out. They told me they had seen in their practice the same problems I was finding in research and that straight husbands had expressed the same feelings straight wives had had.

If not a male–female problem, is this strictly a gay–straight one? I think not. Saying "I think you'll be interested in this," a colleague recently handed me an excerpt from Sekjei and Rabkin's book *The Male Ordeal*. I found myself reading vignettes so similar to those I was in the process of writing, it was as if I had entered the Twilight Zone and was reading my own future material. It was a study of husbands coping with the "liberation" of heterosexual wives. It did not seem to be a "male backlash" book but rather a thoughtful and sensitive description of problems in a changing society that reflected my own concept of "liberation ethics" as an emerging — and emergent — social problem.

I have no patience with "oppressors" of any kind who indignantly cry "Unfair!" the minute they are forced, whether out of anger or necessity, to taste the bitter medicine they have forced on others for centuries. As individuals they may not have deliberately oppressed anyone, but they need to realize that social change will involve individual pain. Nevertheless, if the old "oppressed," even if unintentionally, simply become new "oppressors," we will have hardly made progress. We face hard questions, difficult to answer when the protagonists in the battle against oppression are social groups, even more difficult when they are individuals who have made a lifelong commitment to each other, who presumably love each other, and whose own children will become caught in their crossfire.

In such situations, should an innocent spouse be held responsible for the creation of and solution to society's problems? In this particular situation, is homosexual infidelity any more of a need or right than heterosexual infidelity? Is homosexual arousal so different from heterosexual arousal — so overwhelming — that one cannot — or need not — honor one's marital commitment? Is male arousal so different from female arousal — so overwhelming — that husbands cannot — or need not — honor their marital commitment? At what point does "liberation" end and "oppression" begin? How can professional counselors enable one partner in a marriage to liberate himself or herself without aiding and abetting the oppression of the other partner? Just what is liberation anyhow?

There are no easy answers to these questions, but we need to address them. "Liberation ethics" is emerging as a real and serious phenomenon. It threatens to undermine society's attempts to correct not only the problems of gay/straight couples but of such general problems as racism, sexism, and homophobia. It interferes with the ability to solve issues of marriage and the family in an era when questions of monogamy versus open marriage and nuclear families versus communal living and child care are puzzles for society as a whole. Liberation ethics in gay/straight marriages reflects the need for more attention to the problems that ensue when the needs and rights of one oppressed group (in this case, homosexuals or bisexuals) conflict with the needs and rights of another oppressed group (in this case, women).

Impressions About Crisis

Certainly the study pointed out the need for people in such a situation and their counselors to utilize current information about crisis. One suspects, for example, that some assumptions about wives' "emotional illness" (or for that matter, their husbands') may have been based on failure to recognize acute crisis reactions. Many couples might have been spared considerable time and agony and might have dealt more realistically with problems had they and their therapists realized that many of their feelings and behaviors were part of the crisis-response process and that there were specific steps they could take to ease that process.

At the same time, the study suggests the potential for misuse of crisis theory by forgetting that the steps and stages of coping with crisis are neater on paper than they are in real life, rigidly expecting oneself or one's counselees to feel and behave exactly like textbook examples and assuming "neurosis" or "craziness" if that is not the case.

Given the extreme confusion, the violent emotions and behaviors, and the acute crisis reactions that seemingly lasted longer than the 4-to-6 weeks described in crisis theory, however, questions must be raised about how this crisis compares with other crises and about potential flaws in crisis theory itself. Was this crisis different from other crises of infidelity, divorce, or death? Did these people react differently to crisis than do other people? Or are there lessons to be learned about crisis and crisis intervention?

It will take comparative research with heterosexual couples and other situations to provide the answers to those questions. Except for the specific problems related to stigma and isolation (which are also found in other stigmatized and isolated groups), I found more similarities to others than differences. Certainly such basic themes as loss, love, betrayal, and their attached emotions are not "homosexual" — they are universal problems and emotions, to be found in any counseling caseload, in the love stories of literature, music, and the theater, and in the experience (whether one's own or that of one's friends and loved ones) of most people.

The basic elements of crisis theory were certainly supported in this study, but findings also suggested the need to take a second look at some of its tenets. Since the study, I have become increasingly convinced that study couples' reactions were similar to others' reactions in a variety of crises and that crisis theory itself may have flaws.

For example, is the 4-to-6 week limit for acute crisis states and the call for brief therapy always realistic? The wives' critiques suggest not. Does an "acute crisis reaction" always mean readily discernible emotional distress and total inability to function? Many wives' descriptions of internally erupting emotions and violent behaviors under seemingly calm exteriors suggest not. The question of how distressed people must be or appear in order to be considered "acute" and when "acute" turns into "chronic" may have social, clinical, and even legal ramifications.

Widows, for instance, have often told me how socially unacceptable they felt when they could not control tears after the "official" mourning period. I have noticed that after a few weeks of intensive support, widows have been labeled as "neurotic" and avoided by others until they could either act as if their husbands had never existed or speak of the deceased without any sign of sadness.

Such issues affect professionals' diagnoses, judgments about suicidal or homicidal potential, or simply how fast to move during treatment and when to terminate treatment. In fact, I was pointed toward crisis theory as a framework in which to study this situation, and was perhaps given more sensitive ears with which to "hear" wives' critiques, by Abby, one of my prestudy clients. In her first real step toward reintegration, she began to call her own shots in therapy, telling me she was reading crisis theory, that she realized and appreciated that I was trying to help her build a new life for herself, but that she simply could not "move as fast as the books and I wanted" her to. She needed more time to "lie still and lick her wounds."

Not only was she right about herself (and this perhaps serves as an object lesson to people that they should not hesitate to speak up when they disagree with their therapists), but recent research suggests that she was not unique — recovery from any divorce may take far longer than originally thought.

Personal anecdotes can never replace research, but they can often alert people to possibilities. In an ironic footnote to the study, close heterosexual friends of mine went through a sudden separation similar to many of those found in the study. The intelligent, capable, and self-confident wife was not only attractive, she was a lookalike for one of the country's leading sex symbols. Fewer external problems were faced.

She was given over 2 months of intensive support by her close circle of friends, most of whom were clinicians skilled in crisis intervention, and by several other women who suddenly declared that they were in the same situation. Yet both partners went through most of the same behaviors and feelings found in the study. The wife soon became able to manage attending short social events perfectly groomed and appearing "normal" to the outside world. Yet she was indeed in acute crisis and remained so far longer than had been expected. Her friends, themselves distressed at the breakup, began to feel increasingly helpless and fatigued. Only after about 3 months, when their own lives had long since returned to normal and their support had dwindled to an occasional phone call, did the couple seek professional help and the wife begin to reintegrate.

One might suspect that it is not the victim of crisis who goes in and out of acute crisis in 4-to-6 weeks, but the victim's support group. One might also suspect that the turning to others after a brief period of help (whether that help changes from friends to professionals or the other way around) may be less a sign of reintegration than a desperate measure forced by the loss of support.

There is cause to wonder, then, if inability to get a patient/client back on his or her feet and managing without a therapist within the prescribed "brief therapy" time is due to therapist error, individual needs, or faulty theory. The study findings suggest that there is probably a combination. Human error is inevitable. It is also true that after a few weeks, probably everything has been said that can be said and that the final healing process is a task accomplished only by time and the person's own efforts. At the same time, both the person in crisis and the people who are trying to be helpful need to guard against rigid and unrealistic expectations and the premature removal of support.

There may also be legal ramifications to these issues, for the violent behaviors that occurred in acute crisis reactions were the stuff of which "crimes of passion" and controversial "temporary insanity" defenses are made. One shudders to think what might have happened, for example, if airline security precautions had not created a barrier to Harriet's intent to murder. Marsha's seeming calmness and deliberateness as she engaged in potentially violent and dangerous behaviors was definitely not unique. Such wives would not even have been able to contribute to their own defense had somebody been physically harmed, for not only had they appeared so but they had seen themselves as more rational at the moment than they actually were.

Such stories frequently end up in courtroom battles about whether, for example, a battered wife who finally kills her husband is to be considered a murderer and what sentence should be imposed. One might speculate that an "acute crisis reaction" defense might be more understandable and might lead to more appropriate sentences than many of those we read about today.

Pejorative Labeling

I am in so much agreement with wives' own advice to others that except for one or two small areas of stated differences, my own input into the "advice" chapters was mainly that of providing additional topics and perspectives. Nevertheless, I have noted one potential problem that concerns me enough to give it special consideration. A problem that also occurs with other people and other issues, it is a tendency to misuse professional terminology and concepts, turning neutral and/or descriptive terms into pejorative labels. It often goes along with the tendency to turn recognition of common behaviors or attitudes (that is, "kernels of truth") into stereotypes. In this instance, as in others, it was connected to such words as "neurosis," "denial," and "victim."

I first noticed it in the literature. I became concerned about it when despite their anger at the stereotyping that had been leveled at them, it showed up in several wives' advice to others: "Don't deny, take responsibility for your choice of husbands," "Don't treat yourself as a victim," and "Don't treat us as victims." Such wording usually went along with the statement or implication that the choice of husband had been based on "neurosis," "sickness," or some other "bad" reason, that all failures to recognize homosexuality or to confront a husband were based on "denial," and that denial is always negative, an inability to face reality. It implied that wives had victimized themselves and that to be a victim is not only unfortunate, it is somehow reprehensible. Finally, it implied that these women, by virtue of neurosis, denial, and victimization, were somehow "different," more "abnormal" than other women.

Such wives seemed to take comfort in the thought (as expressed by one such wife) that if they had "created" their own problem, then they could "create" their own solution. It is my own opinion, however, that they had unwittingly become caught up in a guilt-provoking "blame the victim" stance far different from the more common call for responsibility that validated the original choice of husband and asked wives to reassess their needs and options in light of the current situation and to assume *realistic* amounts of responsibility for their future decisions.

There was little evidence from the study that the choice of husbands had automatically been a poor one, that "neurosis," if it existed (and whatever that term means), was particularly relevant, that denial always occurred or that it was always negative when it did occur, or that whatever dysfunctional behaviors occurred were different from those found in other marriages during stressful periods.

One might even argue that society's total institution of marriage rests — and succeeds — on an elaborate denial system in which it is all but taken for granted that most (if not all) husbands "play around" to varying degrees but that one's own husband is faithful unless proven otherwise.

As for the word "victim" — well, I applaud language changes that potentially solve problems, but I worry about language changes that potentially exacerbate them. AIDS patients, for example, view the term "patient" as a derogatory term labeling them as helpless and nonhuman. In doing so, they reinforce in themselves and others the idea that to be under the care of or receiving medical treatment by a doctor (the definition of "patient") is something of which to be ashamed. They increase the chance that "patients" of any kind will indeed be treated stereotypically and in dehumanized fashion.

Rape victims also decry being called victims. They too feel that the term implies that they are passive, pitiable creatures who have, by virtue of their air of helplessness, "asked for it." Some people *are* victims of their own weakness. That is a kernel of truth. But does it mean that everyone who has been physically or emotionally hurt at the hands of another person is passive or that feeling or being powerless is "asking for it?" Or is such a stance merely another version of the very stereotypes we (and they) are trying to break down? Being a victim is neither fun nor desirable, but in my opinion, it is hardly a status to warrant shame, guilt, or even pity.

I also found myself wondering, by the end of this study, about societal and clinical assumptions in other areas. Much has been made of the "unconscious collusion" between husband and wife in incest cases, of the "castrating" wife of the alcoholic who drives her husband to drink and keeps him alcoholic to satisfy her own needs, of the abused child who will most certainly become a child abuser himself or herself, of the battered wife who victimizes herself because of her own battered childhood – these are just a few examples. Could it be that – as in the assumptions about study wives – the desire to find simple clear-cut "answers" has turned "kernels of truth" into stereotypes?

In the final analysis, then, I do indeed consider these wives to have been "victims" of oppression. The questions to be asked are (1) Who is the oppressor and where is anger to be focused? (2) How can a victim overcome oppression without becoming an oppressor himself or herself? and (3) How much responsibility should society take for both preventing and overcoming oppression, and how can it accomplish these goals?

Who Is the Oppressor?

Is homosexuality the oppressor? Is homosexuality simply incompatible with heterosexual marriage? The wives resoundingly said "no," and I agree with them. I am sometimes asked "How can you say that, when all the problems you describe resulted from the husband's homosexuality?'' My answer is twofold.

First, many of those problems and feelings are not found only in gay/straight marriages. Confusion, loss of self-identity and self-trust, betrayal and its resultant feelings, loss of self-confidence, etc. – these are not "gay/straight" feelings and behaviors – they are "human" ones. They are found whenever a marriage of any kind falters or ends, whenever an important interpersonal relationship is ended or betrayed, whenever one is forced to choose between conflicting emotions, desires, and goals, or whenever one faces new and potentially hurtful situations without adequate information or help.

Second, one must differentiate between "intrinsic" biological circumstances that cannot be changed or overcome and social attitudes that can be changed or overcome. If a husband is so totally homosexual in orientation that he can neither give nor receive any pleasure from a heterosexual relationship, homosexuality might be considered a characteristic that precludes the possibility of a satisfying heterosexual marriage. There did indeed seem to be a few such situations in which the husbands probably never should have married. I'll get back to them. The majority of husbands and wives, however, had derived considerable emotional and sexual satisfaction from the relationship for many years. Some continued to do so, and many more might have had they not had to cope with the psychosocial problems of stigma, isolation, and lack of help.

Just a decade ago interracial marriages were "unthinkable" and usually failed not because of the partners' biological racial differences, but because of the isolation, stigma, and lack of support they received. Today they are more accepted and relatively viable. In Hawaii they are so common they are almost the rule rather than the exception. Similarly, it can be expected that as acceptance, information, and support increases, the problems I have described will decrease.

Were Husbands the Oppressors? Where Should Anger Be Focused?

Were husbands as individuals the oppressors? Most wives said no, that they had been treated badly but that husbands should not be the basic focus of anger, for they too were "victims" who were suffering. That stance (with which I also agree) was supported by several formerly married homosexual men who were interested in the study. Expecting defensive rebuttals from such husbands, I instead received comments like the following anonymous one in response to my presentation on a gay radio talk show:

> I just want to confirm your findings. I did and said all the insensitive things you reported. I could tell you even worse stories about how some of my friends treated their wives. My wife and I have a wonderful relationship now, but it's to her credit, not mine. . . . But I also want to underscore the point that the insensitivity is not usually from lack of love or concern for the wife. I loved my wife very much. I still do. I simply didn't know what to do! I was scared and confused! I didn't know where to turn and nobody seemed to know any more about it than I did. Maybe if I'd — we'd — had better help, who knows? Maybe we'd still be married. I applaud studies like this. I hope they help others!

That may be well and good for husbands who really cared, but how about husbands like Harriet's, who deliberately deceived her throughout marriage, who blamed his venereal disease on her and then continued to deceive her after disclosure? Aren't such husbands an appropriate focus for anger?

Yes and no. Certainly they deserve their wives' anger, and certainly their wives deserve our supportive anger at the injustice they received. The purpose of this book, however, is not to indulge in blame but rather to find insights and shed light that will help prevent future tragedies. Harriet herself added to her story an important postscript.

After the reintegration dust had settled enough to allow a civil relationship for the sake of their child, her husband became more sensitive and concerned for Harriet's feelings. Despite all his lies, he told her, he had been honest about one thing. He had sincerely loved her when he asked her to marry him, and he had loved her during marriage. He had often wanted to tell her about the homosexuality but had lost his courage for fear of how she might react. He had been brought up in a devoutly Fundamentalist family. At

19, he had told his parents he thought he was gay. His mother had not said a word in response, but her reaction had been immediate. She had walked swiftly into the bathroom, where she slit her throat.

Did Harriet forgive him or stop being angry at him? Not at all. Does his story justify or excuse his behavior toward her? Certainly not! It does, however, make his fear more understandable. Coupled with the fact that many study husbands and those seen in counseling became suicidal themselves during the predisclosure buildup, it should also, I think, give pause for some collective soul searching.

When our society, no matter how unintentionally, has attached such stigma to homosexuality that it can lead to such feelings and actions, when it has stigmatized both those people who in some way differ from societal expectations and also the people significant in their lives, then it has set the stage for Greek tragedies. Whether unconsciously or deliberately, collectively or individually, society has outlined the plots, written the scripts, and developed the characters. The actors have merely chosen some form of the basic plot and ad-libbed some of their own lines.

True, during the past decade, the gay liberation movement has rewritten some scenes and helped create happier last acts for many people. I would submit, however, that we need to rewrite the entire play, for it is born not merely of homophobia, but of sex-role stereotyping, male chauvinism, and attitudes toward "difference" that invade every aspect of our society.

One might suggest, then, that the real oppressors are bigotry and intolerance, that we are all both their representatives and their victims, and that we all need to change — or at least do what we can to promote change. How individuals do that, of course, will depend on each person's personal convictions, skills, time, and situation. For some it may be simply a willingness to learn, understand, and consider new perspectives. For others it may mean the courage to come out of a personal closet or to open closet doors for others. For still others it may mean a commitment to political activism. For all Americans, however, it should start with a recommitment to the principle that people have the right to pursue happiness according to their own needs and abilities, within the framework of their own religious beliefs. If because of personal or religious reasons a group or individual cannot shine on others' nontraditional parades, he, she, or it can at least refrain from raining on them.

I was recently invited, for example, to discuss my study on a church-sponsored radio station, on the basis that the high number of religious couples in the study would make the topic of interest to listeners. Although I was careful not to offend and the talk show moderator, herself highly religious, was well pleased with the discussion, the station refused to air the tape because my lack of an explicit stand against homosexuality was seen as promoting it and hence offensive to Christian listeners.

I am concerned, however, that people who most want and need the Church's help seem to be the least able to receive it. The ethical dilemmas facing churches that regard homosexuality, extramarital sex, and divorce as sinful cannot help but be difficult. Yet some members of the clergy, even within such religions, have found ways to be more helpful without undermining their religious integrity. The issue cannot be addressed by silence or looking the other way. The closet exists in the Church, in Christian homes, and in the clergy. Sanctioned or not, the people who live in it are part of Judeo-Christian history. Its doors need to be opened.

CONCLUSIONS

If the findings from this research hold true in future studies, there is every reason to believe that:

1. Women who inadvertently marry gay or bisexual men are basically no different from other women. *If* any differences exist, they seem to be "positive" in nature, not "negative."

2. Given any reason to and any help in doing so, women tend to cope remarkably well with learning of a husband's homosexual needs, showing understanding, flexibility, and ability to grow in their acceptance of homosexuality. Both their immediate and future ways of handling the situation depend less on their own personality or attitudes toward homosexuality than on how their husbands handle the situation and how much understanding and help they receive from both their husbands and the rest of society.

3. Not only can marriages survive a disclosure of homosexuality, if the husband remains committed to the wife, they are apt to improve. Not only can homosexuality (or some degree of it) be compatible with heterosexual marriage, if the husband is capable of

some degree of heterosexual satisfaction, gay/straight marriages can be unusually satisfying and stable.

4. Except for the possible need to work out a nonmonogamous sexual contract, the basic ingredients of a happy gay/straight marriage (i.e., mutual love, commitment, trust, shared interests, empathic communication, and some form of shared sexual gratification) are no different than they are for any other marriage.

5. Nevertheless, at the present time this is a complex crisis-prone situation in which wives as well as husbands (and perhaps even more so) are often at high emotional risk. The many marital breakdowns and the severe emotional trauma suffered by so many wives cannot be simplistically attributed to a single cause like homosexuality or infidelity. They cannot be attributed simply to a wife's attitudes toward homosexuality, her ability to cope with the disclosure, or even the nature of an initial disclosure. It was the husband's *ongoing* ability to realistically face his homosexual desires without losing empathy and concern for his wife's needs and rights that was most crucial and that was most often lacking.

Yet problems cannot be attributed solely to a husband's attitudes or behaviors. Rather, they must be attributed to the combined and cumulative effect of all the problems faced in other marriages and divorces, plus societal attitudes toward homosexuality, bisexuality, and nonconformity. This includes unrecognized stigmatization of wives, simplistic, stereotypic, and nonempathic treatment given them by others (including but not limited to husbands and the professionals to whom they turned for help), and lack of the information, guidelines, help, companionship, and general support available to other couples. In short, the problems lay in the combined effects of stigma and isolation, with both partners but especially the wives caught in the political crossfire between the Moral Majority and the gay liberation movements.

These were stories of tragedy and hope. The tragedy lay not only in the marital and personal breakdowns but in the fact that some marriages might never have been made and others might never have broken down had it not been for society's sexism and homophobia and that so much of the pain had been needless. The hope lies not only in the "happy endings" that eventually came to pass but also in the reaffirmation that human beings are strong and resilient, that they learn from and use their own experiences to help others, and that the failures of one generation can hence be turned into the successes of its successors.

These couples were pioneers traveling uncharted trails without the companionship of the wagon train or the leadership of a wagonmaster. Given the handicaps they faced, what seems surprising is not that so many marriages failed or that so many women sooner or later fell apart, but that so many women tried so hard and recovered so well, that so many marriages were still intact with the potential for survival, and that some had not simply survived but were flourishing.

From both partners, the strength, the enthusiastic support for the study, and the high degree of insight and candor about their own shortcomings were impressive. All who participated asked that they be repaid for their time and effort by having the study used to create public awareness and to help ease the path for others. It is my hope that this book will play some small part in granting that request.

Chapter 14

Appendix

REFERENCES

Bell, A., & Weinberg, M. (1979). *Homosexualities: A study of diversity among men and women.* Boston: Little, Brown.

Golan, N. (1978). *Treatment in crisis situations.* New York: Free Press.

Haeberle, Erwin (1977). *The Sexually Oppressed,* Gochros, H. and Gochros, J., Eds., N.Y.: Association Press, 3-27.

Hatterer, M. S. (1976). The problems of women married to homosexual men. *American Journal of Psychiatry, 131*(3), 275–278.

Hays, D., & Samuels, A. (1989). Heterosexual women's perceptions of their marriages to homosexual or bisexual men. *Journal of Homosexuality, 17*(3/4).

Humphreys, L. (1975). *Tearoom trade: Impersonal sex in public places.* Chicago: Aldine Press.

Kinsey, A., Pomeroy, W., Martin, C., & Gebhard, F. (1953). *Sexual behavior in the human male.* Philadelphia: W. B. Saunders.

Klein, F. (1978). *The bisexual option.* New York: Arbor House. [A landmark book, the first devoted solely to bisexuality]

Kohn, B., & Matusow, A. (1980). *Barry and Alice: Portrait of a bisexual marriage.* Englewood Cliffs, NJ: Prentice-Hall.

Kübler-Ross, E. (1969). *On Death and Dying,* New York: MacMillan.

Miller, B. (1979, October). Gay fathers and their children. *The Family Coordinator,* 544–552.

Nahas, R., & Turley, M. (1979). *The new couple: Women and gay men.* New York: Seaview Books.

Skjei, E. and Rabkin, R. *The Male Ordeal*. New York: Putnam, 1981.
Sheehy, Gail (1977). *Passages*, New York: Bantam.

OTHER SUGGESTED READING

The following includes additional books and articles that may be useful, divided into two sections. Some do not deal specifically with gay/straight marriage, but contain useful statistics, information, or perspectives. The titles should be self-explanatory, but I will comment on them as appropriate. Books may be available in or through local bookstores or libraries. All should be available in a university or college library (usually in the social work, psychology, and psychiatry sections), and librarians will be able to help in locating them.

I should note here that two books and one of the articles listed below are starred for special attention. Also published as or in special editions of the *Journal of Homosexuality*, they include several excellent articles on gay/straight marriage by such writers as Eli Coleman, Fred Klein and Timothy Wolf, Dorothea Hays and Aurele Samuels, and David Matteson. Several of these authors have been mentioned earlier, and all are writers to look for in the future. If you have trouble locating them, write The Haworth Press, Inc., 12 West 32nd St., New York, NY 10001, or to order, call 1-800-342-9678.

Professional Books

*Coleman, E. (Ed.). (1988). *Integrated identity for gay men and lesbians*. New York: Harrington Park Press.
Deabill, G. (1987). *An investigation of sexual behaviors in mixed orientation marriages: Gay husband and straight wife*. Unpublished doctoral dissertation, Institute for Advanced Study of Human Sexuality, San Francisco.
Freeman, J. (1975). *Women: A feminist perspective*. Palo Alto, CA: Mayfield.

*Klein, F., & Wolf, T. (Eds.). (1985). *Bisexualities: Theory and Research*. New York: The Haworth Press.
Matteson, D. R. (in press). *Mixed orientation marriages: A six year study*. Boston: Alyson Publications.
Ross, M. (1983). *The married homosexual man*. London, Boston, and Melbourne: Routledge and Kegan Paul.
Tripp, C. A. (1975). *The homosexual matrix*. New York: McGraw-Hill.

Professional Articles

Auerback, S., & Moser, C. (1987). Groups for the wives of gay and bisexual men. *Social Work*, *32*(4), 321–325.
Dulaney, D., & Kelly, J. (1982). Improving services to gay and lesbian clients. *Social Work*, *27*(2), 178–183.
Gochros, H. (1978). Counseling gay husbands. *Journal of Sex Education and Therapy*, *4*(2), 6–11.
*Hays, D., & Samuels, A. (in press). Heterosexual women's perceptions of their marriages to homosexual and bisexual men. *Journal of Homosexuality*, 17(3/4).
Latham, D. J., & White, G. D. (1978). Coping with homosexual expression within heterosexual marriage: Five case studies. *Journal of Sex and Marital Therapy*, *4*(3), 198–212.
Lewis, K. (1980). Children of lesbians: Their point of view. *Social Work*, *25*(3), 198–203.
Ross, H. L. (1971). Modes of adjustment of married homosexuals. *Social Problems*, *18*(3), 385–393.

Popular Books

Clark, D. (1977). *Loving someone gay*. New York: New American Library.

[A warm, compassionate book by a formerly married gay man, particularly helpful to parents, children, and other non-spouse relatives. Straight wives should be forewarned, however, that though some study wives found Clark's comments to wives helpful, others did not. Decide for yourself.]

Maddox, B. (1982). *Married and gay.* New York: Harcourt Brace Jovanovich.
Malone, J. (1980). *Straight women/gay men.* New York: Dial Press.

[Both the Maddox and Malone books are journalists' studies and include accounts of such famous couples as Charles Laughton and Elsa Lanchester.]

Pearson, C. (1986). *Goodbye, I love you.* New York: Random House.

[A sad and moving account of one woman who faced not only her husband's homosexuality and their decision to divorce, but also his eventual death from AIDS.]

Popular Books to Enhance the Marital Sexual Relationship

All of the following are written by leading authorities in psycho-therapy and sexuality.

Barbach, L. (1975). *For yourself.* Garden City, NY: Anchor Books.
Barbach, L. (1982). *For each other: Sharing sexual intimacy.* Garden City, NY: Anchor Books.

[Originally designed for women experiencing orgasmic difficulty, these books have been helpful to other women and their husbands as well.]

Gochros, H., & Fischer, J. (1980). *Treat yourself to a better sex life.* Englewood Cliffs, NJ: Prentice-Hall.

[For both partners, a "do it yourself" step-by-step manual that provides detailed methods for improving communication and enhancing the marital sexual relationship. Includes help for orgasmic, erectile, and ejaculatory problems.]

Zilbergeld, B. (1978). *Male sexuality.* Boston: Little, Brown.

Remember that although these books provide excellent help that may obviate the need for more expensive sex therapy, self-help books do not provide the individual guidance often needed. You needn't be discouraged if they don't seem to make a difference. A professional therapist will be able to help you to pinpoint what is going wrong and to use such books more effectively.

POTENTIAL RESOURCES FOR PEER SUPPORT AND/OR PROFESSIONAL COUNSELING

The following list is essentially a "starting point." Other groups or therapists exist in cities such as Los Angeles, San Francisco, San Diego, Chicago, New York, Boston, Portland, Honolulu, and even in smaller communities across the country. Do be forewarned, however, that all groups often form, disband, and reform again periodically. They may change names and addresses and may not be in the phone book. If you have trouble locating them, an existing gay, bisexual, or lesbian agency or the Metropolitan Community Church in your area may be able to give you information.

I am collecting names of therapists and support group leaders willing to participate in a national (or even international) referral and support network. My list includes therapists (some of whom are or have themselves been in a gay/straight marriage), group (peer and professional) leaders, people seeking therapists, and people who are simply looking for peer support whether from colleagues or from others in such marriages.

I will be happy to hear from anyone who knows about or is willing to participate, whether as a therapist or group facilitator, a counselee or group member, or any combination thereof. Simply specify your interest(s) and enclose a self-addressed, stamped envelope to Dr. Jean Schaar Gochros, 1901 Halekoa Drive, Honolulu, Hawaii 96821.

Bisexual Center of San Francisco and Bisexual Counseling Center. Write Dr. Maggie Rubenstein 1523 Franklin St., San Francisco, CA 94109, for more information.

Bisexual Forum (New York City). Write Chuck Mishaan, 119 E. 84th St., New York, NY 10028, for more information.

Chicago Bi-Ways. P.O. Box A3330, Chicago, IL 60690.

Started originally for bisexual men and women, the group seems to include married couples. Write George Barr at the above address for more information, or write Dr. David Matteson, Governors State University, University Park, IL 60466, for information on the Chicago area.

Institute of Sexual Behavior: Write Dr. Fred Klein, Director, 4545 Park Blvd., Suite 207, San Diego, CA 92116, or Dr. Timothy Wolf, 3549 Camino del Rio South, #D, San Diego, CA 92108, for more information.

GAMMA (Gay and Married Men's Association). P.O. Box 4324, N. Hollywood, CA 91607.

Should have a listing of branches in other areas.

Gay Fathers Coalition. P.O. Box 50360, Washington DC 20004

Will put you in touch with its branches across the country and overseas, with many including support groups for wives and children. Should also have a listing of supportive therapists. You may also write GLPCI Network, c/o Karlin, 5209 N. Ashland Ave., Chicago, IL 60640.

Straight Partners. P.O. Box 1603, Hyattsville, MD 20788

This is a subgroup of GAMMA. Another group (LAMMA) is for lesbian wives and their families.

Married Gay Men's Group. Write Charles Piersol, Group Facilitator, 59 Hartsen St., Rochester, NY 14610.

This group, run by a professional therapist, is also starting a group for wives with its own leader.

ADDITIONAL INFORMATION ABOUT THE RESEARCH

The exploratory research on which this book is based was part of a doctoral dissertation (*When Husbands Come Out of the Closet: A Study on the Consequences for their Wives*), University of Denver, 1982.

Methodology

Thirty-three women from Honolulu, Portland, San Francisco, and Rochester (New York) and their adjacent rural areas were located through nonrandom sampling combining snowball, selective, and convenience sampling. Respondents were given four or more hours of intensive, semistructured interviews, a forced-response questionnaire, and four validated, standardized scales measuring self-esteem, marital satisfaction, sexual satisfaction, and depression. Content analysis and simple descriptive (noninferential) statistics were used for data analysis.

The dissertation itself was confined to those 33 wives (called "the study sample"), since there was more control over the kind and amount of data received than was possible with the 70 "overflow" wives who responded to newspaper publicity and since time and financial considerations ruled out changing the research design. Data from overflow wives were footnoted when they potentially altered the findings.

This was necessary only in the following instances: It was only in the study sample that one wife who eventually came out as a lesbian was found. Only in the study sample was there one wife who had been sexually molested as a child. It was only in the overflow group that two cases of a child's sexual abuse by his father or his father's lover was found. The overflow group provided a wider age range and greater demographic and socioeconomic diversity.

With those exceptions, there seemed no difference in data (including approximate percentages) between the two groups. Hence, although descriptive statistics usually refer to the study sample of 33 women, unless specified to the contrary, all statements are considered generally applicable to both groups — 103 women in total. (At least anecdotally, they also appear generally applicable to people seen more recently.)

Statistical Representation

Medians were used for averages. Although data analysis was mainly qualitative, quantitative support was used whenever possible. There was no difficulty, for example, in specifying how many wives had undergone an acute crisis reaction. Yet even when an accurate account was impossible, it seemed useful to provide some estimate of how common a particular attitude or response might be. To overcome such nebulous terms as "a few" or "many," the following guidelines are suggested. Please bear in mind that actual numbers are based on 33 wives, but that percentages apply to 103 wives.

Term(s)	Numerical representation
"Only" or "all but" 1 or 2	Self-Explanatory
"Few" or "A few"	3–7 (7–20%)
"Many," "Several," "Often"	8–14 (21–44%)
"Almost half"	15 (45–47%)
"Approximately half"	16 or 17 (48–51%)
"Over half"	18 (54–56%)
"Most," "Generally"	19–26 (57–80%)
"Almost all," "All but a few"	27–30 (81–93%)

Copies of the research may be found in the libraries of the University of Denver and the Kinsey Institute. Anyone wishing to purchase a copy may do so through University Microfilms, 300 N. Zeeb Road, Ann Arbor, MI (Dissertation #8315,899).

Index